THE MACS

Published by Delilah Communications Ltd.

Distributed by Putnam Books

Produced by Pilot Productions Limited, London

Typesetting by Phoenix Photosetting, Chatham, Kent

Printed in the United States of America

Library of Congress Number: 81–67645

ISBN: 0–933328–05–2

Illustration credits
While every effort has been made to trace copyright sources, the author would be grateful to hear from any unacknowledged copyright holders. Special thanks to Albert Marion, Bill Harry's *Mersey Beat*, the Lewis Collins fan club, the Daily Express, the Liverpool Echo, Roger Vadim, Noel and Cal Redding, Linda McCartney, Barry Farrell, the Butlins camp photographer, Mike Robbins, Thelma Pickles, Keith McCartney, Dennis Stone, Douglas Eatwell.

THE MACS

MIKE McCARTNEY'S FAMILY ALBUM

Delilah Books
NEW YORK
Distributed By G. P. Putnam's Sons

Dedicated to Jim and Mary

The making of Liverpool

Situated on the west side of England, though almost at the centre of the British Isles, Liverpool enjoys the great advantage of a wide and navigable river, the Mersey. Facing Ireland, the Atlantic Ocean and the New World of America, there was never an exact *start* to 'the Pool' (as we call her).

History has her name coming from the Norse inhabitants who called the place 'Hlither Pollr' (The Pool of the Slopes) and it does in fact stand on the slopes of a low ridge looking down on the estuary. Early 'Liverpudlians' (as we're known to this day) were all the serfs of a lord and were completely at the mercy of their masters. One of the great lords whom Liverpool reveres was King John, the worst King ever to rule England. John was the founder and creator of Liverpool, turning it by Charter, in 1207, from an obscure fishing hamlet into a thriving borough, so that he could use the men and supplies of Lancashire to make a base from which to invade my ancestral homeland of Ireland.

By the middle of the eighteenth century we became the main centre of the most lucrative trade in the world—the slave trade—selling fellow human beings. At first Spain and Portugal controlled the trade, but when us canny Liverpudlians saw how remunerative the flesh BIZ was, conveniently forgetting our own previous serfdom, we soon joined in the fun and by the 1790's we were the main slave port, not only in Britain but also in Europe. Indeed most of our fine buildings were built with the money from the slave and cotton trades.

Along with the first George came the first dock ever built in England, and by the 1920's there were eighty-seven docks covering six hundred acres, including the Gladstone, the largest of its sort in Europe. Even as far back as 1905 Liverpool was among the four greatest ports in the world. She also had the largest cathedral and floating platform in Great Britain, and the largest warehouse in the world (*not*, I may add, above the Cavern).

With the industrial revolution, the volume of trade (particularly cotton) was redistributed and even the South of England had to surrender to Liverpool and the North.

This then was the sort of city and port that Dad was hatched into. He was born on 7th July 1902 to Joseph and Florence McCartney, at 8 Fishguard Street, Everton, a poor district of Liverpool and as a government official recently admitted, 'one of the worst slums in England'. Named, simply, James McCartney and christened into the Church of England, he became agnostic during his life.

Brought up with nine kids, seven of whom lived, Dad developed strong family ties with eldest brother Jack, Joe (who died), Edie, Ann Alice (who died aged one year five months in 1901), Mill, Annie II, Jin and finally Joe II . . . ('If you don't succeed at first, try, try again' . . . old family saying.)

At the age of ten, being accident-prone and a bit of a dreamer, he fell off a back jigger (alley) wall and broke his right ear drum, thus affecting us and the furniture for life, for he would position himself in 'Dad's chair', with his left ear to the majority of the room, in each successive home. He was educated at Steer Street School, Everton, from where he and his brothers and sisters would run into the local grocer's shop asking hungrily, 'Have you got any broken biscuits, Mister?'

'Yes.'

'Well mend 'em!', before departing hastily to avoid any flying groceries.

After 'skewl' the jolly McCartney kids would walk along cobbled Everton streets to St. Margaret's Communal Baths (or 'bayose' as Liverpool slang would have it). There, they would all have a good wash and scrub because nobody had a bath in their home (not even the posh houses) and when clean, would all go for a swim.

C. E. TURNER

Very early family scene at the seaside. How *did* they heat the kettle? Uncle Joe is the little lad with the cap; Grandpa Joe is behind him in the velvet-collared jacket; in the middle is Bert (pipe) Danher, with Grannie Florrie McCartney on the right.

The infants' department of Everton's Steer Str. School. Uncle Joe is the lad with the frown, third from the left on the front row.

THE LIMELIGHT BOY

Times were hard in working class Liverpool around this period, and after school Dad worked at the Theatre Royal, Everton, for a bit of extra cash. He would sell the programmes before the start of each performance, belt up to the top of the theatre where he became the limelight boy, and would then shine the limes on such stars as Maria Martin (yes, *the* Maria Martin, in lavish productions of *Face at the Window, The Betrayal* and *Did she fall or was she pushed?* . . . you may well ask). After the show he would belt downstairs again to collect the programmes thrown on the floor or lost. If they were relatively clean he would take them home, give them a wipe over with a damp cloth, iron them and then sell them again the next day.

Although he could only whistle through his teeth, Dad was an insatiable whistler round the McCartney house (like my middle daughter, Theran, now) and soon earned the nickname of 'duzzy' . . . does he whistle!

In 1916, when he was fourteen, he was employed by A. Hannay & Co., Cotton merchants in a 'job for life', and as cotton played such an important part in Liverpool's growth, let's delve into it in a little more depth.

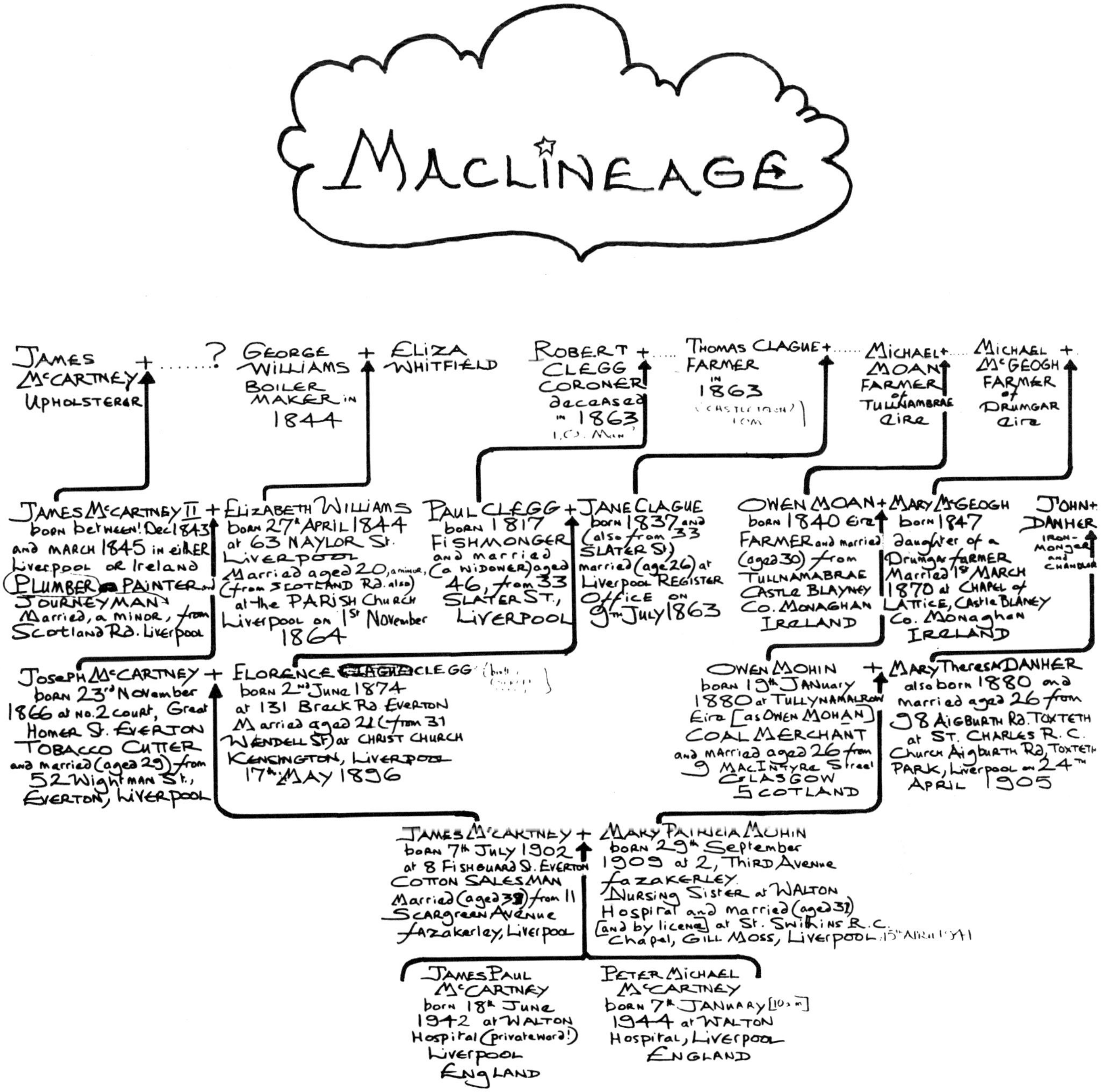

JAMES McCARTNEY + ...? UPHOLSTERER

GEORGE WILLIAMS + ELIZA WHITFIELD
BOILER MAKER in 1844

ROBERT CLEGG + ... THOMAS CLAGUE + ... MICHAEL MOAN + ... MICHAEL McGEOGH +
CORONER deceased in 1863 — FARMER in 1863 — FARMER of TULLNAMBRAE Eire — FARMER of DRUMGAR Eire

JAMES McCARTNEY II + ELIZABETH WILLIAMS
born between! Dec 1843 and MARCH 1845 in either Liverpool or Ireland
PLUMBER & PAINTER and JOURNEYMAN
Married, a MINOR, from Scotland Rd. Liverpool
born 27th APRIL 1844 at 63 NAYLOR St. LIVERPOOL
Married aged 20, a minor, (from SCOTLAND Rd. also) at the PARISH Church Liverpool on 1st November 1864

PAUL CLEGG + JANE CLAGUE
born 1817 FISHMONGER and married (a WIDOWER) aged 46, from 33 SLATER ST., LIVERPOOL
born 1837 and (also from 33 SLATER St) married (aged 26) at Liverpool REGISTER Office on 9th July 1863

OWEN MOAN + MARY McGEOGH
born 1840 Eire FARMER and married (aged 30) from TULLNAMABRAE CASTLE BLAYNEY Co. MONAGHAN IRELAND
born 1847 daughter of a Drumgar farmer Married 1st MARCH 1870 at CHAPEL of LATTICE, Castle Blaney Co. Monaghan IRELAND

JOHN DANHER + IRON-MONGER and CHANDLER

JOSEPH McCARTNEY + FLORENCE ~~CLAGUE~~ CLEGG
born 23rd November 1866 at no. 2 court, Great Homer St. EVERTON
TOBACCO CUTTER
and married (aged 29) from 52 Wightman St., EVERTON, LIVERPOOL
born 2nd June 1874 at 131 Brack Rd. EVERTON
Married aged 21 (from 31 WENDELL ST) at CHRIST CHURCH KENSINGTON, LIVERPOOL 17th MAY 1896

OWEN MOHIN + MARY THERESA DANHER
born 19th January 1880 at TULLYNAMALROW Eire [as OWEN MOHAN]
COAL MERCHANT
and married aged 26 from 9 MACINTYRE Street GLASGOW SCOTLAND
also born 1880 and married aged 26 from 98 AIGBURTH Rd. TOXTETH at ST. CHARLES R.C. Church Aigburth Rd, TOXTETH PARK, Liverpool on 24th APRIL 1905

JAMES McCARTNEY + MARY PATRICIA MOHIN
born 7th July 1902 at 8 Fishguard St. Everton
COTTON SALESMAN
Married (aged 38) from 11 Scargreen Avenue Fazakerley, Liverpool
born 29th September 1909 at 2, Third Avenue Fazakerley
Nursing Sister at WALTON Hospital and married (aged 31) [and by licence] at St. Swithins R.C. Chapel, Gill Moss, Liverpool 15th April 1941

JAMES PAUL McCARTNEY
born 18th June 1942 at WALTON Hospital (private ward!) Liverpool England

PETER MICHAEL McCARTNEY
born 7th January [10 am] 1944 at WALTON Hospital, Liverpool ENGLAND

GOOD LORDY PICK A BALE OF COTTON

The cotton trade between England, America, Egypt and the West Indies was prodigious, and with the invention of the Spinning Jenny and the building of so many cotton mills, Lancashire and Liverpool soon became richer and more populous than at any time in their previous history. With all the cotton at *their* disposal, America had neither the facilities for spinning, nor the market to get rid of the stuff, and that's where Lancashire, Liverpool, and the Cotton Barons came in. They had the new machines and the labour (including six-year-old children working in steam heat of ninety degrees from five in the morning until nine at night) to mass-manufacture it and become millionaires in the process.

Beware! Dad's at work, sampling the grades of cotton in the Cotton Exchange. The longer the staple, the better the cotton.

A job for life

The Liverpool Cotton Exchange, where Dad worked, was described in the 1925 *Illustrated London News* as having 'a very real meaning to the markets throughout the world that hold their hands till Liverpool has spoken'. Every other day he travelled by train to Manchester's Royal Exchange, the largest commercial exchange in the world. His job is described in the club booklet of the day: 'No more wonderful assembly gathers together than at high change. They are a unique type, unbeaten in shrewd judgement and mother wit, liberty-loving descendants of the men who stood by Abraham Lincoln over the issue of slavery when it was against their interests so to do. Transactions representing vast sums are just noted down in a pocket book (Dad always carried one); their word is their bond and no sentiment is talked. These plain men are the tried leaders of an industrial folk numbering ten million or more. Here the world's cotton trade is virtually controlled.' So *that's* what Dad did at the office every day!

Starting as a sample boy in Hannays he earned six shillings (thirty pence) a week. But in 1930, after fourteen years' hard labour, he was made cotton salesman (not usual for a 'working class chappie' at the time) and his wages rose to the grand sum of five pounds a week. Whilst 'resting' in between cotton ships unloading on the River Mersey, he became house-gardener to the cotton bosses 'over the water' in the unthinkably posh district of Heswall, Cheshire, and started his life-long love of gardening.

LITTLE FLUTTERS ON THE GEE GEES

One of Dad's hobbies at this time was betting. Not that Dad was an insatiable gambler, it's just that he didn't know when to stop. So one day when he decided that his Mum, Flo, needed a good holiday, he took the quickest course available to raise the money . . . the race course! After a series of disastrous 'little flutters on the horses' he became seriously in debt to the bookies and was hauled before Mr. Hannay at work: 'Well Lad, you're really in hot water this time.'

In training for 'a little flutter on the gee-gees', is Dad on the right, with Uncle Albert on the left, and Uncle Albert's father in the hat.

'Yes, sir.'

'What made you gamble so much?'

'Well sir, it was to send me Mum on her holidays, she hasn't had one for years and she needs to get away.'

This bizarre family logic seemed to impress Mr. Hannay (a 'gentleman') and he agreed not only to pay off Dad's debts but to send Flo on a tour of Devon, on *one* condition, that Dad paid back the money as soon as possible. Dad readily agreed and for the next twelve months he walked the five or six miles from his home in Scargreen Avenue, West Derby to the Cotton Exchange in the City to save on the tram fares, and also smoked Woodbines instead of Capstan or Players cigarettes.

Encouraged by father Joe, another of Dad's great loves was music, and after teaching himself chords on the second hand 'Nems' piano, given to 'the Macs' during World War I, he formed the Masked Melody Makers (Mmm!). As the title suggests, they used to wear black highwayman masks, but one night when the joint was really jumpin' their masks melted all over their faces. Quickly changing their name to Jim Mac's Band they performed such ragtime classics as *Ama Pola My Pretty Little Poppy, The Birth of the Blues* and Dad's favourite, *Stairway to Paradise.* Dad also wrote and played his own composition, *Eloise*, around this period. They were all in their late teens when they played local dances at such salubrious Liverpool venues as Oak Hall, Deakons and St. Catherine's Hall.

Years later, after the start of the Second World War, Dad met Mary Mohin. Mary was a nursing sister at Walton Hospital, Liverpool and was staying with Dad's sister Jin McCartney and her new husband Harry Harris. Jim bumped into her at the McCartney's 11 Scargreen Avenue home and because of a sudden air raid blitz, they had to stay the night together downstairs and (boom!) fell in love.

MUM

Mum, Mary Patricia Mohin, was born on 29th September 1909, to Owen and Mary Teresa (Danher) Mohin at No. 2, 3rd Avenue Fazakerley, Liverpool. She was christened a Catholic along with elder brother

Jim Mac's Band. Dad is third on the right past the drum (looking like a young Paul!). Immediately left of the drum is Bert Danher; next to him is a straight-faced Uncle Jack; sitting down behind Jack is Annie McCartney and Aunt Millie. Later, Annie married Bert Danher and produced Bett (who married Mike Robbins, the man responsible for my first and only stage performance with Paul—at Butlins, no less).

Wilf, younger sister Agnes (who died aged two at the end of the First World War), younger brother Bill, and finally the baby who died with her mother in January 1919. When Owen re-married, Mum acquired a step brother and sister Jack and Vera. Although not the strictest of Catholics during her life, she stayed loyal to the Faith to the end.

Mum couldn't accept her step mother, Rose Mohin, and, aged about thirteen, she moved to her Danher relatives in their Litherland chandler shop. At fourteen, she entered into nursing at Alder Hey and then Walton Hospital. A devoted nurse, at twenty-four she became a sister, and at thirty-one she met, fell in love with, and married my Dad, Jim. Dad was thirty-nine when they married at St. Swithens Roman Catholic Chapel, Gill Moss, Liverpool, on 15th April 1941, and then moved to furnished rooms in Sunbury Road, Anfield.

Not marrying until he was nearly forty, Dad had presented a few problems to his proud parents, and some time prior to his marriage, when 'Freda's flighty sister' came down from Arbroath, Scotland, to 'set her cap' at Jim, Father Joe wasn't too happy. He politely referred to her as 'the whore's robber from Arbroath' and was so anxious for this woman and Jim not to get spliced, he even kept the date of her arrival in his diary. No fool our Joe (ref. any future hanky-baby-panky from Freda's sister).

Due to his grade C ear and the fact that he was over conscription age, Dad was luckily spared the blushes of death in Europe, but neverthe-

Mum, dressed as a nurse, but looking more like a nun on the cover of my first solo album.

less became an automatic setter-lathe turner in Napier's aircraft factory during the day and a fire-fighter at night. During the war there was a short respite to sing-along activities in the McCartney home as the piano had been stuffed full of sandbags.

When she got married, Mum gave up nursing at Walton Hospital to have her first child.

The McCartney family

James Paul McCartney was born 18th June 1942 in a 'private ward' of Walton Hozzy, 107 Rice Lane, Liverpool, (not that Mum's previous position as sister of the maternity ward led to preferential treatment, you understand).

Brother Paul was born on a balmy 18th June, the same day Norma (Marilyn Monroe) Jean was married to Jim Dougherty, three weeks after her sixteenth birthday, and in the same year which saw Japan invading Burma; British Commandoes raiding St. Nazaire; the end of white bread in Britain; Czech patriots assassinating Gestapo chief Heydrich; Rommel taking Tobruk from the British; British budget doubling entertainment tax; the RAF raiding Hamburg; Hitler launching his V2 rocket; the British retaking Tobruk from Rommel; E. Fermi splitting the atom in Chicago; magnetic tape being invented; Gilbert

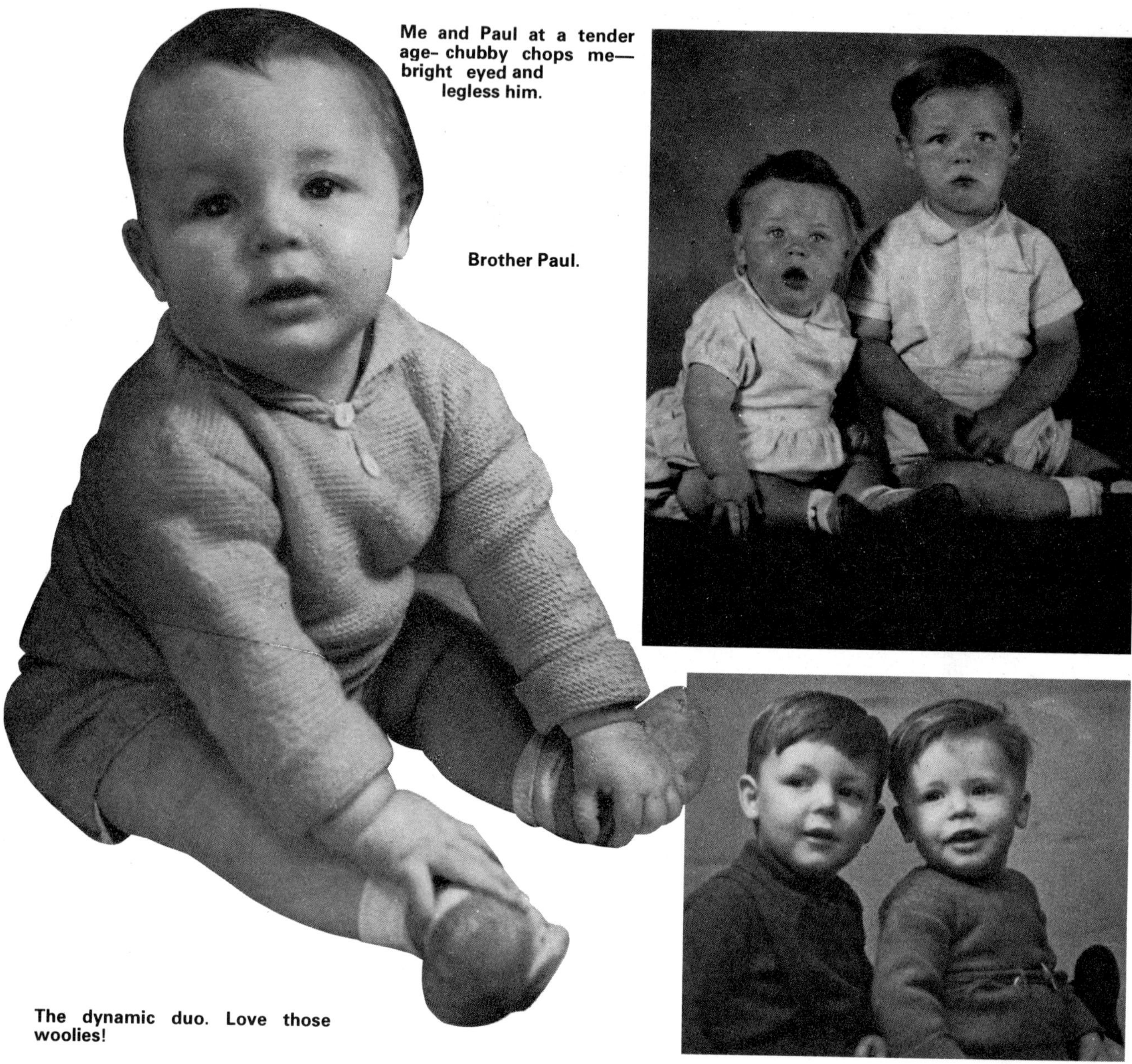

Me and Paul at a tender age- chubby chops me— bright eyed and legless him.

Brother Paul.

The dynamic duo. Love those woolies!

Murray founding Oxfam; the Alaska Highway opening; Tommy Hanley starring in BBC Radio's ITMA; Britain building over 23,000 planes and 8,000 tanks, and losing over 3,000 ships.

Because Napiers was classified as Air Force, Jim got a small house for himself, Mother Mary and child over the Mersey water at 92 Broadway, Wallasey, away from the bombs for a while.

Just 18 months after Paul's birth, I chose to be born, and preferring to be brought up in Liverpool, Jim and Mary accommodatingly moved back across the water. Just in time too; Auntie Jin was discussing the bombing with a woman on a Liverpool bus when she was informed of a bomb which missed the docks at Birkenhead ('over the water') and scored a direct hit on a house in St. Vincent Road, Claughton—Auntie Mill's road! When the two sisters finally contacted each other, much nail-biting later, Milly informed the family that she was indeed in her own Number 35 house at the time a stray bomb hit the house opposite, wiping it out. All that were found of the occupants were various arms and legs scattered about surrounding gardens!

Brother Mike.

ME

Arriving at ten o'clock on the cold morning of January 7th 1944, also at Walton (registered number 190), I was named Peter Michael McCartney and promptly taken home to our new prefab bungalow home in Roach Avenue, Knowsley Estate, Liverpool. Mother Mary, however, was taken back to hospital with mastitis, a disease affecting the breast. 1944 was the year after Frank Sinatra became the first teenage pop idol; the German Army was driven from Russia; the Communist Party won the by-election at Skipton; the allies dropped 81,400 tons of bombs on Germany (slightly less than Mr. Nixon, who dropped nearly seven million tons of bombs on Vietnam and Indo China in later years) and occupied Europe in one month! The Fifth Army entered Rome; the D-Day landing was successful in Normandy; de Gaulle re-entered Paris; the first V2 rocket landed in Britain; Roosevelt won the US Presidency for the fourth time; North Burma was cleared of Japs and quinnine was synthesized; painter Edvard Munch died aged eighty; and the first non-stop flight from Canada to London was made.

So there we were . . . the Macs, a complete little family unit. Well nearly complete. . . .

GRANDAD MAC

Unfortunately brother Paul and I never had the privilege of knowing our grandparents, or calling them Grandad and Grannie, as Dad's father Joe died before we were born and his mum Florrie in 1945, the year after my birth.

Joe McCartney, was born on 23rd November 1866 in Everton and for the whole of his life worked at Cope's tobacco firm, St. Vincent Street, Liverpool, as a tobacco cutter and stover. He played big brass double bass in both Cope's and the Territorial Army brass bands, whose

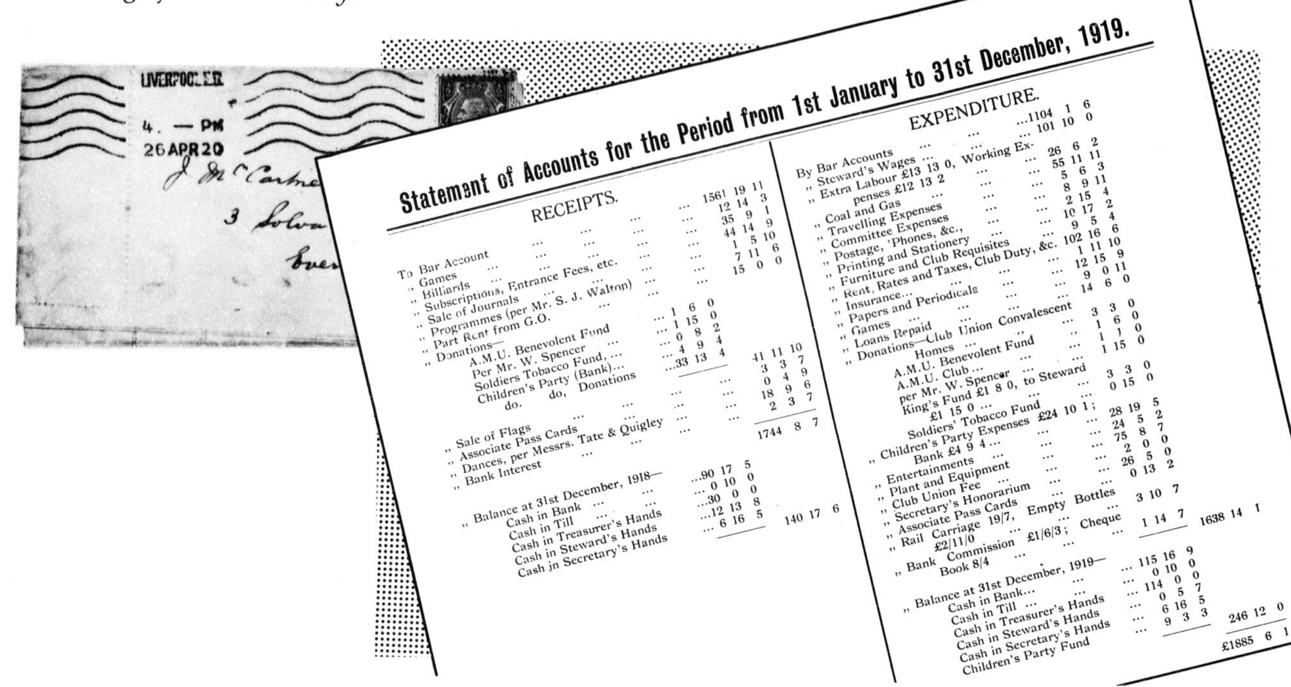

Statement of Accounts for the Period from 1st January to 31st December, 1919.

RECEIPTS.

	£	s.	d.	£	s.	d.
To Bar Account …				1561	19	11
,, Games …				12	14	3
,, Billiards …				35	9	1
,, Subscriptions, Entrance Fees, etc. …				44	14	9
,, Sale of Journals …				1	5	10
,, Programmes (per Mr. S. J. Walton) …				7	11	6
,, Part Rent from G.O. …				15	0	0
,, Donations—						
A.M.U. Benevolent Fund	1	6	0			
Per Mr. W. Spencer …	1	15	0			
Soldiers Tobacco Fund, …	0	8	2			
Children's Party (Bank)…	4	9	4			
do. do, Donations	33	13	4	41	11	10
,, Sale of Flags …				3	3	7
,, Associate Pass Cards …				0	4	9
,, Dances, per Messrs. Tate & Quigley …				18	9	6
,, Bank Interest …				2	3	7
				1744	8	7
,, Balance at 31st December, 1918—						
Cash in Bank …	90	17	5			
Cash in Till …	0	10	0			
Cash in Treasurer's Hands	30	0	0			
Cash in Steward's Hands	12	13	8			
Cash in Secretary's Hands	6	16	5	140	17	6

EXPENDITURE.

	£	s.	d.	£	s.	d.
By Bar Accounts …	1104	1	6			
,, Steward's Wages …	101	10	0			
,, Extra Labour £13 13 0, Working Expenses £12 13 2 …	26	6	2			
,, Coal and Gas …	55	11	11			
,, Travelling Expenses …	5	6	3			
,, Committee Expenses …	8	9	11			
,, Postage, 'Phones, &c., …	2	15	4			
,, Printing and Stationery …	10	17	2			
,, Furniture and Club Requisites …	9	5	4			
,, Rent, Rates and Taxes, Club Duty, &c.	102	16	6			
,, Insurance…	1	11	10			
,, Papers and Periodicals …	12	15	9			
,, Games …	9	0	11			
,, Loans Repaid …	14	6	0			
,, Donations—Club Union Convalescent Homes …	3	3	0			
A.M.U. Benevolent Fund …	1	6	0			
A.M.U. Club …	1	1	0			
per Mr. W. Spencer …	1	15	0			
King's Fund £1 8 0, to Steward £1 15 0 …	3	3	0			
Soldiers' Tobacco Fund …	0	15	0			
,, Children's Party Expenses £24 10 1; Bank £4 9 4 …	28	19	5			
,, Entertainments …	24	5	2			
,, Plant and Equipment …	75	8	7			
,, Club Union Fee …	2	0	0			
,, Secretary's Honorarium …	26	5	0			
,, Associate Pass Cards …	0	13	2			
,, Rail Carriage 19/7, Empty Bottles £2/11/0 …	3	10	7			
,, Bank Commission £1/6/3; Cheque Book 8/4 …	1	14	7	1638	14	1
,, Balance at 31st December, 1919—						
Cash in Bank…	115	16	9			
Cash in Till …	0	10	0			
Cash in Treasurer's Hands	114	0	0			
Cash in Steward's Hands	0	5	7			
Cash in Secretary's Hands	6	16	5			
Children's Party Fund	9	3	3	246	12	0
				£1885	6	1

open-air park concerts and walks through city streets in smart khaki uniforms created quite a thirst, as the statement of accounts for the period of January–December shows:

To sale of journals	£1. 5s. 10d.
To dances as per Messrs. Tate & Quigley	£18. 9s. 6d.
To bar account	£1,561 19s. 11d.

Joe always practised and played his instrument at home and encouraged his children to do likewise on their chosen instruments. He was a quiet, reserved man with a good sense of contained humour (much like our Dad), and also had a very good singing voice (much like Dad's brother, Uncle Joe) which he unfortunately kept to himself. An old lady who knew of Joe's secret voice asked him to sing *The Old Rugged Cross* for her when she was ill, and when she died she left Grandad forty pounds in her will, a fortune in those days, so he *must* have been a good singer. Joe went to bed at ten o'clock every night, and his only swear word was 'Jaysus'. Although he never drank, he would buy pints of beer for friends, and have a glass of lemonade himself.

GRANNY MAC

Grannie Mac—Florrie McCartney.

Dad's Mum, Florrie McCartney, was born 2nd June 1874, also in Everton, as Florence Clegg. After marrying Joe at Christchurch, Liverpool, in 1896, she became 'Mum' to the McCartney seven in their successive Fishguard Street, Lloyd Street, Solva Street (Everton), and Scargreen Avenue (West Derby) Liverpool homes.

A matriarch, she ruled with a rod of love. Whereas Father Joe appeared to be stricter, Mother Florrie actually kept the family together, was more easy-going, and always had a joke to tell. She was so broad-minded that she even told her young kids smutty jokes, always with a twinkle in her eye. As the head of the family you always went to Flo with any troubles (much like Auntie Jin today), and later on in life all the children in her neighbourhood grew to love her as 'Granny Mac'. In fact, just before her death, on VE Day at the end of World War II, she said, 'If it's the last thing I do, it's hang that flag out!' referring to an Edward VII 'give away' flag in a packet of peas. She tied the flag to the end of a brush, hung it out the window, and was dancing round the bonfire in the street below with the local kids when her maker tapped her on the shoulder and asked for the pleasure of the last dance.

THE ELDER MACS

Dad and his brothers and sisters remember various stories of their parents Joe and Forrie McCartney . . . like the time Joe spotted a new girl scrubbing the stone steps of her newly acquired home in his own Whiteman Street, Everton. Although seriously engaged to another girl at the time he enquired, 'Hey Mam, who's the new girl opposite?' He'd fallen in love with Florence Clegg, but unfortunately had already bought his bottom drawer (dowry) for his other fiancée, so times being hard, Florrie had to suffer the indignity of the 'other woman's' Welsh dresser in her home until the time came to move from Solva Street (their third home). Then everything went with them, *except* the bottom drawer. In the early years, money being in short supply, one drawer of the dresser was always full with apples and oranges, due to the school doctor's observation that the McCartney kids appeared 'improperly fed'. Florrie Mac hadn't taken too kindly to the suggestion at first, and had marched up to the school to sort the doctor out with 'murder in her heart and dandruff in her moustache', as Uncle Joe later recalled.

To supplement his meagre income Father Joe McCartney invented various ways of increasing the family fortune. One weekly method was the 'turnup turnout'. As he worked in a tobacco firm, and tobacco was highly sought after in the war, bless me if the tobacco leaves didn't fall off the workbench down into Joe's turnups. What a surprise when he got home at the end of each week to discover all that illicit substance nestling round his ankles! The baccy was then turned out onto the *Liverpool Echo* (echo, echo) newspaper and used as barter to buy potatoes, turnips, etc.

In Whiteman Street, Everton, Joe and Florrie lived next door to a family who couldn't pay the rent (times were often *that* hard), but when the bailiffs came to throw them out into the street, this Liverpool family was more than prepared. The entire contents of the chamber pot were poured over the poor official's head. Furious at this indignity, he threatened to take the family to court, but found that he couldn't because of a small legal technicality—the contents of the pot had been 'dirty' as opposed to 'clean' water.

SOLVA STREET

When she was a child in Everton, Auntie Jin remembers the 'big woman from Solva Street' (sounds like the title of a Western), whose voice used to fade to nowhere in the middle of a conversation; for example, 'Hello Mrs. Mac, have you heard about our Hermioney, she's got herself in . . . fourteen bags of potatoes.' Her favourite saying was, 'Give us a hand to throw me Ma out,' and in between silences she came up with such gems as, 'I've bought some lovely shoes, you know, the ones with cupid 'eels' (cuban heels?), and finally, 'My daughter-in-law's a wonderful pianerist. She can accommodate ANYONE.'

Then there was the local abortionist who practised on herself, and could do anything with a crochet hook . . . *but* crochet.

Solva Street brings back some of the fondest MACmemories. Although they referred to it as 'a bit of a dump' and, when kids, wouldn't tell people where they lived, they spent thirteen happy, sometimes hungry years there. Victorian cobbled streets outside, it was the sort of mad-house where you could turn any accident to advantage. For instance, when a bottle of sauce was dropped on the stone floor one day, it quickly became a slide. But not content to stop there, the happy Macs soon turned it into a jam, oil, sauce slide to be enjoyed by all.

As it was a large family, the door was seldom closed and when my Dad (plus anyone else who could pick up an instrument) started rehearsing, it became an excuse for the whole street to join in. Every night some twenty cups of tea and endless Welsh rarebits (before they could afford bacon butties) were religiously made, and people would dance to the music outside in the street. It was such a happy, relaxed atmosphere that the youngsters Joe and Jin can never remember going to bed without the assistance of home-made music.

Just like our Dad with rock and roll music, Joe McCartney, a brass band man at heart, never understood the modern big band music of the day and always referred to the Henry Hall and Tommy Dorsey Bands as 'a load of old tin cans'.

'Your lips look like a pillar box, Jin. I'll give you half a crown if you'll let me rub a banana in your face'.

The happy, hungry years

'POUND NIGHTS' . . . SPIRITS AND PILLAR BOX LIPS

As *everybody* was poor, the McCartneys used to have 'Pound Nights' (not pound *notes* but *lb* pounds) when friends and relatives would arrive with a pound of sugar, a pound of tea, a pound of cheese etc. In those days there was always a 'jockey' on a pound of cheese, which meant that the grocer would cut an extra bit from the block to make the weight up. One evening when Florrie Cannon brought her pound of cheese round, the eldest brothers Jack and Jim undid the paper in the kitchen, took out the jockey and replaced it with a mousetrap. Luckily they didn't set the trap and when Florrie Cannon opened her paper in the parlour, she didn't exactly explode (as her name suggests she might have) but simply blushed, which was the cue for everybody else to explode laughing (Explode—laughing—cannon: it went down a bomb!). (No more, Michael, please.)

Lord knows where the Mac lads got their sense of humour from, but another evening Annie and Mill McCartney had some friends round who believed in 'spirits'. The seriousness of it all tickled Father Joe no end. At his usual ten o'clock bed-time he retired upstairs, put a white sheet over his head, gathered some chains and keys about him, and descended spiritually down the stairs. He did it so badly that everyone collapsed laughing, so he was sent back up to bed. This time with no supper.

Another Solva Street remembrance comes from Auntie Jin, who would get 'all dolled up' to go out for the evening and elder brother Jim would comment admiringly, 'Your lips look like a pillar box,' and add, 'I'll give you half a crown if you'll let me rub a banana in your face.' The alternative was to put shrimp heads down her back. A half-crown being a fortune, Jin would let him have his little joke, collect the money, wash the mess off and then go out, a little wiser and a little richer (no relation to *the* 'Little Richar').

Shsh!

Entertainment in the 1920s wasn't just a simple task of turning on the television. There *were* no tellys. In fact, there were no radios in working class Liverpool till one day in 1900 when the Macs got their first crystal set. Just imagine the effect of a wireless on half a dozen sparsely educated, poor Liverpool children—a box without wires which you turned on to hear music floating up from London through the air!

The McCartney radio consisted of a cat fascia whose whisker you had to place on the crystal for your reception. When *purr*-fected you could even get foreign, over-the-sea stations. As there was only one earphone to appreciate such wonderment, silence was imperative for peaceful listening. The constant 'shsh! . . . shsh!' to his girls as they curled their hair with crinkly bread paper finally led Joe to give all his children sixpence to go to the pictures when his favourite programme came on . . . Opera.

La Traviata wasn't exactly the kids' cup of tea. They preferred to listen to Auntie Vi on 2 LO, who would tell stories and play the piano. And not to forget the popular Enoch and Sheenoch (indeed, who *could* forget Enoch and Sheenoch?).

Early Dada-style pic of Uncle Jack, the gentle giant.

JACK THE GENTLE GIANT

Uncle Jack, the eldest Mac, was a gentle giant of a man with a soft whisper caused by laryngitis, who worked for the Liverpool Corporation. You had to listen carefully to catch his conversation but the words were well worth catching as Jack was one of nature's true gentlemen and had a beautiful way of telling jokes, always with a twinkle in the eye. His repertoire was endless and when there were ladies in the company he would always moderate his language with a store of clean jokes. It was a sign of maturity when Jack told you a dirty 'Corpy' joke.

GET KNITTED

Uncle Jack was a city council rent collector for a while, and one day found a rather upset householder on the end of his knock.

'Mr. Mac, do you think I'm going mad or wha'?'

'What seems to be the trouble, Mrs. Woman? You look as white as a sheet.'

'I've had a terrible shock Mr. Mac. I've caught a mouse in the trap. Come and see.'

'That's nothing to get worried about love. There's lots of mice in this street.'

'I know that Mr. Mac, but *this* one's fully clothed.'

And sure enough there in the mousetrap was the deadest, but nicest-dressed mouse he had ever seen (knitted hat, dress, the lot). Uncle Mac eventually discovered the culprit to be a lonely old lady down the street who 'felt sorry for the poor things' and confessed to catching them, knitting their woolly little clothes, dressing them, and finally letting them go. (Now I know what they mean by dressed crabs.)

HOLD TIGHT—CLANG! CLANG!

Jack was once a tram conductor on the 46 tram, or 'boneshakers' as they were known locally. In those days it cost just twopence to go one way as far as you liked and fourpence for a day return, which meant the unmitigated luxury of going *anywhere* all day. Jack used to whisper stories about his passengers, like the pretentious Liverpool lady whose precocious daughter was reluctant to mount his Corporation chariot and remained standing in the muddy street. Her mother solved the problem by demanding in her hupper class scouse haccent, 'Gloria, come in out the muck,' and then asking for 'Two to Tagartavarnew please,' which roughly translated means 'two tickets to Tagart Avenue'.

And there was the woman who kept his tram waiting ages while she taught her child to walk down the top steps: 'Come along darlin', Mummy's waitin',' at which Jack looked up and said, 'And so is Jackie,' with that twinkle which prevented any further comment.

THE CHIPPY BY THE HIPPY

In 1942, when ITMA was one of BBC radio's biggest successes, the host Tommy Handley (ex-Liverpudlian) used to tell jokes about 'the chippy by the hippy'. The 'chippy' was the french fried establishment belonging to one of Tommy's relatives; the 'hippy' was scouse for the Hippodrome Theatre, West Derby Road, Everton. And a big treat for the younger McCartney kids was to stay up late on a Saturday night for eldest brother Jack to return from the Hippodrome and listen with bated breath whilst he relived the show by mimicking all the turns. One of the Music Hall jokes he told was about the old Liverpool lady who joined a long, posh, well-to-do queue, waiting outside the Empire Theatre.

'What are we waitin' for love?' the old dear enquired.

'*The Tales of Hoffman*,' she was poshly told.

'Well you've got to eat something these days haven't you?'

THE MOHIN—HAN—MOANS

As our beautiful mum died so early in life, less is known about the early Mohins, but what I *have* learnt is that Dad, Owen Mohin, was born on 19th January 1880, in Ireland, as Owen Mo*han*.

The extraordinary reason for such a quick name change (as told by only surviving brother Wilf) was that in the small Irish village where Owen went to school, the Mohan clan were so prolific in number that whenever the school headmaster asked questions of a Mohin, ninety per cent of the classroom's tiny hands shot up. After a while he decided to reduce the confusion by literally halving the class.

'De children on the left shall remain MO*HAN* . . . de children on de right shall henceforth be called MO*HIN*.'

Not only that! . . . Owen's father (another Owen, natch) was christened Owen MOAN! Please don't ask why.

When he was twelve, Owen (Mo*hin*) left for Glasgow, Scotland, and at the age of twenty-five settled down in Liverpool where he married Mary Teresa Danher (aged twenty-six) in St. Charles R.C. Church, Toxteth Park. After the death of his wife in 1919 he took his three children (Wilf, Mum and Bill) back to Eire where his attempt at farming collapsed, not helped by his great love of gambling. Like Dad and his family, it's not hard to see why gambling was so popular in those days. It must have seemed the only way out of an otherwise dead-end, poverty-prone existence. Unable to benefit from an education, and with hard work being no solution, what else was there? Back he went to Liverpool, where the coal business proved lucrative and, in 1921, on a return trip to Ireland to buy horses for the coal carts, he was introduced to his future wife Rose by her brother. A marriage (of convenience?) was arranged, with a dowry of one hundred pounds dangled in front of his betting nose by Rose's brother. (Money inducement was offered with the women in Ireland round this time so that the men could have sole ownership of the farms . . . no fools us Micks.) The new Mohin family returned to Liverpool, Fernside, but not with the blessing of the eldest children Wilf and Mary (Mum).

The main remembrances of the early Mohins seem to centre around the coal business or 'on the coal' as it was usually called. At the height of Owen's career he had five horse-and-carts (coal—one shilling and sixpence per cwt.) which was considered rather grand and enabled the family to live in the posh end of the slums. Then Owen decided to expand to Manchester, which in those days was a round trip of three days . . . it now takes under three quarters of an hour by car. Meanwhile Mary Teresa became the proprietor of a furniture shop in Aintree, Liverpool, where part of the business was to buy old clothes pegs in the cold, wet, off-season, clean them up and sell them in the warm weather as new. (She should have gone into partnership with Dad and

his theatre programmes.) Later on, with the help of spare horses and carts, the Mohins started a furniture removal business. At the peak of his success Owen had four racehorses, which son Wilf rode at the Sealand and Bidston race courses. But as Wilf says, although he never drank or smoked, Owen's biggest snag was gambling, and sure enough in the end he lost all his money on the gee gees, with the result that life at home for mum and the lads wasn't *that* rosy.

Dad and Mum memories

If it's true that we all choose our parents before we are born, then I reckon that Paul and I made a damn good choice with Jim and Mary. They were all and more that parents could be. Dad was a man of his word, proud, hard-working, less serious than Mum, just and loving, but stern when the need arose. It's always harder for men to show other men affection except when they're children or old people such is our society ('all arse over tit' as Dad would say). But Dad gave us plenty of love when we were kids and tried to give more towards the end of his life, but the constant boring pain of arthritis made it hard for love to shine through. Whereas Mum was the affection-giver (not over-demonstrative, though, as she'd had little love given to her as a child), Dad's chosen role was the arbitrator. He had the last word and the ultimate warning from Mum was 'Look out you two, or you'll get a smacked bottom from your father'. Although basically serious, as he worked in 'the City', Dad always had a subtle, underground, bubbling sort of fun which could explode at any second like a geyser (with a farting, raspberry sound or the pulling of the tongue).

MEMORIES OF JIM

When we were boys Dad used to give us piggy backs round the house . . . Smoke the Havana cigar we bought for him every Christmas—rolling it in his fingers to feel the leaf, clipping it with a cigar cutter, spitting the end out into the hearth and then lighting it up until the smoke filled the house . . . 'Race us to the bus stop,' which meant giant strides but 'No running!' and inevitably he'd beat us . . . Show us how to deep-breathe, in through the nose, hold, out through the mouth, to be repeated *ad nostrium* . . . Shout 'Quiet!' for the football results each Saturday afternoon (just like his Dad, Joe, for opera), and woe betide you if you moved an inch . . . Strap his bicycle clips on before taking us on long country bike rides . . . Take us with him round the Liverpool Speke estate with bucket and shovel to hunt for horse manure to spread over his beloved garden . . . Play the piano, cross-handed (one hand over the other) with joy in his heart . . . Approach one arm bandits with alarming intent . . . Do the crossword every day, and if we helped, but didn't know a word, he'd say, 'Look it up in the dictionary' (which might explain my love of words . . . any words!) . . . Apologise for not holding our stomachs when we were being sick (like Mum used to do) as it would make him sick too . . . Let us smell his fingers after crushing the flowers of his favourite dried-out lavender into an ash tray and then set fire to it, allowing the smell to meander through the house . . . rub his stubbly chin against our smooth cheeks, and blow 'raspberries' against our skin . . . Take us to the

Dad and his beloved piano. I drew this much later on when we were at Forthlin Road. Whenever any of the family sees it, they immediately recognise it as 'Uncle Jim' . . . even from the back.

Mum and the boys at Squire's Gate Holiday Camp.

Dad, although outwardly quite serious, had an underlying, bubbling sense of humour that could explode at any time. Pulling tongues on New Brighton beach—a family trait.

barbers in Penny Lane where the tonsorial artist would clipper up the back of our necks over the ears, army style (and it wasn't half cold on the back of your neck when you got outside) . . . Show us how to press our trousers under the mattress to get a good crease in them . . . and later on, he'd teach us how to drink in pubs under age and give us the money to get a round in . . . Make marvellous custard, rice puddings and Yorkshire pud (he was proud of it an' all) . . . Pour quadruple, four-finger measures of neat alcohol for each and every guest (a Jimacmeasure) . . . Tip the tunnel toll man who collected your money to get under the Mersey by car (who else but Jim McCartney would tip the tunnel man?).

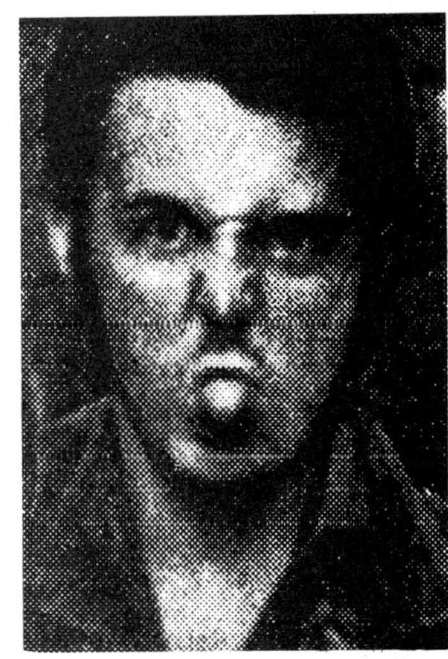

But Dad's biggest personal predicament came after Mum's death when he had to decide to be a father *or* a mother to his two growing (one teenager) lads. Luckily he chose to be both, a very hard decision

These were taken at a farm in North Wales where one of the sheep ate sweets!

when you've got used to being the man around the house, but he made an amazing job of it. As with Mum, our pubescent period didn't bring out the best in us McCartney lads, and we gave Dad very little help plus a lot of cheek through these very difficult times. He just bit his lip and carried on, day after day, and night after lonely night. He could have cracked up, got drunk, beat us up, brought women home—he had every justification for doing so, but he just 'soldiered on' (family saying) until we were big enough to 'fend for ourselves' (another family saying). In fact whichever way you look at it, life is one long family saying.

MEMORIES OF MARY

Mum was my love, perhaps because I was the youngest, perhaps because I was a holy little lad, perhaps because we had the same temperament or perhaps it was just a silly phase we were going through. Up till her death I think I identified more with her, and Paul more with Dad. In terms of physical resemblance I favour Mary, and Paul, Jim, with both sets of our children bearing some of the same magnificent McCartney features. I certainly needed Mum more than Dad, whereas Paul tended to be more independent. Since Mum's death I've somehow stored most of her memories in a private, sealed box in my heart, but every now and then the lid flies open and beautiful pictures come pouring out . . .

Pictures . . . of helping in the kitchen by slowly stirring cake mixture in a giant bowl with a wooden spoon—fawn coloured outside, white inside—before licking spoon and bowl clean of the sweet dough . . . of guiding wet clothes through the mangle while Mum turned the two

finger-crunching rolling pin mangles . . . of her sneaking us first cuts of a hot Sunday joint before serving the main meal onto the plate . . . of pushing meat down into the mincer and withdrawing little pink fingers just before they, too, became mincemeat . . . of waiting, mouth watering, for hot scones from the oven, the waft of hot air in the face when the door was finally opened, and the feel of thick melting butter and hot scones in hungry mouths . . . of playing ships with Paul in the bath, being flannelled, scrubbed, and pumice-stoned when the dirt was deeply ingrained, then lifted out and towel dried as only Mums (and Dads) can do . . . of her buttoning our shirts, tying shoe laces, trying tying ties, going to the 'dreaded' dentists and Mum buying me a brown lead toy cart horse to take away the pain . . . of having Vick rubbed on our chests when a cold was attached . . . of Mum flicking the thermometer professionally (just like a nurse) putting it under my tongue and then taking my wrist-held pulse . . . of feeling her concern and love for our illnesses through walls, round corners and upstairs . . . of swaying to and fro on the Singer sewing machine's carved steel foot pedal whilst Mum sewed above . . . of the smell of small hand-sewn bags filled with Dad's lavender that nestled amongst shirts and sheets in cupboards, and Mothaks moth balls dangling from dingling wardrobe clothes hangers . . . of resting my head on her lap whilst listening to the radio at the end of the day . . . and finally, pictures of being tucked into freshly aired beds and cuddling down with cold feet touching hot rubber water bottles. ('I want the orange one.' 'No, *I* want the orange one, you had it last night.') . . . of being kissed goodnight on the lips and then, 'Go(d) bless' from the door as all but the landing light went out (just in case of the bogey men).

The 'Macs' at New Brighton when it had a pier.

Later in life we both took Mum for granted as most kids approaching puberty probably do, but I tended to *over*-love her, and my love sometimes manifested itself as aggression. Recriminating remembrances include the time I got her so upset she boiled over and chased me upstairs in our 20 Forthlin home (she *never* lost her temper, so I must have said something terrible to her). I locked myself in the toilet until she cooled down.

One afternoon, just before she died, I caught her upstairs in Mum and Dad's bedroom crying to herself. She was holding a crucifix and a picture of one of her Catholic priest relatives.

'What's up, Mum?'

'Nothing love.'

Being a nurse she'd guessed what was wrong with her. Soon afterwards they confirmed cancer of the breast and within a month she was dead. It was that quick. One minute a loving, warm, hugging mother, the next—nothing.

Just writing this brings tears trickling down my nose onto the paper. (We McCartneys always did have our bladders too near our eyes.)

Mum's death affected us more than we'll ever know. Without knowing what a soul was, her death touched it, reaching right down to the bottom of my heart. I was twelve and Paul was just fourteen.

Either before or after the end (probably after) I had a recurring nightmare of Mum being on a bus platform with her hand outstretched and me running for the bus. My legs were moving like lightning and I could have run forever, but I stayed on the same spot—just out of reach of her hand.

Before she died she received the last rites and allowed the Catholic head of the clinic where she worked to tie rosary beads round her wrists, and admitted to Brother Bill's wife Auntie Dill, 'I would have liked to have seen the boys growing up.'

Owing to the fact that I was only 3, I don't remember much about Sir Thomas White Gardens where we were domiciled when Mum became a midwife. But oh, the hard reality of going back to your roots—when I returned to take this pic I stepped out of the car right into a pile of dog muck!

KIDSTUFF

Looking back and *going* back are two entirely different kettles of fish. One is the easy, eyes-closed joy of the mind's reminiscences, the other is the hard reality of the changes which life and times bring. People departed, different or dead, houses somewhat smaller, whole streets missing, and gentle summer fields where butterflies fluttered, turned into three-laned motorways packed with foreign cars, driven by grey-haired English dads, speeding nowhere. Past and present all mangled into that which 'is' . . . here and now.

But let's go back to the relaxed, inward reflections of times gone by when we were all knee high to a grasshopper, and (as Dad would say) life was just a lavatory bowl of cherries.

On closing my eyes, the memories simply flood back . . . memories of childhood Speke, the overflow estate from Liverpool's catholicly expanding centre.

After the birth of her first son Paul, in 1942, Mum gave up nursing at Walton to become a health visitor, but health visiting being too 'nine to five, office jobbish' Mum turned to midwifery, which meant domiciliary homes for her, Jim, Paul and me in the ground floor flat of Sir Thomas White Gardens, Liverpool City Centre, then out to 72 Western Avenue, Speke, near the banks of the upper Mersey, where most of my memories start.

The front of 72 Western Avenue, Speke. My earliest childhood memories.

At the Welsh farm again with Mr. Jones, the farmer. My legs were too short to reach the pedals!

Schooldays and holidays

My *earliest* memories grow less hazy around the time of our first school and my first day at Stockton Wood Road Infants School, which opened in June 1940, and grew to be the largest infants school in England with over 1,500 kids!

Although Paul and I were baptised Catholics (and circumcised Jewishly) our parents preferred a non-Catholic education, as Dad in particular believed there was too much religion and not enough education in Catholic schools. On the Big Day, in her blue and white starched midwife's uniform and cap, Mum walked me from our home to the school where elder brother Paul was already ensconced. We met the teacher, had a little chat and everything seemed settled, so Mum waved 'bye bye' and set off home. She'd forgotten one thing . . . me! My nearly five-year-old mouth opened up and all hell was let loose, but to no avail. Through a sea of tears and a set of thick prison bar school railings she slowly disappeared from view. I don't know what all the fuss was about, our house was only one hundred yards round the corner! Nevertheless this was the Freudian introduction to my first few years of school incarceration. But after the initial nightmare (or should I say daymare) had worn off, it wasn't half as bad as I thought.

Stocky Wood school yard. The building jutting out, on the right of the picture, is where I levitated a brick onto the school bully's head.

It was at Stocky Wood (badge—black and yellow, with a picture of a Spitfire flying over the River Mersey) that Paul and I saw our first film. We were seated on long wooden benches watching Crime Buster Dick Barton, a great radio hero of ours, when it all became too much for Paul. In the flickering half light I watched with *great* amusement as Big Brother stumbled over me and his pals to exit screen left, scared out of his tiny mind. He wasn't scared when it came to smaller things such as bullies, however, and many's the time he came to my rescue in the school play yard. 'Big brothers have a use after all,' I thought. Just before we left Stocky Wood, the balmy summer days proved far too alluring for little lads, and Paul and I would 'sag from school' (play truant) past war-camouflaged rubber factories, through the stately grounds of Speke Hall and down to the banks of the river Mersey where we much preferred to strip off and swim nude in the then unpolluted waters.

My memories of brother and I are of two independent little chaps, but Uncle and Auntie's remembrances are of 'two right little swine', always up to mischief, or with their backs to the wall saying, 'We won't . . . WE WON'T!' I'm sure they're just a might confused. I do remember a few instances, however, which might give their memories *some* validity. Like the memory of Paul and me in 72 Western speeding up the growth of next door's apples by throwing stones at the apple tree, and then vigorously denying it. The stones on the other side let us down!

Memories of being boss of my own gang in the later Stockton Wood years and charging against the 'enemy' across the school yard in full war cry (obviously why the headmistress Miss Margaret A. Thomas, who used to make the school toys herself, advised the world that one day I would be a 'Leader of men').

And there came an older bully unto the yard who hit little girls and maketh them cry, and it behove me to teach unto him a lesson:

Seeing that I was far too young and weedy to challenge him personally, I chose a friend to talk for me . . . (no, not Paul) . . . a housebrick! Being, as I've said, a holy lad it wasn't too difficult to levitate the brick up into the air . . . over the Bully's thick head . . . and cut (snip!) the invisible strings. After this bloody, awful incident, he didn't bully little girls, or anyone else for that matter, ever more. And here endeth the first lesson.

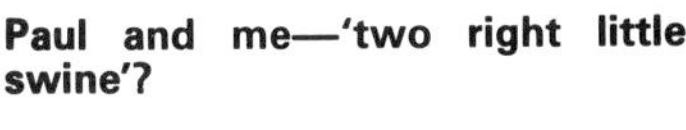

Paul and me—'two right little swine'?

Paul and his earliest fan, sitting in the back garden where we threw stones to speed up the growth of our next door neighbour's apples.

Memories of 'darling' brother swinging me head first above the back door of our 72 yard, keeping hold of my ankles . . . tight! 'Let go.' 'No.' 'Let go.' 'No.' 'Let go, I'm going to fall!' 'No.' 'Let go-o-o O-Oh,' as I pancaked, full facial onto the concrete below. Luckily nothing was broken, except bits of my front teeth, and in between sniffles, profuse apologies were offered from darlin' brother lest I might spill the beans (and teeth) to Dad.

Memories of walking through Speke, dying to go to the toilet but only half way home, when suddenly the unbelievable (but natural) started to happen. Unable to take cover and too shy to knock on a door, nature took its course and with the feeling of a thousand housewives' eyes on my every step, I walked slowly the rest of the way home with my (off) white knickers swinging proudly against my grey trousers. A job well done.

As it was not long after the war, most luxury commodities were scarce but the black market was still rife. No wonder then that there was a look of smugness on Dad's face when one evening he came home from work and produced two of the strangest objects we'd never seen.

'These, children,' said Dad, 'are bananas.'

'Bananas,' said we. 'What are bananas?'

'Bananas are delicacies,' said Dad.

'What are delicacies?' said we.

'Delicacies are bananas,' said Dad as he unzipped the pair and presented them to the pair. We dutifully took discerning mouthfuls.

'Yuck,' said I.

'Ugh,' said he. Dad nearly stuffed them up our . . . memories are made of this.

Me showing off the results of Paul dropping me onto the concrete of our back yard (and, incidentally, my birth mark—till now known only to a chosen few).

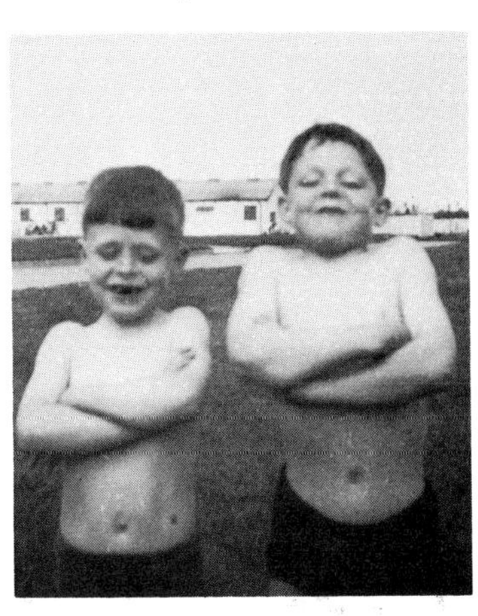

THE FAMILY SAYINGS

Then there were the family sayings. As a welcome . . . 'put it there if it weighs a . . . ton', to be announced on the full extent and a tight squeeze of the hand . . . 'When I was knee high to a grasshopper' . . . 'Never use two words when one will do' . . . If a joke failed, 'it'll go better second house' . . . 'Every mickle makes a muckle' (which means every penny counts) . . . 'As snug as a bug in a rug' . . . 'In goes your eye out' . . . 'It's no good having a dog and barking yourself' . . . And as the answer to an unanswerable or unknown question, 'because there are no hairs on a seagull's chest'. Plus the famous Dadism, 'moderation and toleration, sons', and not to forget his and Auntie Mill's immortal 'here we are, where are we?'

Needless to say being dads ourselves these days, Paul and I are still keeping up the family tradition with our own unfortunate children. Abbi, my youngest, still has trouble with some sayings however, and for ages it was 'put it there if it weighs a . . . tunnel', until the day I asked her to repeat it again 'for Uncle Paul' and she changed it to 'if it weighs a . . . TONGUE'.

Uncle Albert and Auntie Mill—'Here we are, where are we?'

NAPPY NIGHTMARE

Being the district midwife had its pros *and* cons. On the one hand there was a house supplied by the Council and the respect, plus the occasional gifts given to Mum from parents. She was looked up to, and indeed was, in fact, a sort of local doctor.

On one occasion a distraught mother arrived on our doorstep in Western Avenue with the present of a baby boy screaming its tiny head off. 'I've done something terrible nurse,' said the mother, not knowing which way to turn. On unwrapping the baby, Mum discovered a large nappy pin stuck through his small penis (Ow! I can almost feel it). 'I didn't know what to do for the best nurse.' Mum pulled the pin smartly out, dabbed 'the body' (as Abbi, my daughter, calls it) with TCP disinfectant, and returned the baby to its parent without a blink. Unable to thank Mum enough, exit one smiling patient plus soothed child. (At least he'll be able to water the flowers easily when he grows up.)

Mum as I remember her in her midwife's uniform.

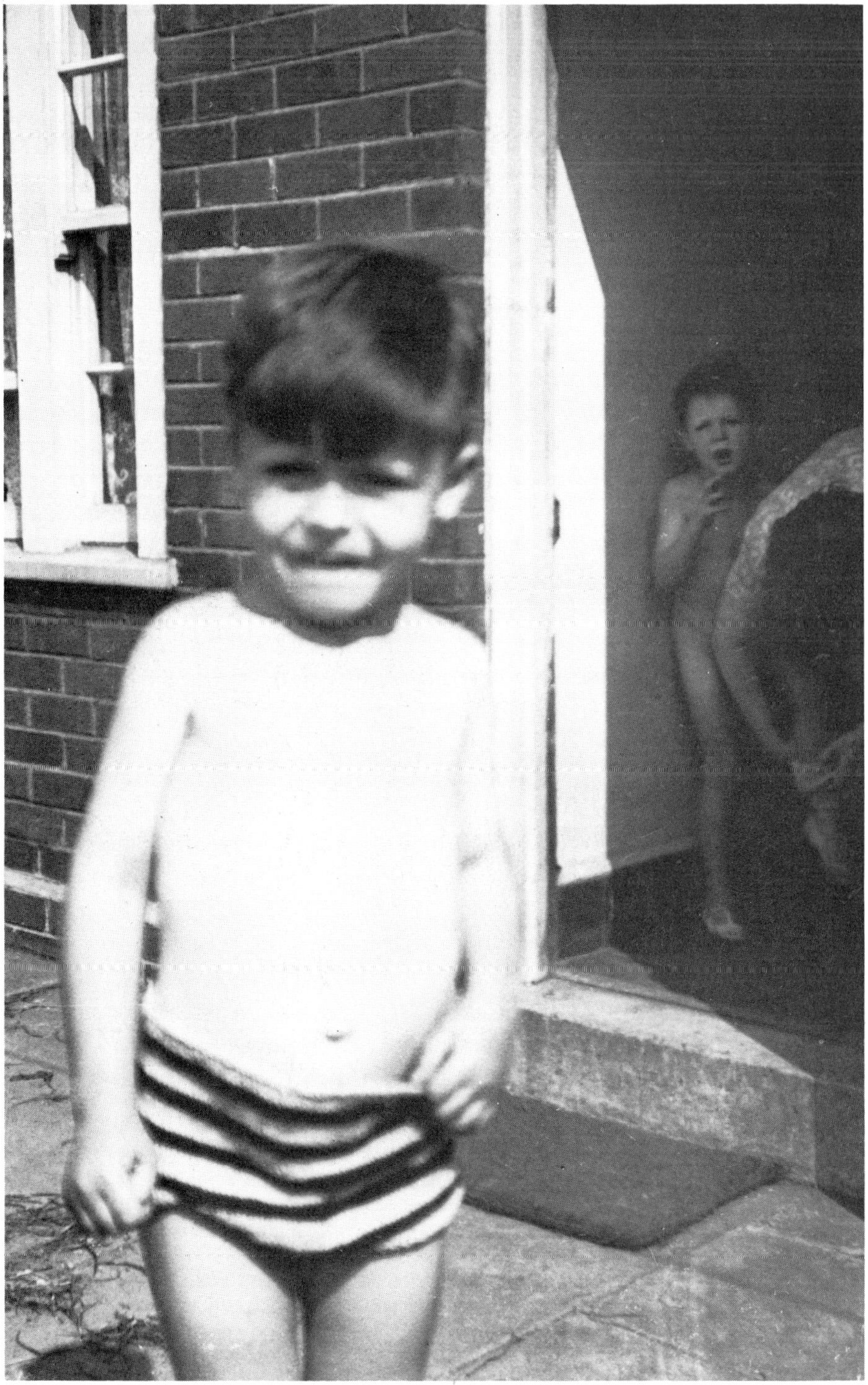

Me-posing in the garden of Western Avenue, with brother upstaging me in the background (even then).

12 ARDWICK ROAD

Most working-class people were, and still are, trying to achieve higher standards for their families, and our parents were no exception, but in our family it was mainly Mum who wanted us to 'better ourselves'. So when the opportunity arose to move to a newer estate on the outskirts of Speke it was quickly seized. When I say newer estate I should say extremely new estate; in fact Ardwick would have been better named Western, because when we moved there the roads weren't even finished and when it rained it resembled a muddy Wild West frontier outpost.

12 Ardwick Road, Catbush City Limits of Speke.

LIME PIT BLUES

Opposite our new house was an open area destined to become a playing field, but at first it served as a builder's working dump and in the corner of the 'field' was a lime pit which was immediately banned by Dad. Unfortunately when it rained, the lime pit turned itself into a rather attractive swimming pool-cum-shark-infested ocean for us two little lads, and the presence of a stout 'pirate' wooden plank across the water made it even more enticing. One day when Dad was safely at work, Mum was at the shops, and we were on school 'hols', Paul and I just happened to find ourselves in the vicinity of the lime pit. Big brother was leader of our expedition and bravely led me across the plank which suddenly wasn't as stout as it had seemed and began to wobble. Paul panicked, and just as he was about to plunge into the water grabbed onto the nearest thing—me. 'Splish! splosh!' went the fully clothed little chappies into the cold wet limeade, twice the height of themselves. On surfacing we screamed for help, but soon realised there was nobody about. When we tried to climb out we just burnt our hands and slipped back down the wet lime and under the water. Matters weren't helped by the fact that neither of us could swim! And Paul was beginning to panic. Just when things were looking serious, I caught sight of the stump of a tree protruding from the side of the pit which I grabbed onto and with my other hand managed to grab hold of Paul. For what seemed like an eternity we both treaded water like two drowning rats. Finally a passing workman heard our plaintive squeals and yanked us out.

Not surprisingly, when Dad came home and discovered two shivering wet rats who'd been swimming around the banned lime pool all day, he took offence, and we were duly, nudely bashed and sent up to bed with no supper (tails between our legs). Later that evening Dad was passing the bottom of the stairs when he overheard Paul whispering to me, between sniffles, 'And I'm going to dig a big hole (sniff) and fill it full of water (sniff) and then I'm going to take him (Dad) up in a plane, thousands of feet high (sniff), and push him in.' Shortly afterwards Mum crept upstairs with some supper telling us 'not to let Dad hear.' As we munched our illicit food in the dark, little did we realise that he had sent her.

DICK BARTON—SPECIAL AGENT

As we had to share the same bedroom in 12 Ardwick Road it was not uncommon for Paul and me to come to disagreement every now and then. So, to keep us out of mischief, Dad rather ingeniously rigged up a set of earphones from the downstairs wireless to our beds. As the earphones were made of hard bakelite stuff we used to put them under the pillows so that we could drop off listening to our favourite programmes . . . 'The time is quarter to seven, this is the BBC light programme, time now for *Dick Barton, Special Agent* with Snowey (White) and Jock (Anderson) . . .' A fifteen-minute crime busting, very 'British' detective serial, broadcast every evening until 7 o'clock when the *Devil's Gallop* signature tune posed the questions, 'Can Dick get to Von Luger's dastardly bomb in time? . . . Will Snowey set him free? . . . Does Dick dare defuse de . . . dan da ran dan . . . Listen to the next instalment of . . . *Dick Barton Special Agent*.' . . . and of course 'Music . . . Music . . . Music . . . into our dreams.

TICKLE TORTURE

Not that we used to fight *all* the time, just most of the time (like most healthy one-and-a-half-year differential lads do). But once Paul went just that little bit *too* far, and instead of the usual half-hour wrestling bout of strength he decided to speed things up with an elbow in the back (the trials and tribulations of being a 'younger brother'). For quite some time I staggered around the room gasping for air, not the most pleasant of sensations. Always a courteous lad, Paul quickly apologised, but this time apologies weren't enough. There and then I swore that when I grew up and was bigger than him I was going to KILL him, but until that fateful day arrived I had to be revenged. So that night I waited for dear brother to drop off to sleep and then set about my terrifying retribution. From my pillow I plucked the biggest feather available and slowly approached his bed. When I was about three feet away I suddenly froze. He was looking straight at me! After an eternity I realised that my brother sleeps with his eyes just slightly open. Undeterred, I moved closer until I was a few inches from his nose. Then the torture began . . . just a little tickle at first up the nostril, then the other nostril and then the ears and then eyelids . . . the lot. Some of the facial expressions he was forced to make nearly made me blow it and laugh out loud, but my desire for revenge was so great I forced myself on . . . and on. No matter which way he wriggled, I was there when he settled. The tickle torture was kept up all night and only when day broke did I finally relent and just like Dracula I sunk back into my coffin bed, feather in hand . . . deliriously happy.

TURNIP BOMBS

Kids' games in Speke were the usual ones for our age (around ten). There were conkers (horsechestnuts soaked in vinegar to make them harder so you could SMASH your opponent's conker to smitherines—someone even had a 'hundred and twoer') and ollies (Liverpool slang for marbles) to be played on pavements, in gutters, through fields etc., always with the statutory 'ollie bag' hand made by Mum. Then there were ciggy card and bus ticket collecting and train spotting, or I should say it *started off* as train spotting.

On barmy summer holiday mornings, 'our gang' would collect outside our 12 Ardwick home before setting off into the wide open prairie fields surrounding Speke.

When all were present, 'Prince' (our trusty, scruffy, half-breed sheep dog and Paul's favourite) would appear from nowhere, dead on time, to lead us past the bus depot on the outskirts of Speke into Bluebell Woods. This was aptly named because in the appropriate season the floor of the whole wood (now the Ford Factory in which Mum's stepbrother Jack works) would be covered in 'knee high to a grasshopper' bluebells.

After charging through the blanketed bluebell beauty we would continue over the fields past Chinese Farm to our destination—the main Liverpool to London railway-line and Tabletop Bridge.

The latter was a concrete air raid shelter built in the middle of the bridge during the war and used by dogs, tramps and passing drunks (by the smell of it). Here, train spotting would commence, but possibly due to the fact that the trains would thunder past at some 90 m.p.h., actual 'spotting' became difficult, so little inventive minds set about remedying the situation. It started off with farthings, and then half-pennies, and then pennies, then twigs, then stones, then branches and finally half bricks(!) placed on the railway lines to see what effect the 2.05 from Lime Street to London, Euston would have on them. The possibility of train derailment was secondary somehow. But the *pièce de résistance* was the turnips. Just by coincidence, and there's no such thing as that, the field next to the railway was full of turnips and after hungrily sampling the raw vegetables, 'turnip time' began. The gang would get into position, the 'player' with his row of turnips on the top of Table Bridge and the 'judges' further down the line. In those days the trains had steam engines with open cabins (for the driver to breathe) and the art was to wait for a train, take a deep breath, hold your turnip over the bridge and, as the train thundered underneath, drop it with split second timing through the swirling grey smoke fumes onto the train driver's head! Your eyes by this time were in no fit state to see if a direct hit had been scored, but the judges further down the line marked you a 'direct' or 'near' hit by the choice of expletives used by the train drivers as they disappeared into the distance . . . 'What the 'ell was *that*, Bert?' or 'You bleedin' little b . . . . .ds!' etc. etc. Luckily the enclosed cabs of today's expresses are protected from any present-day trained killers, but the thought of what we actually *did* for kicks those days still sends a shiver down the spine.

CAT BUSH CITY LIMITS

When you've been one of seven kids raised in the cobbled streets of Liverpool, you learn to appreciate Mother Earth when she comes your way. Dad was no exception. His love of gardening grew until it reached the heights of his becoming the Secretary of Speke Horticultural Society. So it was with great joy that he tended the small but productive front garden of 12 Ardwick Road. Roses, snapdragons and dahlias grew in profusion but the pride of Dad's garden was his lavender bush . . . long, low and laden with light blue flowers.

Everything was coming up roses until one day Dad stormed into the house. 'Those bloody toms have peed on my lavender.' We all trooped out of the house to witness one long luscious bush with patches of cat-soaked dying lavender. But what to do, Blue? The garden gates kept the dogs out all right, but the moggies (Liverpool terminology for our feline friends) simply jumped up, climbed along the top of the lavender bush and settled down for a little relief. Dad scratched his brain and all sorts of cat repellants were tried . . . newspapers, netting, cellophane and even little bells, but all to no avail, until one day he came in rubbing his hands and said, 'Right, that ought to do it,' with no further explanations. Happy that he was happy at last, we retired for the day and the family McCartney were all tucked up as snug as a bug in a rug until the middle of the night when, 'Miaow, MIAOW!' hit the silent night air. One tom cat was not at all happy with the seating arrangements in 12 Ardwick Road, and next morning we all found out why. Dad had strategically placed, throughout the lavender bush . . . inverted knitting needles! MiaOW!!

JOSEPH WILLIAMS

When the post-war Speke birth explosion reached the epidemic level of 1,500 infants, we were moved from Stockton Wood across Liverpool

Joseph Williams Primary, Gateacre.

to the relatively modern Joseph Williams Primary School in Gateacre (pronounced Getaca). This meant being put on to a bus each morning at 9 o'clock and shuttled off on a daring half-hour journey along the 'wet nelly route' as we called it (don't ask me why) to Belle Vale and 'Joey Williams'. (We Liverpudlians have a terrible habit of abbreviating everything!) But it also meant that we could have a ball on the top deck of the bus—singing songs, and changing the number of the bus as we rode merrily along. Normal school hours were nine to four, and we thought we had made it when we arrived at 9.30, but they were ahead of us by letting us out at 4.30.

Like Speke, Joseph Williams was on the edge of the countryside so headmaster Mr. (Pop) Gore organised nature rambles along peaceful farm lanes and beside tiny streams, where one day we even saw an otter* swimming under the water's surface! Deep water joy! They even had a rabbit hutch with *live* rabbits!

It was while we were at Joseph Williams that Paul went through his 'fat' period, the only time that anything outwardly affected him. And I remember the feeling of sheer one-upmanship whenever we had an argument, to counter with a lightning 'Fatty!' before running like hell to escape the ensuing wrath.

In contrast to chubby chops, I was skinny and good at Physical Education (P.E.). The highlight of Mr. Gore's headmastership was when he discovered that I could hang upside-down from the apparatus by my toes! God knows how I didn't fall and bash my brains out in front of the whole school but I didn't and was preparing to star in Mr. Spiller's school gymnastic film when I made a slight *faux pas*. For a laugh I changed round all the wellies (wellington boots) in the cloak-room and as everyone had forgotten to put their names inside them, nobody knew which ones were theirs. For this slight bending of the rules I was suspended from the film on the day of shooting, and although the teachers had to admit 'he was never the athletic type', Paul got the job (yar boo . . . skinny). Someone, somewhere, must still have the movie of this historic event.

* Now an endangered species in Britain.

THE LITTLE WHITE MOUSE

One of the highlights of our school term was when Kenny Carhill, a friend of Paul, brought his white mouse to school. Before the assembly bell he sneaked into class, took the pet carefully from his pocket and hid it in his desk with only his best friends allowed 'a look'. During lessons, to the class's suppressed delight, the little white mouse got fed up with nibbling the ruler in the dark and started poking his head out into the fresh air. Completely oblivious of the fun Mr. Wallard, the teacher, was reminiscing about 1066 and all that, when he decided to rest on Kenny's desk. Unable to say, 'Sir, you're going to squash my illegal white mouse under your big BUM,' Kenny and class watched in silent horror as the desk lid closed on the (not so) white mouse.

PLAYS AND PRETTY PLAYERS

After the excitement caused by Pop Gore's coloured magic lantern shows he decided to monopolise the hysteria and organise two plays for us toddlers. The first was *Autumn Leaves* (music by Schubert) and the second, over which Pop took personal control, was a pirate play which starred 'Fatty Fred Protheroe' and brother Paul (his first taste of true theatre). All they seemed to produce was a lot of 'yo ho ho' shouting and the CLACK of wooden swords, but what an excuse to get out of homework!

It was in Joseph Williams that I fell hopelessly in love with Margaret Lansbrough (or was it Gaynor Fairhurst?), a pretty young thing with fair hair (or fur hur as I still say, even with my mid-Mersey accent). Of course I didn't tell *her*. I just used to wait for the barn dancing in the main hall so that we could touch innocent pink palms together in the 'Gay Gordons' Barn Dance. With my short-sleeved, open-necked white shirt, fawn corduroy shorts, knee-length grey socks, which kept falling down, and white, or usually 'off white' pumps, I must have cut a dashing figure.

Me mates, Ian on the right, Geoff on the left, and me (hopelessly in love with Margaret Lansborough at the time) outside the entrance to Joey Williams. Cut quite a dashing figure didn't I?

On a recent 'drive down memory lane' I discovered with horror that our old country school is now in the middle of a concrete 'Clockwork Orange' complex. The countryside, like the otter, is rapidly becoming extinct.

NEWTON'S LAW OF . . . RELATIVELY SPEAKING

On summer days, for some 'exercise,' Dad, Paul and I would cycle from Speke past Joseph Williams and across the peaceful countryside to Auntie Jin's 147 Dinahs Lane, Huyton home. One such afternoon, after receiving our customary thirst-quenching refreshments, Paul and I were sniffing round the back yard of Jin's large semi-detached house and discovered a big can of petrol. Our fresh thirst for knowledge posed the interesting scientific question: Would it or wouldn't it burn up a wall?

'Of course it will.'

'Bet you it won't.'

'How much?'

'Bag of ollies.'

'You're on.'

One tin of Uncle Harry's best petrol was unscrewed and the stupid one that made the bet laid a trail along the back yard up the wall of the garage and onto the tarpaulin roof. Once on the roof I made sure that

I'd collect my winnings by staying there to verify the results of the experiment.

'OK, let's prove it,' said the sceptical scientist below, setting fire to the gasoline.

'Whoosh!' went the trail.

'See!' I shouted, happy for scientific verification (and a bag of marbles), 'What a gas!' but not too happy with the now fiercely burning garage roof which blocked my exit to the ground.

Just then, who should be pushing his blue serge bike along Dinahs Lane but the Local Constabulary. Calling on my relative's door he enquired, 'Excuse me, madam, but is that your son setting fire to himself on your garage?'

Our scientific enquiry was soon settled by Newton's Law of relatively speaking . . . a hand falling onto a bottom . . . repeatedly!

FROGS LEGS AND CHINESE FARM

When Dad saw us take an interest in nature study at Joseph Williams, he was so keen to foster it that he asked brother-in-law Bill Mohin for one of his empty beer barrels, and somehow got the heavy wooden container from the Eagle Hotel near the city docks back to the rear garden of our 12 Ardwick home. There he dug a large hole in the ground, lowered the barrel down and filled it full of water, thus providing a home-made pond.

Paul and I searched the surrounding fields and ponds for 'water life' and returned with plankton, weeds, water lilies and our prize joy—masses of frog spawn with hundreds of tiny black eggs. As usual with children, we took intense interest in our 'pond' at first, and every morning and evening would check to see if any tadpoles had hatched out of their gelatinous home. After a while our interest waned, but when someone in school was boasting about how many frogs he now owned, we dashed back to our pond to find that our tadpoles had not only hatched out but had grown legs and 'hopped off'! We were hopping mad and decided to take revenge.

That weekend we assembled our gang, and trusty Prince led the charge through Bluebell Woods down to Bluebell Stream. Here we caught the biggest Bluebell frogs we could find and hung them by the legs on the farmer's barbed wire fence (ugh!) to dry.

'That'll teach 'em,' we said and headed for Chinese Farm. We had forgotten one thing . . . the Great Bull-frog in the sky.

When we reached Chinese Farm, Prince was sent ahead to check that the orchard was clear, and when no barking took place, we swarmed up the apple trees and proceeded to fill our pockets with succulent Cox's Orange Pippins. I don't know why we called it 'Chinese' Farm, but suddenly two of the most unoriental looking farm labourers appeared out of the East. Like ripe fruit we dropped from the trees and pelted for the orchard gate, whilst Prince put up a very impressive smoke screen of barks. I cleared the gate like a gazelle and was half way into freedom when I heard a familiar squeal. The huge farm lads had taken the undignified method of ploughing *through* the thick hedge and had caught brother Paul at the top of the gate. I don't know whether it was because of his chubbiness or the heavy apples, but there he was like a suckling pig with one arm being twisted behind his back.

'Come back yous lot,' shouted the twister.

I looked round and noticed that the gang, including 'trusty Prince' had disappeared in the general direction of Speke.

'Come back or oil brake 'is arm!' Twist . . . 'Squeal!'

Being one of nature's gentlemen I agreed to be caught—'But only if you let him go.'

They agreed and the two McCartneys were 'frog marched' through the orchard (heavenly croak croak) and brought before the even less Chinese-looking farmer with our bulging pocketed stolen wares.

'There's been too much of this goin' on, oil have to teach you two a lesson,' threatened the rustic mandarin giant. 'Throw them in the black 'ole, oil get the law this time.'

With that we were slung into a potato-smelling outhouse and plunged into darkness by the banging and bolting of a large wooden door.

After what seemed like a lifetime, two voices were heard approaching our dark dungeon. One was Dad's! The gang must have told him what had happened.

'And you were just about to call the POLICE, Mr. Hewson?'

'Well there's been too much of this goin' on and these two was part of a big gang with a vicious dog.'

'And you say they stole your apples, Mr. Hewson?'

'Caught them red 'anded, pockets bulging with the things. Mind you, one of them did come back for the other.'

(My heart swelled with pride.)

'But you're thinking of calling the POLICE?'

(My heart skipped a beat.)

'Well, you say that these two are your boys?' asked the farmer.

'That's right, Mr. Hewson.'

'And you say that they'll never do it again?'

'I promise, Mr. Hewson.'

'Well, just this once moind . . . Open the door Jack.'

The massive door creaked open to disclose two sad sacks of humanity shielding their eyes to the bright sunlight. 'I'm not calling the police this time because your Dad 'ere says you won't never come pinching my apples again.'

'Do you promise?' asked Dad.

'We promise,' we unisoned.

'Say you're sorry to Mr. Hewson.'

'We're sorry, Mr. Hewson.'

'Just moind you never do it again, that's all.'

Dad had brought our two bikes with him, and as we mounted up he said, 'Say goodbye to Mr. Hewson.'

'Goodbye Mr. Hewson.'

'And moind you tell your gang friends not to come round 'ere 'an all.'

'Yes, Mr. Hewson.'

As we turned the lane out of the farm Dad turned to us and whispered, 'Silly old Sod.'

'SKIDADLE'

One lovely summer day in 1953 (weren't they all lovely when you were a kid?) Mum asked Paul and me, with a twinkle in the proverbial eye,

Paul on his 3-speed, drop-head Raleigh sports bike in front of 12 Ardwick.

to 'skidadle' for a couple of hours. Sensing something was afoot we readily agreed. So, jumping astride our drop-head, 3-speed Raleigh sports bikes, we headed for the rhododendron woods near Speke shore. Wondering how we could stretch out TWO whole hours until the coming surprise, we soon got fed up with swinging through the rhododendron bushes with Tarzan and headed for the Oggie (Oglett) shore cliffs. We walked along the top of the cliffs with our bikes, entirely disregarding the magnificent view over the River Mersey to the Wirral and Welsh Wales, preferring instead to look down into the grass for any lost money. The top of the cliffs was the spot where loving couples met and did all that 'rolling round' on the ground. (Never could see the sense in it meself, but at least it *did* buy the sweets.) Not much money later (it had been raining) we joined a gang of Garston lads playing 'chicken' on their bikes. All one had to do was ride one's bike down the sheer cliff face and stay on. Evel Knievel would have been proud of the Evil McCartney brothers as they risked death numerous times. It was either that or get beaten up by the Garston 'they-played-tick-with-hatchets' gang. Luckily one of the thugs fell off first and was carried home legless. Although the couple of hours weren't up, we could contain ourselves no longer and rode home at break-neck speed. There in the lounge, was our first black and white television, with grinning parents to boot. We didn't, however, as we were so overcome with happiness. Instead we watched the Coronation of Queen Elizabeth II with all the neighbours (because not only was it *our* first telly, it was the first one in the road).

BALL BACK BUTT

One day Paul and I were playing outside No. 12 with a ball I'd just 'found' in the next road, when a little lad came up to me and demanded,

'Ay yous, that's our ball.'

In those days you seldom ventured out of your own road or 'territory' and if you did it was at your own risk. So it was with great interest that I looked down on the little man. For one, he wasn't from our road, for two he was alone, and for three he was half my size.

'You what?'

'You 'eard, yous have got our ball.'

'So?'

'Well, give us it back.'

'No,' said I, holding it tantalizingly above his head.

'Give us it back!'

'No,' I taunted.

'Give us it back, or I'll butt you.' (Butt not being short for butty, a Liverpool sandwich, but for the hitting of one forehead by another.)

'Try it,' said I.

With that, in one of the quickest moves I'd never seen, the half pint grabbed the lapels of my jacket, pulled himself up and landed his head 'Thud' right between my eyes. Momentarily everything went pitch black, until slowly, normal vision returned, only to find that the ball and half pint had completely disappeared. All that was left, was one highly amused brother rolling round the floor with laughter.

THE ELEVEN PLUS!

In the educational system of the 1950s a lot of emphasis was placed on the eleven plus, the examination which divided eleven-year-old children from brothers and sisters into either Grammar (High) Schools (with the possibility of graduating to higher education, universities and so on), or the definitely more infra dig Secondary Modern (Lower) Schools (with the probability of specialising in woodwork, cooking, metalwork, etc. As it happens, I now think that I, and perhaps Paul, would have been far better suited to the latter education system as we were both stupid—sorry more artistically inclined—but at that time the eleven plus was definitely the major hurdle to be faced and you only had one jump at the fence.

Not surprisingly, Paul, being a good applier, sailed through the course. In fact he even reached the second recall of the Margaret Bryce Smith Annual Scholarship. This was a trustee-set-up exam on the 'tough' side, with a small £5 gratuity for the winner. Then he settled into the Liverpool Institute High School, City Centre. Michael on the other hand was a different kettle of fish, as his early skool reports confirm . . .

Art/~~Woodwork~~	85	80	Excellent. He has worked very well
German/~~Spanish~~	59		Fair. He must learn to think and not make silly guesses

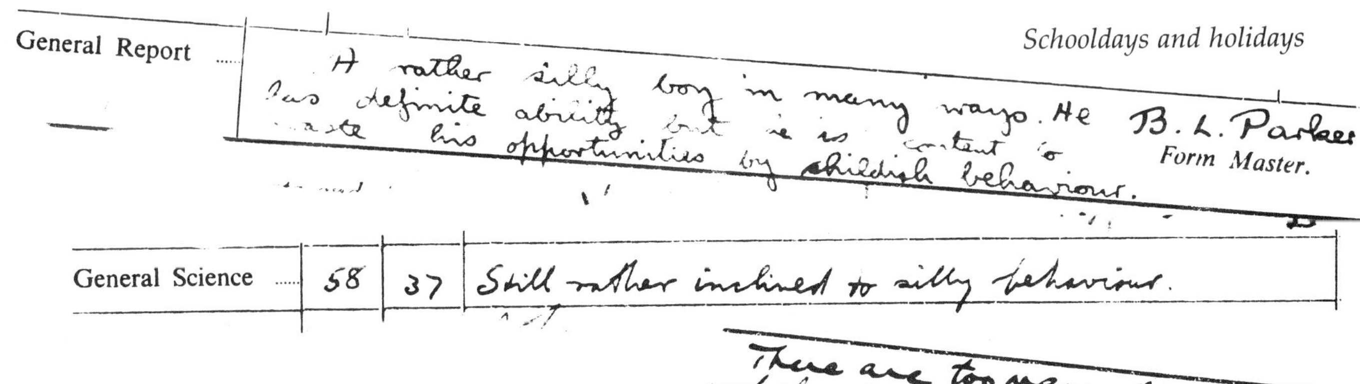

General Report — A rather silly boy in many ways. He has definite ability but he is content to waste his opportunities by childish behaviour. — B. L. Parker, Form Master.

General Science | 58 | 37 | Still rather inclined to silly behaviour.

Could be good but is often very inattentive & silly.

There are too many signs of silly behaviour for this to be a satisfactory report. J. R. Edwards. Beware! — Headmaster.

School report. 'Too many signs of silly behaviour . . .'

Although nothing was said out loud I had the distinct feeling that we all thought that I was a non starter in the coming race. So imagine my feelings when the results were finally announced and I came home to tell the family the fateful news. Mum was cooking in the kitchen when I delivered the blow:

'Mum.'

'Yes, love.'

'I've passed; I'm going to the Institute too.'

Time froze for a second. Suddenly she grabbed me up in her arms, hugged me tightly and wept with tears of joy. Her little lad had passed the post.

No tie (a rebel even then!). The day I passed the eleven plus.

20 FORTHLIN ROAD

As I've explained, Mum was mainly responsible for our moves to 'better positions'. It was a bit of a pain for us as we'd just make friends and then . . . whoosh(!) off again. Her final move was to the relatively

'Lower' school (April 1956): Me in the front row with bezy mate Howell Moore on the right; Paul in the back row and George Harrison in second-to-back row. The Baz in the centre, plus 'Chopper', 'Squinty' and gym-towel-flicker teachers. With Ivy, (the lad who introduced Paul to John) Vaughan, Peter 'newscaster' Sissons, and can I spot Neil 'roadie' Aspinall?

posh area of 20 Forthlin Road, Allerton, where she continued her health visiting vocation, taking on an extra job in a clinic not far from Ringo's Admiral Grove home.

It was exactly the same house . . . only different. The differences being a 'through' door from the lounge to the dining room (which meant in effect you could run 'round the house'), a back garden, which overlooked Mather Avenue Police College Training Field instead of other houses, but, best of all, the luxury of an INSIDE toilet. (No more lowering of warm pink bummies from overcoat clad bodies onto ice-cold winter bog seats!)

It was here, at 20 Forthlin, that Mum developed chest trouble (for which she used to take bisodol to ease the pain) and soon after died of breast cancer in Northern Hospital, Liverpool, on the Halloween eve of October 31st 1956—All Saints Day (which in the Catholic religion means that all her sins were washed away and her soul went straight to heaven, which it did).

At least she saw both her boys attend 'Big School' for a year.

The Liverpool Institute High School for Boys was founded in 1825 after the Napoleonic Wars, and opened on 15th September 1837, Queen Victoria's coronation year.

Charles Dickens lectured from its main hall in 1844, just after completing his *Pickwick Papers* . . . no less.

The Art College was part of the Institute until 1890, when the doors linking the two establishments were bricked up.

Great heights of scholastic achievements were reached by the eminent jurists Lord Mersey and Sir Charles Lumb, the famous Physician Sir MacAlister of Tarbert, and chased Chemist Sir Henry Enfield to name but two.

With such an eminence of old Liobian* boys in the professions, commerce and industry, you were made overpoweringly aware of the 'tradition' of one of *the* centres of Liverpool Education. 'The Inny', as we lovingly called it, was a fee-paying establishment until

* Liverpool Institute Old Boys Association.

1944 (they must have heard about my birth) when the local authority changed it to a Grammar (eleven plus entrance examination) School.

A 'Public School Type' attitude prevailed to churn out the more reliable sorts of chap, until the seeds that our working class fathers had sown started to grow and we were introduced into the very concrete of the pillars of the 'institution'.

'Thou shalt not build they dwelling on sand, lest thy dwelling fallest down' Isaiah, Chapter V, platform nine.

Very much in the 'old school' tradition, our Churchillian Headmaster, Mr. 'The Baz' Edwards, seemed reluctant to accept the lower standards which our generation of new wave, lower class yobos threatened. In retrospect who can blame him? After all, we were the beginning of the end.

But we were blissfully unaware of any of these historical, sociological or political problems. We had passed the eleven plus and *we* were going to a GRAMMAR School . . . 'The Liverpool Institute!' (Skool Motto—Non Nobis Solum Sed Toti Mundo Nati—Not just for playing solo but for truant too).

What a 'to do' . . . into town with our dutiful parents, off the bus, into an outfitter's, appointed to the Innys to buy the compulsory blazer, cap, tie, shorts and socks. It was either Ravenscroft and Willis 'robe makers and heraldic shield specialists', or Watson Prickard *official* agents for Old Boys' ties, scarves, hose etc. ('Please call to see our new model railway'). Then, out of the infitters onto the bus and home to be fully attired in 'the uniform'.

With statutory fresh leather-smelling satchel, containing ruler, rubber, pencil bag, compass, slide rule etc., faces scrubbed spotless, hair combed immaculate conception, shoes highly black leather polished, and new satchel placed firmly on both shoulders . . . off we went back to town, up the Greek facade, stone-stepped entrance for the last time (from now on . . . 'side entrances and gates only', unless you were in the 6th Form (or late!)), into the last bastion of a bygone era for the next seven years . . . the Inny!

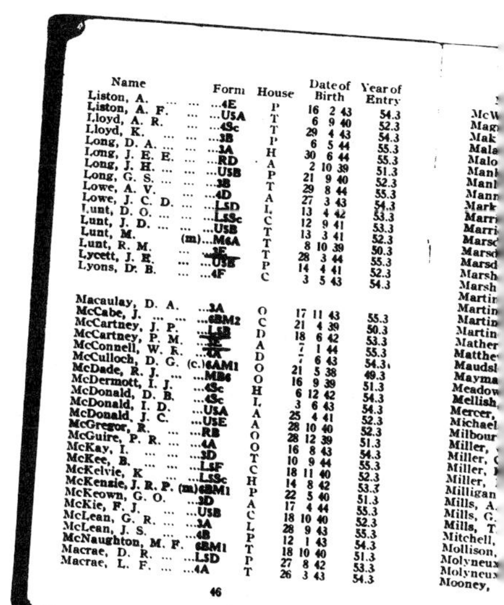

Name	Form	House	Date of Birth	Year of Entry
Liston, A.	...4E	P	16 2 43	54.3
Liston, A. F. ...	...USA	T	6 9 40	52.3
Lloyd, A. R. ...	...4Sc	T	29 4 43	54.3
Lloyd, K.	...3B	P	6 5 44	55.3
Long, D. A.	...3A	H	30 6 44	55.3
Long, J. E. E. ...	...RD	A	2 10 39	51.3
Long, J. H.	...USB	P	21 9 40	52.3
Long, G. S.	...3B	T	29 8 44	55.3
Lowe, A. V. ...	...4D	A	27 3 43	54.3
Lowe, J. C. D. ...	...LSD	L	13 4 42	53.3
Lunt, D. O.	...LSSc	C	12 9 41	53.3
Lunt, J. D.	...USB	T	13 3 41	52.3
Lunt, M. (m)	...M6A	T	8 10 39	50.3
Lunt, R. M. ...	...3E	T	28 3 44	55.3
Lycett, J. E. ...	...USB	P	14 4 41	52.3
Lyons, D. B. ...	...4F	C	3 5 43	54.3
Macaulay, D. A.	...3A	O	17 11 43	55.3
McCabe, J.	...6BM2	C	21 4 39	50.3
McCartney, J. P.	...LSB	D	18 6 42	53.3
McCartney, P. M.	...3E	A	7 1 44	55.3
McConnell, W. R.	...4A	D	7 6 43	54.3
McCulloch, D. G. (c.)	6AM1	O	21 5 38	49.3
McDade, R. J. ...	...MB6	O	16 9 39	51.3
McDermott, I. J.	...4Sc	H	6 12 42	54.3
McDonald, D. B.	...4Sc	L	3 6 43	54.3
McDonald, I. D.	...USA	A	25 4 41	52.3
McDonald, J. C.	...USE	A	28 10 40	52.3
McGregor, R. ...	...RB	O	28 12 39	51.3
McGuire, P. R. ...	...4A	O	16 8 43	54.3
McKay, I.	...3D	T	10 9 44	55.3
McKee, B.	...LSF	C	18 11 40	52.3
McKelvie, K ...	...LSSc	H	14 8 42	53.3
McKenzie, J. R. P. (m)	6BM1	P	22 5 40	51.3
McKeown, G. O.	...3D	A	17 4 44	55.3
McKie, F. J. ...	...USB	C	18 10 40	52.3
McLean, G. R. ...	...3A	L	28 9 43	55.3
McLean, J. S. ...	...4B	P	12 1 43	54.3
McNaughton, M. F.	6BM1	T	18 10 40	51.3
Macrae, D. R. ...	...LSD	P	27 8 42	53.3
Macrae, L. F. ...	...4A	T	26 3 43	54.3

46

Liverpool Institute Book of Criminals. Lunt is now a caravan salesman with more money than all of us put together! . . . A & B forms were good, but E (that's me) were pretty dumb!

Paul in Inny uniform, during his chubby period.

The seven year itch

A typical beginning of term consisted of being wakened by parents . . . pulling blankets over heads and going back to sleep . . . staggering out of bed and dressing in the freezing cold, as we couldn't afford electric fires . . . downing breakfaster than most, as inevitably we were late . . . belting to catch the 86 bus . . . sprinting into school just in time for the bell . . . slowing down into prayers and opening your goldfish mouths, miming to the hymns you hadn't learnt . . . walking back to your form, arm in arm with your best mate . . . roll call . . . 'Lunt?'—'Present Sir', 'Makin?' —'Present Sir', 'McCartney?'—'Here Sir' (pause), 'Morgan?'—'Present Sir', 'Moore?'— 'Here Sir' (longer pause as he thinks, 'So *they're* the two!') 'Poole?'— 'Present Sir', etc . . . becoming a compulsory member of the Sports and Arts Club and writing out your term timetable . . . off to Geography, Latin, German, Maths or Art classes . . . short break for milk and straws . . . more lessons . . . bell for dinner . . . bell for end of dinner-hour . . . line up in the yard . . . march to your classes 'in orderly fashion' . . . next lot of lessons till four o'clock and, *magic*, the end-of-day-blues-bell . . . homework in satchel next to half finished sweets . . . cap-holding dash to bus stop . . . pushing onto the 86 Garston Bus . . . cap off . . . do homework on top of bus, nod off or chat up fellow school girl . . . off bus at Forthlin Road (or Garston if you fell asleep) . . . key in door of No. 20 to meet either the smell of Mum's yummy teas (for a year) or, later, a cold dark house whose fire had to be emptied, ash bucket dumped in the bin fire set and lit . . . huddle till you got warm . . . watch 'children's hour' on the black and white telly or mime to Elvis Everley 78s . . . wash hands—have tea . . . complete unfinished homework . . . supper . . . brush teeth, comb hair, pyjamas on, kiss parents or 'Night night Dad'—'God bless sons' . . . snuggle down in beds and go to sleep with earphones under pillows.

The Inny taken from John Lennon's art college, showing the upper and lower yards.

The next day the whole procedure over again.

No one could forget the sound, when the 'break' bell rang, of over a thousand boys racing along wooden corridors, down stone staircases and OUT into the yards. There were two play yards: 'the lower yard' which contained the fives courts (a glorious, old-fashioned game of bashing a small leather ball against a brick wall with heavy, smelly, leather gloves), drinking fountain, toilets, and acres of concrete expanse, *but* which was overlooked by the Baz's study . . . and 'the upper yard', which contained Paul and the older boys, the notorious 'smokers corner' (to which my brother later graduated) and which was overlooked by the adjoining Art College (and Lennon). Both yards were surrounded by wrought iron railings and the whole school was overshadowed by the unfinished end of Liverpool Cathedral—the biggest in Britain.

When it rained, which in Liverpool it does quite a lot, we were allowed into the assembly hall where we quickly learned to play 'shove 'apenny' (shuv ½d) on the highly polished-by-little-boys'-bums benches. This game consisted of shoving a penny (your man) to strike a half penny (the ball) into your opponents goal (two books)—all with your ruler . . . Oh the gay abandon of it all!

In the upper yard, at the end of the long brick building, is smoker's corner—blind to all but my eagle camera eye. Taken in my Lowry period.

But woe betide you if you were late in the morning; they locked the gates. You then had to walk up the front entrance steps and try to sneak through the office to your class or the bogs—anywhere to hide until prayers had finished. And if you were caught . . . look out! They made you go downstairs to the dining hall with the 'minority religions'. Then, when prayers were coming to an end, you were shepherded upstairs into the assembly hall, pulling the sheep's clothing over the headmaster's eyes by trying to look Catholic, Jewish, Buddhist . . . anything! One of my class mates, Harding (the Nazi doodler), who had been late for five consecutive mornings, tried this ploy. He got away with it for four days but on the fifth the Baz demanded in front of the whole school, 'You boy, are you a Jew or a late?' 'A late sir,' replied the rich Devon accent. 'See me after prayers.'

You may have guessed by now that the main person to keep away from was the Baz, and the ultimate detergent was for our form masters to wash their hands of us and take us to the Baz's study. If the headmaster was otherwise engaged you had to stand there until he came out and then you had to con your way out of a caning.

If you couldn't bluff your way out of it, or if the master had gone in to see the head before you, the 'inevitable' consisted of bending over the Baz's desk and getting from one to six 'of the best' whacks (more, or less strokes, depending upon the severity of the offence) with long canes of various thicknesses, the thin one being the real killer.

The cute ones amongst us used to put exercise books down our underpants but if the Baz caught you he'd make you take them out and you'd get a double dose.

Trying hard not to cry like a cissy, you'd then walk out of his study, slowly down the rear stairs, stroll casually across the yard into the outside toilets, and SCREAM bloody murder down the bogs. If it was a *really* bad 'un, you'd go into the inside wash room and examine the stinging wheels in the mirror for blood. The Baz never drew any from me or Paul . . . but by god . . . did he hurt!

You may have guessed by this last sentence that brother wasn't exactly a paragon of virtue. In fact when I arrived at the Inny Paul had established quite a reputation with the masters as being 'a bit of a lad' and when they heard that another McCartney was coming, they were on the alert. I didn't let them (or him) down, falling right into the 'go on then I dare you!' syndrome from my fellow classmates. Silly bugger that I was, I dared . . . and got caught . . . and got bashed, over and over again, for amongst other things, not wearing my cap (regularly) . . . going to the out-of-bounds chippy . . . throwing 'water bombs' (brown paper bags filled with fountain water) over the upper yard wall onto kids, prefects, or masters! I once got half a prefect (the ones with minigowns and green flashes). Although nobody would admit to having thrown it, Peter Sissons (one of our nation's television news readers) guessed it was me right away, so, 'off to study' again. Another favourite adventure was to stick milk bottle tops into the light sockets, replace the bulbs and when the master came into the classroom, switch the lights on . . . snap, crackle, BOOM! The whole school's lights would fuse!

Oh yes, I nearly forgot, one belting that was actually worth it was for catching a cheeky Blackburn House schoolgirl in the winter and stuffing ice cold white snow down the front of her nice warm white blouse.

Apart from the Baz's cane there were other disciplinary measures which included raps across the knuckles with the master's ruler, chalk and wooden blackboard dusters thrown at you with uncanny accuracy. And one big, healthy Latin monster-master (they were always the healthy ones) with slicked back, Brylcreamed hair and pencil thin moustache (like a failed Hollywood movie star) would get us eleven year olds to bend over and touch our toes in front of the class, then he would raise his size fifteen pump high above his head and with the full weight of his grown-up, healthy body he'd run across the room, releasing the arm trigger and (whoosh!) knock us kids (cheeky sods agreed . . . but still only kids) quite a few feet across the classroom floor. I hope one of his own children gives him this to read in his old folks home.

Another more amusing teacher nicknamed 'Chopper' used to bore his knuckle, the one with the wart on, into the side of your cranium whilst telling you off, and once when I objected to my best mate Howell Moore being harassed (Howell was cowering on the floor in

mock fear at the time), 'Chopper' reciprocated, 'Oh you don't think it's right eh McCartney?' 'No, sir.' 'Well come down here lad.' I was up in the Science benches and answered, 'No thanks you'll hit me.' 'No I won't lad, come down here.' 'No sir, you'll hit me,' said I, edging down. 'No I won't lad come *here*.' 'No sir, you'll hit me sir,' getting the nearest I dared. 'No. I won't lad.' CRACK! He caught me with the full force of his open hand and knocked me unconscious. He'd gone too far this time and he, plus the whole class, knew it. When I came round I threatened to 'Get me Dad on you' and ran from the school with my face burning. When I told Dad he simply said, 'Don't be silly son, the masters are always right,' and went back to his crossword.

Paul's taking the picture by pulling a length of cotton attached to the family box camera on a chair in Forthlin's back garden. (Nearly every time he pulled it the camera'd fall off!) Ted & Jean (Auntie Edie's daughter) stayed with us for a while after Mum died. And there's 'Scampi Dogs' which I 'lost' one day at the shops, to everyone's great concern.

Finally there was the healthy gym master whose job it was to make us even healthier, and the climax of his afternoon was to order us into the cold shower after our gym joggings. If you preferred not to freeze to death, his particular cheap thrill was to flick you on your bare bum with a wet towel (no wonder we were such rebels with all those lunies around!).

A CAREER IN CRIME?—THE INSIDE STORY

For some reason he had it in for me, so to get my own back on Mr. Healthy I used to wait until he was taking another class. Whilst they were gyrating in the gym I would sneak into the changing rooms and pinch money from their hanging clothes. The sheer criminal thrill of patting blazer and trousers to see which ones jingled, taking out the money (sometimes a pound note(!) came with the change) then exit from the gym, thinking 'let the b . . . . . flick that one out'.

With the 'loot', I would sneak down to Ma Gee's tuck shop where the whole shop became my Aladdin's cave. Crisps with blue salt packets, bubbly gum, gob stoppers (and your mouth was so small in those days it really *did* stop your gob) yellow tongue-colouring sherbet, penny liquorice to dip in the sherbet, sticky lice (a sort of twig thing you chewed), Uncle Joe's mint balls, sweet cigarettes with cards of famous footballers and the favourite drink of the time . . . Black Brew. The name sounded good enough but the taste . . . heaven. I'm sure the manufacturers spiced it with something illegal because it certainly had a kick.

I think the Baz must have had the concession on Ma Gees because, instead of being allowed out to another two local sweet shops, we had to queue outside the matronly Ma's.

My career in crime escalated from gym pockets to pinching sweets from the two out-of-bound shops, and then on into town where the *pièce de résistance* was thieving books from Charles Wilson's bookstall. Harding (the nasty doodler) started that one, but I was soon behind him (and the bookstalls) with my open satchel on the floor, reading a book with my right hand whilst knocking other books off into the satchel with my left. (So that's why they call it 'knocking off'.)

In the middle of all this childish skulduggery my ego received a sudden shock. Best mate Howell was 'borrowing' some very cheap jewellery for his Mam in Chester Woolworths when he was caught . . ! Just like that. We'd just been to a scout jamboree, when the next thing I knew, a large hand attached to a giant uniformed policeman was taking my Bezzy Mate away to the Cop Shop. (With me watching from a *safe* distance.) He was duly charged, judged and fined at Chester Crown Court. 'There for the Grace of God go I,' thought young Michael and ever since that day I haven't had the slightest desire to touch anything that isn't mine, even when there's no chance of getting caught.

In the end, even the daring had to stop. I suppose it was a sign of sixteen year old maturity but one day when someone said, 'Go on you do it Maca,' (a nickname which both Paul and I shared) I suddenly twigged. 'No. This time *you* do it, squire,' and never looked back. It's not the things you do in this world, it's the things you leave out.

All through my Grammar School career I stayed in the lower echelons of the system while Paul managed by animal cunning, superior intellectual application and a lot of nouse, to stay in the higher half of the school. Not that he cheated (he just never got caught) but he was always good at applying situations and people (and still is).

Michael on the other hand would have been better off going to a school where he could have applied his 'more artistic' nature and not mangled through a system to which his every nerve end was alien.

As can easily be seen from my school report card the only subject in which I excelled at school was art, and the climax of an otherwise undistinguished school career was to receive a 'first' in that subject. So it was with great pride and joy that I took Dad to see my first prize on the School Hobbies Open Day. A Liverpool Institute Hobbies Day was quite a spectacular affair with the whole building transformed into a Bacchanalian orgy of scholastic achievement by both the masters and the boys. After Dad had seen my number one, Paul and I showed him round the rest of the exhibits but I kept nipping back to the art room to bask in my own glory and overhear what people thought of my painting. The last time I excused myself from Dad, the art room was empty except for two very Liverpool ladies. I was going through my surrealist period at the time so the painting consisted of a self-portrait profile, against a red white and blue sky, a pair of army boots on a carpet and, naturally, one solitary Magrittian index finger sticking through the carpet. As the picture had been given the highest award in the room, the ladies stopped to admire. No they didn't say 'Whar is it?' . . . They were obviously far too intelligent for that. 'It's very good', . . . 'But what is it?', said one, 'It's obvious . . . it's a pair of boots and an 'ead,' said the other.

'But what's the finger doing?'

'That's obvious an' all.'

'Well?'

'Er? . . . It's tryin' to pinch the boots.'

George Handsome and John 'Ted' Lennon

When we lived in 12 Ardwick I vaguely remember a lad who lived in Upton Green, a couple of roads away from us.

George in *his* school uniform.

The next time I saw the same lad was in and around the 'Inny', but as he was a year ahead of me, he was immediately classified as one of the 'big lads' and therefore unapproachable.

He was obviously one of those working class rebel chaps and towards the end of our school days together he got more and more outrageous. The compulsory school uniform was outvoted by his extrovert dress sense and his hair was the longest anyone could possibly get away with in the Inny, all 'Tony Curtis'd back', with a school cap perched on the top rear like a rabbi's skull cap.

When his guitar playing affinity with Paul was established in end of term skewl koncerts, he'd visit our new Forthlin home and we slowly became friendly.

His dress by this time was even more interesting . . . full length, skin-tight drainees down to his bright fluorescent socks, even brighter lime (Upton) green waistcoat under his blazer which he would flash at me in the school corridors (followed by a wink). He had the first blue suede*, winkle picker shoes which together with incessant chewing of gum all became his trade marks.

My Sweet Lord knows who he was, but his Mum must have loved him.

OLE FOUR EYES

Around the same 'Elvis' era, in the same year that Mum died, I used to see John 'Ted' Lennon (drainees, sidees, suedees, the lot) walking to and from the art college past our school with other teds or a blonde girl. When Paul had been introduced to this other, older, rebel by Ivan (Ivy) Vaughan we too became nodding acquaintances . . . when he had his glasses on that is. Both he and his girlfriend Cyn were as blind as bats without them and it was highly amusing to shout 'Hello' to one or the other, or both of them in Mount Street and watch them try to focus on pillar boxes, lamp posts, passing policemen . . . anything, in order to return the greeting. In the end they both used to shout 'Hello' back, with a royal wave of the hand in your general direction.

Before Cyn, John went out with Thelma Pickles (who later married Roger (colleague) McGough) and because he was so paranoid about his thick lensed glasses he refused to take them out with him, not even on a lead. This back-fired on him, however, when they went to see Elvis films. In the middle of Elvis's classic *The Reno Brothers* (later re-titled *Love me Tender*) John mumbled 'What's he doing now Thel?' and 'What happened then Thel?' . . . and BANG! . . . 'Who got shot Thel?' Too late . . . Presley lay dying.

In later years, when people started taking fab pics of him, Johnny would always remove his glasses before they got their lens caps off . . . except for me of course, I got the exclusives! On reflection I am convinced that this was because of my true to life artisticly viable camera work and not the fact I was Paul's sister.

I don't know what it was about Lennon, but I seemed to share a certain affinity with him, even right up to the last time I saw him in 1974 in New York.

Maybe it was because his Mum had just died too, and with shared death you don't have to *say* anything, you just *know*. Maybe it was his failure at academic school, or his obvious natural artistic talent. Or

* Elvis was 'in' in 1956 with *Heartbreak, Don't be Cruel* and *Hounddog*.

John, top row left, in his art school days, given to me by his girlfriend Thelma Pickles and taken in Gambia Terrace, where John later shared a flat with Stu Sutcliffe. It was a real artist's flat which was turned over one day by journalists they then took pictures of the 'beatnik's' flat, which made it look even dirtier than it was.

maybe it was because he was one of nature's born rebels . . . I don't know.

Dad certainly didn't take too kindly to him: 'He'll get you into trouble son'—advice to Paul.

But as dad actually *lived* his 'toleration and moderation' adages, Johnny 'moondog' wasn't exactly *banned* from 20 Forthlin, at least when dad was at work John used to come round and rehearse. (Not that I would stay off school to sit in on rehearsals, you understand).

I got the exclusives of 'old four-eyes'.

Back at the factory, a 'satisfactory' school career was summed up in my final report by J. R. Edwards, Headmaster . . . 'and I'm not too happy about his chances of success, he has played football for the school during the last two years, and his character is reported to me as being satisfactory', which shows you how far they were away from it all. You see I never played football for the Baz . . . . .d *or* the School.

On the other hand, Dad's end-of-term report from Steer St. School on 5th July 1916, was more promising . . . 'Has attended this school since infancy and is now in VII. He is a boy of good character, nice quiet disposition and manners: his work is up to the average. Nothing whatever against him. Fred H. Brodley (M.A.) Headmaster'.

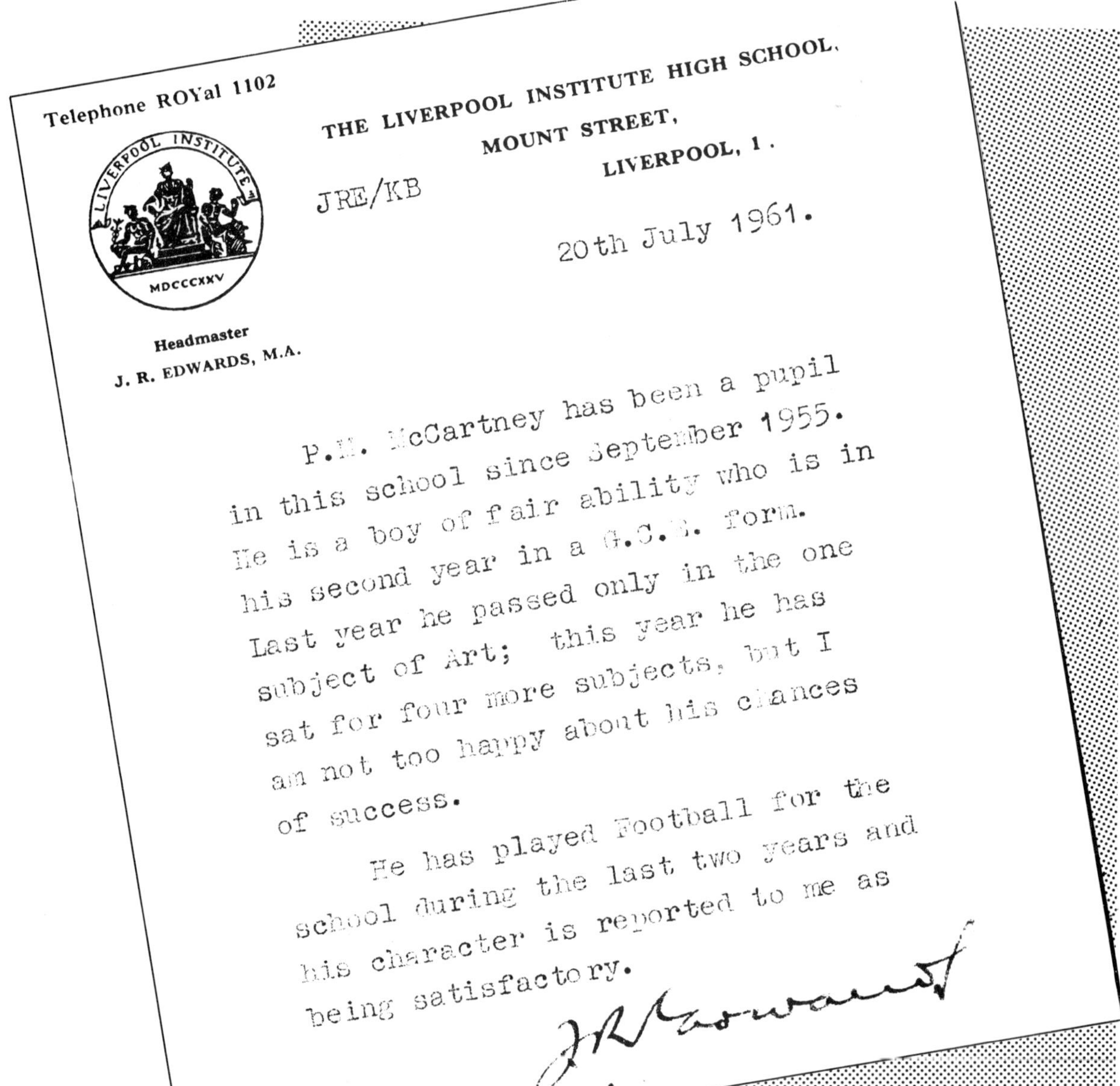

Telephone ROYal 1102

THE LIVERPOOL INSTITUTE HIGH SCHOOL.
MOUNT STREET,
LIVERPOOL, 1.

JRE/KB

20th July 1961.

Headmaster
J. R. EDWARDS, M.A.

P.M. McCartney has been a pupil in this school since September 1955. He is a boy of fair ability who is in his second year in a G.C.E. form. Last year he passed only in the one subject of Art; this year he has sat for four more subjects, but I am not too happy about his chances of success.

He has played Football for the school during the last two years and his character is reported to me as being satisfactory.

J R Edwards

Dad Muso, and 'Purse the lips son'

Having been a gay eighteen-year-old gadabout pianist himself playing at home, parties, dances and even backing silent 'chariot-race' movies at the local 'flea pit' cinema (with 'here comes the buggy ride' music) Dad was only too keen to introduce both Paul and me to his exclusive 'musicians only' club.

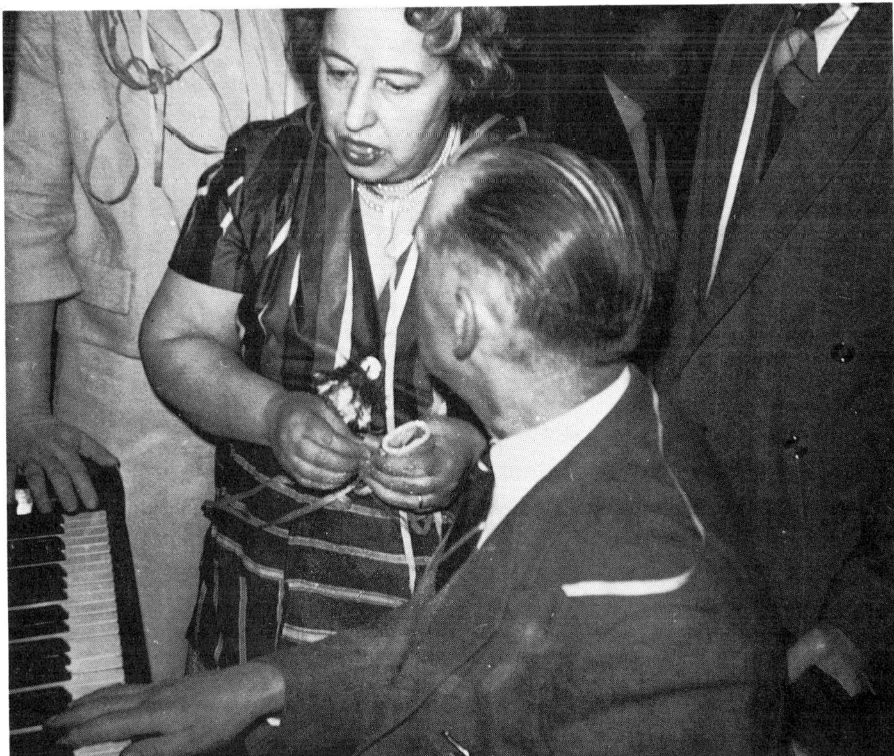

Playing a musical instrument was a passport to popularity in Dad's eyes.

Playing a musical instrument was a passport to popularity in Dad's book, so passing his secret on to us seemed only natural. The only problem was that neither of us was interested! True, he had paid for us to have piano lessons across the main road from Forthlin in Mather Avenue, but we were both bored out of our tiny little minds with the monotony of the 'practice makes perfect', even though the young piano teacher was himself interested in us. The fact that summer was calling to us outside didn't help.

'Hi Paul and Mike are you coming out to play?'

'Sorry summer . . . got to practice . . .'

Our reluctance to tackle the piano didn't deter Dad however. Whichever musical instrument took our interest (*any* instrument) it was quickly followed up by Papa. But here again we didn't fancy an instrument until one day at Auntie Jin's when elder cousin Ian was having trouble getting a tune from his trumpet.

'Here Paul, see if you can get anything out of that,' challenged Ian. '. . . it's B flat.'

'I can hear that,' brother could have said, and was only too happy to oblige. After a few tries (Dad had played the cornet in Jim Mac's band and had advised, 'Purse the lips son, purse the lips'), he played a passable toon.

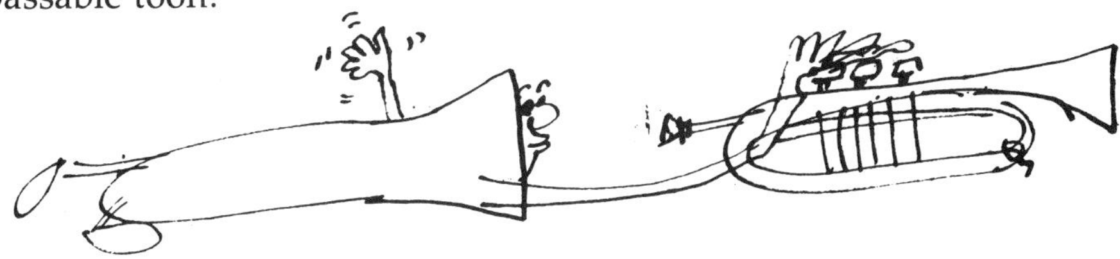

'OK Sunshine I give in—it's yours,' offered cousin Harris.

An offer, needless to say, which wasn't refused and the first step on Dad's 'Stairway to Paradise' had been taken.

SKOOL SCOUTS, BROKEN BONES & BUTLINS BY THE SEA

Before we exited skewl left, Paul and I joined the Nineteenth City School Scouts.

In the first North Wales summer camp before Mum's death, we ignored our patrol leader's friendly advice to keep our shirts on in the hot sun and both immediately got sun stroke. Typically English (or should I say Welsh) weather, it then proceeded to rain, not just ordinary rain . . . but monsoon, continual, torrents of rain until the river banks burst and flooded the camp. By some extraordinary coincidence Mum and Dad just happened to be passing our waterlogged field the next day and witnessed two bright red lobsters twisting and turning in an attempt to find some peace from the burning pain. Mum professionally tended our scalds and we continued our holiday, swimming from tent to tent as only two little lobsters know how.

The second scoutastrophe occurred on 29th July 1957, after Mum's death, on the first day of our two pounds fifteen shillings (including transport) summer camp at Hathersage, Derbyshire, near Sherwood Forest . . . Robin Hood land.

PARENT'S PERMISSION TO CAMP FORM

The Summer camp of the 19th City Troop will be held at Hathersage between 29/7/ and 7/8/ 1957

POSTAL ADDRESS 19th City Scout Troop, c/o "Callow Farm", Hathersage, Near Sheffield, Derbyshire.

TELEGRAMS As Above

DEPARTURE: Those attending will parade under Troop arrangements at Central Station at 11am on 29/7/ [Monday] 1957

Cost: The total cost of the camp, including transport, will be £2 : 15 : 0 which should be paid to S.M. before .... 195....

PERSONAL GEAR.

For each Scout.

Complete Scout Uniform including hat (and staff.)
At least 2 blankets or Sleeping Bag.
Pyjamas or change for the night.
Sweater, Jersey or Old Coat.
Spare shirt, shorts, stockings & underclothes.
Spare shoes and plimsolls or sandalls.
Bathing trunks, Towel.
Soap, comb, brush, toothbrush, etc., in toilet bag.

Handkerchiefs.
Mending materials.
Mackintosh or greatcoat.
Two enamelled soup plates.
Enamelled half pint mug.
Knife, fork, spoon in bag.
Groundsheet.

Pack in Rucsac or kitbag marked with name.

Everything should be clearly marked with name.

For each Patrol. Mirror, boot brushes and polish, clothes brush, electric torch.

I shall be pleased to provide you with any further information that you may desire, and should be glad if you would return to me the attached form at your earliest convenience.

Please accept my personal assurance that everything will be done to ensure that the camp is run in such a way as to secure the safety, health and happiness of your son.

Date 12/7/ 1957 A. Evans
Scoutmaster.

S.M.'s permanent address 131, Blackmoor Drive, Liverpool, 12. (STO. 7517)

A pulley system had been built to haul camp fire logs up a cliff from a solid oak tree to our field at the top of Callow Farm. On the pulley rope was a cylindrical drainpipe from which the logs were hung; this was lowered down to the tree.

After a suggestion (from Paul or I?) that a young scout could be easily lowered on the pipe instead of the logs, a volunteer (called *me*) stepped forward and after grabbing hold tight, they (and he) pushed me off the cliff top. It started off smoothly enough, but half way down, the handlers at the top of the cliff (Paul?) suddenly realised just how fast I was actually going and instead of slowing me down, panicked, and pulled the other way to stop me. The only thing that stopped was my heart. I sailed through the air with the greatest of . . . SPLAT . . ! straight into the oak tree (not unlike Tom and Jerry).

'We thought you were going to crash into the tree,' helpfully explained my brother picking me up. Amazingly I was still alive but my left arm wasn't, it was screaming, 'You stupid b . . . . .d!' to my brain in enormous pain. I was taken to one of the merry men of Sherwood, a drunken horse doctor, who diagnosed a broken arm and offered to set it on the spot. 'You won't feel a thing . . . jusht a little snap! That's all . . . hick.' But I decided to try the Royal Hospital, Sheffield instead, where they X-rayed me, pronounced 'a severe broken humerus' (not very) and offered to anaesthetise me whilst they set it. Not seeing the sense in unnecessary pain I chose to 'go under' and after the operation, emerged in a bed with my left arm firmly encased in plaster . . . forced to salute 'Hitler style' to the Arthur Jackson ward.

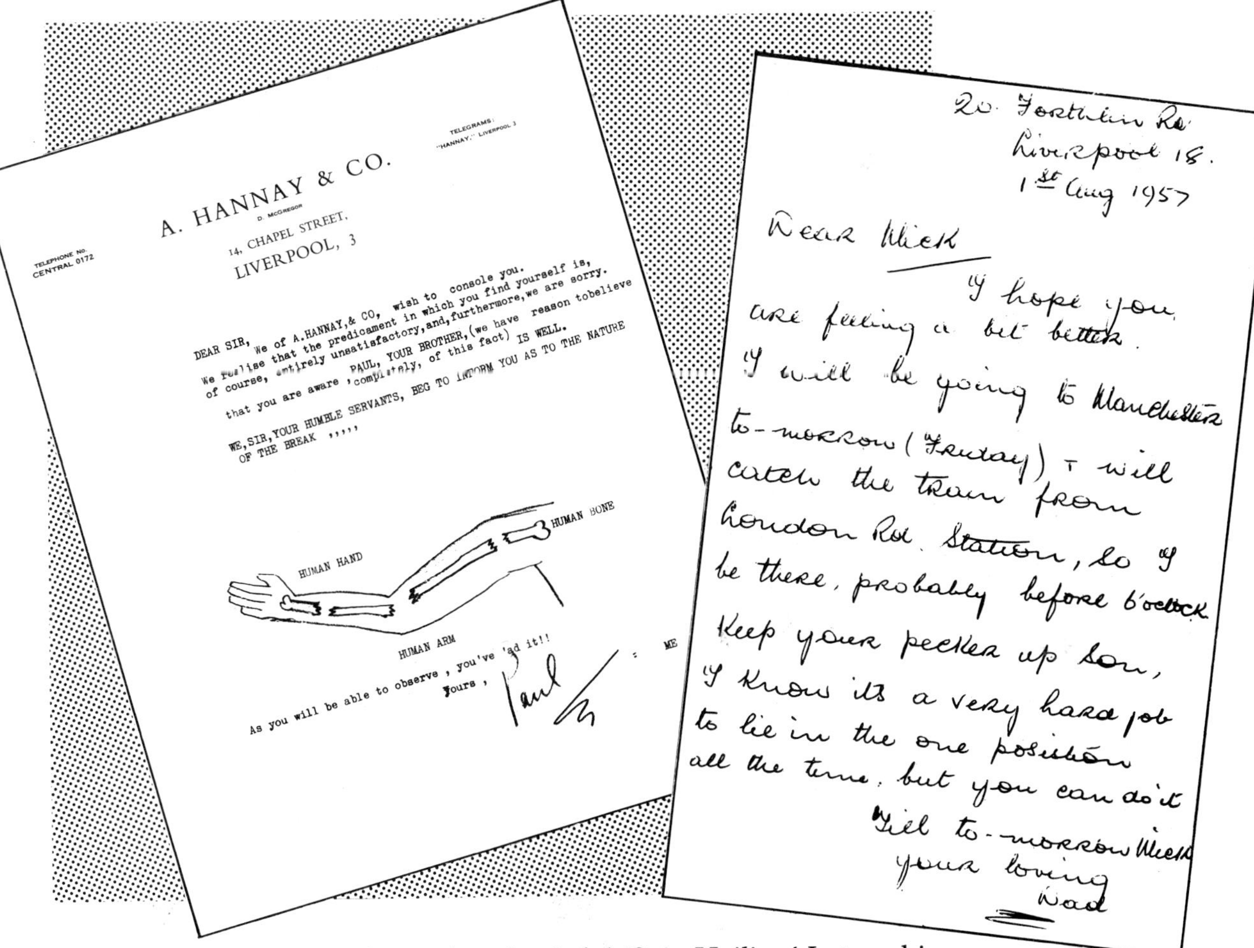

A. HANNAY & CO.
D. McGREGOR
14, CHAPEL STREET,
LIVERPOOL, 3

TELEPHONE No.
CENTRAL 0172

TELEGRAMS:
"HANNAY," LIVERPOOL 3

DEAR SIR,
We of A.HANNAY,& CO, wish to console you.
We realise that the predicament in which you find yourself is,
of course, entirely unsatisfactory,and,furthermore,we are sorry.
PAUL, YOUR BROTHER,(we have reason tobelieve
that you are aware ,completely, of this fact) IS WELL.

WE,SIR,YOUR HUMBLE SERVANTS, BEG TO INFORM YOU AS TO THE NATURE
OF THE BREAK ,,,,,

As you will be able to observe , you've 'ad it!!
Yours ,
Paul

20 Forthlin Rd
Liverpool 18.
1st Aug 1957

Dear Mick
I hope you are feeling a bit better. I will be going to Manchester to-morrow (Friday) I will catch the train from London Rd. Station, so I be there, probably before 6 o'clock. Keep your pecker up son, I know its a very hard job to lie in the one position all the time, but you can do it.
Till to-morrow Mick
Your loving
Dad

For the next four lonely weeks of painful 'Seig Heiling' I stayed in this infuriating position with as many visits that Dad could fit in from Liverpool or Manchester (Sheffield was a hell of a distance from our house). So you can imagine my relief when the doctors announced that my plaster could come off and Dad wrote to say that he and Paul were coming to take me to Butlins Holiday Camp, Filey, Yorkshire (where cousin Bett and hubby Mike were working the summer season).

When they cracked open my arm it hurt like hell and further complications arose when the nerves went in the top of my arm and my wrist dropped (what a gay day that was!). But they assured me that the paralysis would disappear with regular physiotherapy and constant exercise, plus small rubber balls (for the gripping thereof).

When the day for my departure from Sheffield Royal finally came, I was well ready. Dad and Paul arrived with my clothes and I was amazed and overjoyed to find that Dad had allowed the concession of 'drainy' (tapered to the leg) jeans in my wardrobe, which he'd refused to let Paul and I wear at home. Paul found a rather ingenious way round this rule by taking his trousers to a little Jewish tailor's every week and having just a fraction taken off each time.

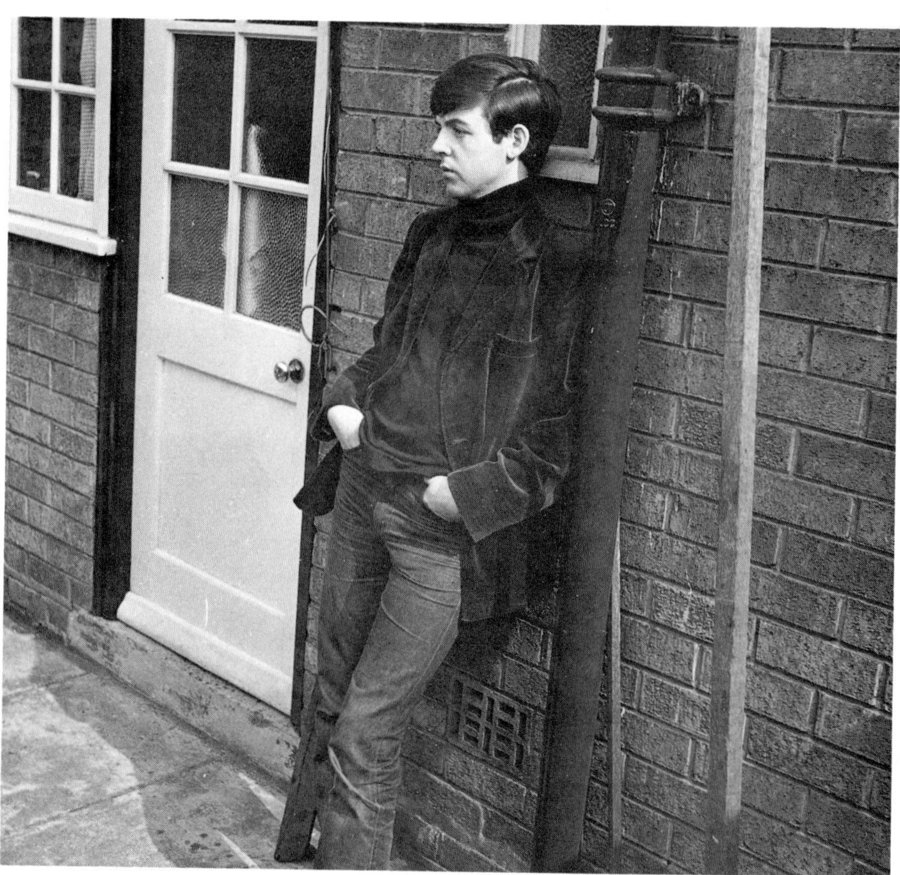

Paul, envious of John's skin-tight, drainies, got round Dad's rule not to wear tapered jeans by taking them to a Jewish tailor who'd take them in a bit each week.

'Paul! Have you been buying those Teddy Boy trousers?'

'No, Dad they're the ones *you* bought me, . . . look there's the label.'

'So they are, that's funny, they didn't look that narrow in the shop.'

In the end Paul's drainees were as skin tight as John Lennon's, our rebel hero.

But I digress . . . changing into 'civvies' after four weeks of pyjamas seemed quite strange, particularly with one arm, but Paul helped me on with undies and vest, check shirt, green tweed sports coat (plus white hanky out of top pocket) and my brand-new drainees . . . not quite skin tight, but great! The nurse hung my loose wrist in a white sling over my sports coat, and as I was rather 'wobbly on my pins' the other two felt quite sorry for me. My skin looked as white as the sling, but 'sod all that' as the dynamic trio set off for Filey, fresh air, fun and frolicks by the sea . . . not forgetting my little rubber balls.

BUTLITZ

On arrival at Butlins we quickly settled into our chalet (no. 9,989$\frac{1}{2}$a) and flipped through the entertainment programme 'spotlighting some of the star events for your holiday' . . . The Sunday Variety Show . . . The Most Glamorous Grandmother of Great Britain' 57 . . . Dancing to Fred Percival and his Orchestra . . . Television! . . . Miss Rock 'n Roll Tattoo Contest . . . Football and Cricket Coaching (gave that a miss) . . . Holiday Lovelies and Tarzan Competitions . . . and the *People* National Talent Contest. We then headed for the cavernous Windsor and Connaught dining hall where we discovered that the first, five thirty p.m., and the second, six forty-five p.m., meal sittings had LEFT-legged chickens on every plate. Close scrutiny through the week disclosed that *all* chicken meals had left legs and we could only surmise that Butlins had the concession on a one-legged chicke farm somewhere in the wilds of Yorkshire.

With Dad just before I was 'invited up' onto the stage of the Gaiety Theatre with a face as white as a sling.

Mike Robbins arm-in-arm with the Blighty 'Pin up' girls and Des O'Connor (famous British comedian and personal friend to Morecambe and Wise).

The Butlitz Girls.

The most glamorous grandmother of Great Britain 1957

The Blighty "PIN UP GIRL"

The next morning to the merry alarm call of cousin Bett singing, 'Wakey, wakey, rise and shine campers' over the PA, we set off round the camp past the Rock 'n Calypso Ballroom . . . Pig and Whistle beer garden and Welcome Inn (get it) bars . . . sick bay . . . Empire and Gaiety theatres . . . and finally the table tennis and games room which housed the one armed bandits! Not that we took after our dear father who was a slot machine addict, it's just that we had discovered a machine which kept paying out, without putting another penny in! The only slight problem was that it was manned by a girl. In the end the sight of all those pennies escaping from heaven became too much for Paul and me. We circled dangerously near the Yorkshire lass, 'Will you be long?' 'Nay lad' . . . clunk . . . dring . . . dring . . . dring.

'It's twelve o'clock, nearly time for first sitting.'

'Nay lad, not hungry,' clunk . . . dring, dring, dring.

'Don't you fancy a game of table tennis . . . on your own?'

'Nay lad,' dring . . . dring . . . dring.

'Get off!'

'Nay lad,' clunk . . . dring . . . dring . . . dring . . . three Bell Fruit Gums . . . jackpot! Clatter of tiny pieces.

For centuries Yorkshire and Lancashire have been heated rivals and this Yorkshire lass was in no way helping to cool the duel. All that lovely filthy lucca slowly disappearing, and *not* into our pockets. Klunk . . . dring . . . dring . . . clatter. Our temperatures were by now near boiling, when an old wise Yorkshire saying suddenly came to mind 'if there's owt (something) to say—say it, if there's nowt (nothing) to say—shut up!'

Paul and I positioned ourselves on either side of the girl and, not saying nowt, kicked her in the ankles . . . hard!

She immediately saw our point of view, and tears welling up in her eyes she stumbled from the games room.

The two Liverpool vultures descended on the one armed bandit and stripped it bare.

(But really we were 'armless . . . 'onest to God.)

Radio Butlin—'Wakey, wakey, rise and shine campers!'

"THE PEOPLE"

NATIONAL TALENT CONTEST

Organised in conjunction with

Butlin's LTD.

CASH PRIZES OF OVER

£5,000

MUST BE WON

I wish to enter the above Contest. Completion of this Entry Form implies acceptance of the Rules and Conditions governing the Contest.

NAME

ADDRESS AGE

Date of Holiday Week

Insert name of Camp or Hotel at which you will be competing

SECTION

VOCALIST ☐ INSTRUMENTALIST ☐

COMEDIAN ☐ SPECIALITY ACT ☒

This Entry Form (when completed) should be handed to the Entertainments Manager of the Butlin's Holiday Camp or Hotel at which you are staying.

NOTE: If you have not already booked your holiday, this Entry Form can be sent with your Booking Form to the Camp or Hotel selected.

'Ladies and gentlemen . . . the McCartney Brothers!'

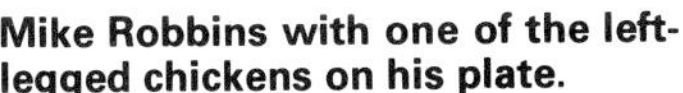

Mike Robbins with one of the left-legged chickens on his plate.

In the camp, our unquestionable hero was Mike Robbins, compere producer, Red Coat extraordinaire. The fact that he could introduce us to passing superstars, was Cousin Bett's husband AND the host of the *People* National Talent Contest with its five thousand pounds cash prize, had nothing to do with it.

'Why not enter and let us discover you!' shouted the posters. 'Auditions, Monday, Tuesday and Wednesday, ten thirty a.m. in the Gaiety Theatre. Entry forms available at reception. Cash prizes of over £5,000 *must be won*.' Who could resist?

Paul had been rehearsing a Little Richard number and before my arm episode we both did a very passable Everley Brothers *Bye Bye Love* impression at home, which Dad was very proud of. But as for going up on a stage in front of people . . . no chance. I was only thirteen and not quite ready to take the showbiz establishment by the horns. Paul on the other hand had just turned fifteen, a veritable old man and seasoned performer.

Paul sitting on Cousin Ted's pram, brushing up his Little Richard act, down on the beach.

'Ah come on, let's do it Mike.'
'No way.'
'*Bye Bye Love*'s great.'
'Yeah but I'm not, I feel dead weedy.'
'No, you're not, is he Dad?'

Dad added fuel to the fire, 'Of course not son, anyway it's only a bit of fun. What have you got to lose?'

'No thanks, maybe next year.'
'OK,' said Paul. 'But you'll come with me won't you?'
'Of course.'

On the big day, Paul slung his guitar over his shoulder, I slung my sling over mine, and together we stepped out into the early morning sun and headed for the Gaiety Theatre.

Once inside, Mike Robbins lost no time in getting to the point.

'Ladies and gentlemen, every now and then you come across outstanding musical talent and today is no exception, so put your hands together for a young man from Liverpool . . . Paul McCartney!' Applause, applause.

Our kid stepped bravely up onto the stage and whispered something to the producer compere.

'Well, how about that campers,' Mike announced. 'We have with us in the audience today Paul's young brother Michael who only yesterday came out of Sheffield hospital with ninety-seven fractures after breaking his arm up a mountain, and the *two* brothers are going to give us a little number, will you welcome please . . . Mike McCartney.'

'You B . . . . .rother,' I swore to myself. The blood drained from my face leaving it whiter than my fresh white sling, but as in all good showbiz films 'the show must go on' so I joined my elder brother on stage to Mike's covering quips, 'A big HAND for young Mike now,' and 'This could be your BIG BREAK,' and 'What are you going to start off with, lads?

'*B. . .B. .B.B.Bye Bye Love*' (it was nearly 'Bye Bye Mike').

'Ladies and gentlemen, for the first time on any stage, a really warm welcome for . . . the McCartney Brothers,' and into an extraordinary version of the Everley Brothers classic stepped the real one-armed bandit and close relation.

When the applause died down (Dad always was a good clapper), Paul launched into *Long Tall Sally*, and that was the first and last time the McCartney Brothers ever gave a live stage performance together. Good job really, when we got off stage, I was ready to puke up!

As we were both under the minimum age limit of sixteen we didn't exactly win a penny of the five thousand pounds, but more important, when we got outside into the fresh air we discovered our first fan . . . Angela of Hull.

Paul holding Dot, his first real girlfriend, in Forthlin's back garden.

'OUR' FIRST FAN AND THE LETTERS

The only small problem was that Angela Hull fancied *me*, and the fact that a girl could see beyond my rugged, mountain-man appearance into the inner core of my sensitive soul became too much for my 'good looking' brother. On the day of her departure we both walked her to the camp gates where she caught her bus home to the East Coast. Later she wrote from Gypsyville, Hull, pouring her love for me all over the pages, and passing on her 'regards' to Paul. I only got the one letter.

Paul sneaked down to the letter box in Forthlin Road for each successive one, took them up to his room, opened, read and then hid them! Later on, this performance was repeated with a beautiful German girl called Ursula Milczewsky who came to our house a Beatle fan, and left a broken shell of a girl, hopelessly in love with yours truly. Paul could never understand how such good looking girls could fall for such an ugly duckling as me and I personally don't know what made me so irresistible (well I do but I'm not telling you). Suffice it to say that it was too much for the boy and even to this day I'm convinced he has a drawer full of my first love's correspondence which he reads over and over and over to himself (tragic really).

Ursula Milczewsky, whose letters Paul hid in his secret drawer upstairs, pictured during my 'depth of field, tree' period.

LUCKY RINGO

Just prior to my 'humourous' arm, Dad had *again* been on about taking up a musical instrument and I thought I'd have a bash at the drums, to placate him. Who knows, I might back someone famous one day. Not that there was anything suspicious about Paul unloading my light blue speckled drum kit from the back of a lorry, or the fact that the Quarrymen's drum kit got mislaid at the same time. But what a coincidence!

Being considerate chaps we at once thought of the neighbours (our house being in the middle of a tightly packed box of terraced homes), so we decided on a 'noise level' for them. This consisted of me sitting at my drum kit and bashing the hell out of the skins whilst Paul walked away from our house to see how far he could get down Forthlin Road before the banging subsided completely. *Unglücklicherweise* for the neighbours he ended up in Mather Avenue, a hundred yards from our house. Now *that's* what you call a sound check . . . Keith Moon would have been proud.

When I returned from Sheffield and Butlins, gripping my little rubber ball had little effect on my upper arm nerves, and the possible permanent paralysis of my left dead hand was pretty real. The worst

Paul with my light-blue speckled, off-the-back-of-a-lorry, Quarrymen drum kit which suddenly became the 'Beatles' drum-kit . . .

aspect was holding it up (my left hand, that is) with my right hand, only for it to flop down again like a cold, dead fish. It might as well have been cut off. After many electric shock sessions with pretty Sefton General physiotherapists and the strapping on of a hand iron of which 'cripple' Lennon would have been proud, my dead hand slowly Frankensteined back to life and things returned to comparative normality, but not after many childish attempts to hide my 'crippledom' from the eyes of the world. Fortunately for the neighbours (and Ringo) the desire to return to drumming left me. Let's face it, with my way with women and obvious drumming talent Ritchie would have stood *no* chance. Mind you our kid must have got some nifty rehearsals in whilst I was away, as on my return I couldn't fail to notice just how good he was. For proof just listen to the drumming on *Band on the Run* and *McCartney II*—all his own work.

'Drainies on drainies'. Paul in his 'David Frost' shirt. Even the girl fans used to wear them. We used to shin up the drainpipe and thro' the toilet window of Forthlin Road when we lost our key to the door.

Paul getting some nifty rehearsals in whilst I was away. See too the moody, magnificent Pete Best.

IN A WORLD OF HIS OWN

When the skiffle era came in with a *Rock Island Line* 1956 bang and Lonnie Donegan ruled (OK), Paul desired a guitar at the subtlest level of consciousness and suddenly HEYPRESTON there it was, all covered with emotion. Dad didn't need to be asked twice.

Although our grand, stand-up piano was just waiting for us to fall in love with her, neither of us fancied a romance just yet, but Dad more than made up for that when *he* was in a 'Joanna playing mood' . . . he wouldn't leave it alone.

The next on the scene were 'my' drums and finally a banjo manifested itself 'For Mick', which I tried to master but my tender left hand eventually gave it up (that's my excuse and I'm sticking to it).

But the guitar was Paul's chosen instrument. When he picked it up he would get lost in another world, particularly after Mum died. It was useless talking to him. In fact I had better conversations with brick walls around this period. He even took it with him to the bogs, and sometimes paddled round the bath in it. But people he *could* converse with were fellow musos . . . George from school and rebel Johnny 'Moondog' Lennon the original punk rocker personified . . . and why not, they were nice people who also loved music.

Paul, with his 'Cliff/Elvis' hair, lost in a world of his own.

The earliest pic of John, Paul, George and Dennis playing together in Auntie Jin's Dinah's Lane back room during the Elvis era.

POST CARD

CORRESPONDENCE

Dear Mike,
Hope you're OK [illegible]
[illegible] – Bett + Mike send
love. Playing on Sat.
– billed as the Nerk Twins.
May be serving behind
bar. Rocking etc. fun,
[illegible] & [illegible] again
Get well soon time.
Rock, Paul

ADDRESS

Michael McCartney
WARD 14
SEFTON GENERAL
Hospital
LIVERPOOL,
LANCS.

XXXXXXXXXXX

THIS IS A REAL PHOTOGRAPH

Postcard from Paul to me in Sefton General Hospital (I was always in there for something or other). Paul and John had gone down to Mike & Bett's pub in Reading and were playing there, billed as THE NERK TWINS. (courtesy of *The Goon Show*).

1960, the Casbah . . . and Hamburg!

Oblivious to the realities of 20 Forthlin Road.

Six months after Buddly Holly, Ritchie Valens and the Big Bopper were killed in their '59 aircrash, the Casbah opened with about three hundred fans of the Quarrymen squeezed into the (still wet) painted, spider's web cellar. John, Paul, George, Stu Sutcliffe (learning bass) and Pete Best (Mona the owner's son) played their hearts out in the bowels of the large semi-detached Haymans Green, West Derby home of Mrs. Best.

For some extraordinary reason I was a member of the Crosby Green Methodist Youth Club in the road parallel to Haymans Green (it was our green period!). *Extra*ordinary because both places were miles from Forthlin Road and it involved three bus changes for both of us.

Paul, Stu Sutcliffe and Pete Best at 'Mona the owner's' club, The Casbah. Stu was very intense with a very strong presence, but thin and weedy so our kid looked down on him a bit. But what a mind—I think that's why John liked him so much.

Peroxide bouffant fan at the Casbah straining to see a joyous George and Paul with his Solid 7 bass guitar (upside down), strung with three piano wires.

On the hot August night of the opening, I sagged off my Christian Methodist duties to attend the premier of the Casbah and private party afterwards, with a warning from Mrs. Best to all of us not to use her personal living quarters upstairs.

The Big went down fanobviouslytastic and the party was in full swing with Bo Didley's *Rhythm and Blues* EP . . . 'all you purdy women brang (bring) it to Jerome' (eat your heart out Jagger) . . . 'Oh you purdy thing' and . . . 'I'm a man, spelt MAN . . . oh', turned up to full blast, when suddenly the beer and heat hit my fifteen-year-old head, calling for cooler air and a light refreshment. I went upstairs to the private, out-of-bounds living quarters of Mrs. Best and quietly opened her front lounge door. There on the sideboard in the soft firelight was, heaven upon heaven, a lemonade bottle three quarters full! The top had been opened and pushed back on, so it was no sweat ripping it off with my teeth and gulping it down my parched throat. But as the liquid hit my numbed tastebuds and the inside of my esophagus I realised, 'Ah!' it was HAIR LACQUER! The rest of the night was spent puking up my guts, all fifteen years of them, in the not so best toilet.

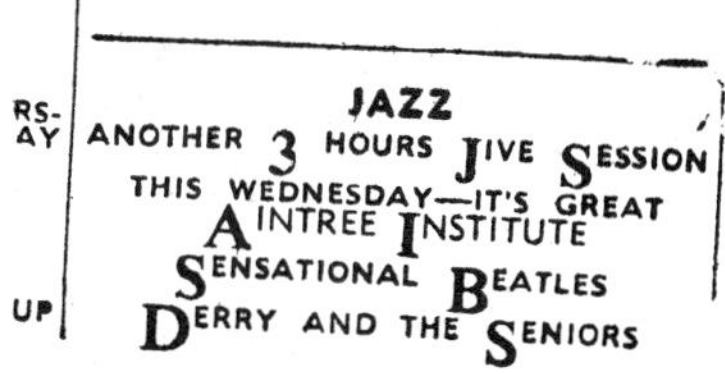

RS-
AY
UP

JAZZ

ANOTHER 3 HOURS JIVE SESSION
THIS WEDNESDAY—IT'S GREAT
AINTREE INSTITUTE
SENSATIONAL BEATLES
DERRY AND THE SENIORS

OFF TO THE FRONT . . . KAMERAD AND INTERNATIONAL SMUGGLER

After his first taste of super-stardom in 1960, backing Johnny Gentle

I should like to apply on behalf of the group for an engagement at your holiday camp. The group mentioned is known as the 'Beatals' and is led by John Lennon. The boys, whose ages range from 18 to 20, have a good deal of experience behind them (Ardwick Hippod, Manchester, L'pool Empire, many local ballrooms & clubs too numerous to mention) &, as they having been working together for 4 years, have acquired three very important things – competence, confidence, & continuity. I am sure that the group will completely fulfil your requirements.

Yours Sincerely

J. P. McCartney.

Just before the war Paul, on behalf of the group, wrote this daft draft letter to Butlins to try and get a gig. Note Beatals(!) led by John Lennon, no less. Read it . . . what a superb bullshitter . . . lines borrowed from our Dad . . .

EXCLUSIVELY AT THE CAVERN
Central 1591
THE HIVE OF JIVE
HAMBLETON HALL
Page Moss, Huyton.
TO-MORROW! YES! TO-MORROW!
!!! THE BEATLES !!!
MR. SHOWMANSHIP
RORY STORM AND THE HURRICANES
MR. BIG DADDY
DERRY AND THE SENIORS
YOU CANNOT AFFORD TO MISS THIS FABULOUS ROCK GROUP.
LINE UP — ONLY 2/6 BEFORE 8 p.m.
Be Early and Tell Your Friends.
ONLY THE TOP ROCK GROUPS AND BOB "BIG BEAT" WOOLER
JIVE TO-NIGHT JIVE

What to call yourself? Bob Wooller, who put their ads. in the Liverpool Echo (echo . . . echo), was the guy who loved to build up their advertising with !!!! of all sorts . . . the SENSATIONAL . . . the AMAZING . . . go early and TELL YOUR FRIENDS!

NIGHT OF THE WEEK, with Hal Graham & his Orchestra, 6/-. To-morrow: Whit Sunday Club Special.
IT'S THE BIG BEAT AT THE GROSVENOR BALLROOM
WALLASEY
WHIT MONDAY: 2 STAR Rock Groups, THE SILVER BEETLES & GERRY & THE PACE-MAKERS
Non-stop 8-Midnight. Adm. 3/- Come early
REECE'S
Proudly Announce their NEW BALLROOM with its CONTINENTAL STYLING
5/6.

on the Larry Parnes package tour of Scotland (they must have been superstars: the postcard from Inverness said they were 'going down better than Vince Eager or Duffy Power'), Paul was waiting for his Art and English 'A' Level results and as Dad though, all set to 'make an honest living by getting a steady job'. As I was the proverbial younger brother he didn't usually confide in me, so you can imagine my surprise when on top of the 86 bus taking us to our 20 Forthlin home, he suddenly said, 'I've had some amazing news, but I don't know whether I can tell you.'

'What news?'

'Well it's just that . . .'

'What?'

'They've asked us to go to Hamburg!'

'Blimey!'

'For stacks of money.'

'You mean you'll be famous?'

'Oh yeah. Lots of money and famous, *and* I can buy you lots of things too, but there's just one thing . . .'

'What?'

'Dad!'

'That's a point. He'll never agree (long pause for thought transference to work) unless . . .'

'What?' said Paul, all interested.

'Unless we persuade him TOGETHER.'

'Wow, that's a great idea, why didn't I think of that, thanks Mike.'

'OK Paul.'

Dad wasn't that easy to convince, however, as he really wanted Paul to go to Teachers Training College and this is where, if Mum had been alive, the end of the start of the Beatles (and later on my group, Scaffold) would have been nigh. Mum wanted us in one of the 'professions' when we grew up. I can see it now: 'Doctor McCartney?' 'Coming nurse?' . . . or 'Excuse me Father?' 'Yes my son?'

Portentous headlines from the Observer!

To stamp the seal of approval on things, Paul brought Alan Williams, their small, gregarious energetic, enthusiastic Welsh 'Manager' to the house. He extolled the quality of Hamburg's top (mercy) wages and luxury conditioned fun clubs to Dad, and with Dad's latent desire for one of us to follow in his father's footsteps, it wasn't that hard for Uncle Al, the kiddies pal, to get pater's consent.

So off they tripped to Hamburg and off I tripped to Amsterdam and Cologne for my summer holidays (within spitting distance if you had a good yoka*). It was in Köln that I bought my first Pop Out Camera with mock leather case† and also became part of an international smuggling ring. It wasn't so much the camera I'd bought . . . more the other Minolta 'spy camera' my nice German friend asked me to bring back to England.

'Just take zis camera through ze customs, Kamerad, zen place it in ze left luggage locker and drop ze key in ant envelope to zis address, yah?'

Rockin' on the Rhine with my Köln pop out camera.

* Liverpool spitting slang.
† Up till now I'd taken pics with the family box-camera. I used to develop and print my own film in our little back bedroom after reading it all up from library books.

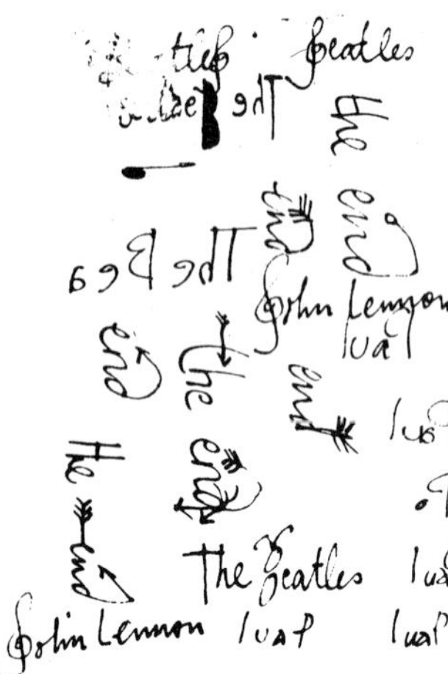

'Warumnicht . . . how much?'

'Five pound—pfunds.'

'You're on . . . viederschauen.'

It was only when I was facing the customs officers' 'anything to declare' board that I suddenly realised what I was doing.

Tiny beads of perspiration broke out as the poker-faced customs officer said, 'Have you got any money to change son?'

'I think s-s-s-s-so officesir.'

'Well go and change it.'

When I got back I noticed that my case had been well and truly turned inside out, but didn't think to complain as they might just search me and find the spy camera in my inside pocket.

He ticked my bag and let me through (good job it wasn't Japan!). I put the 'hot property' in the locker and posted the key c/o 'International Smuggling Ring, Balham'. When I got home I wondered if being arrested on spy charges and locked in the Tower of London for the rest of my young life was really worth £5. I decided it wasn't but at least I had my Köln Pop Out Camera and started shooting straight away, getting plenty of practice before brother returned from Deutschland with his new group.

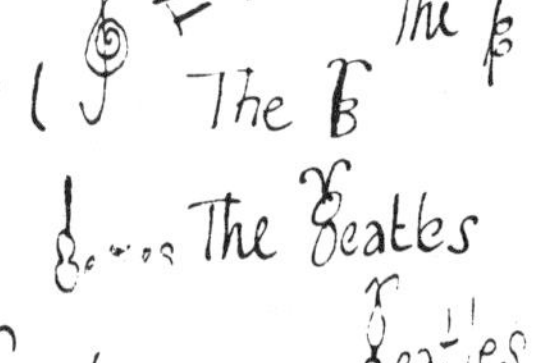

Paul doodling in search of a Beatles logo.

WE'RE JUST 'THE BEATLES'

After settling back in school, just before Christmas 1960, I answered the knock on the front door of our 20 Forthlin home. There stood an emaciated skeleton that was once my brother. 'Happy Christmas Mike, I've got your blue plazy (plastic) mac . . . it's gear.' After four months hard labour in the Indra and Kaiserkeller Clubs, Hamburg, (eight hours* a night with Monday off and a standard diet of cornflakes and milk) he and Pete Best had been deported for accidentally trying to burn down the Bambi Kino (cinema) with french letters. (mistake No. 1 . . . they should have used Bundespost). I brought little Nell into the lounge to let Dad see, and the usual distractions followed. 'We've been working really hard and I've got a new watch, boots and overcoat; we've dropped the 'Silver' now, we're just 'the Beatles' and we've all got group jackets with leather collars and a gear pleat in the back . . . and a new 'lecy' (electric) razor and blue velvet shirt with short sleeves . . . and—wait for it—a fab new Spanish guitar . . . only £2! . . . honest.' But nothing could detract from the fact that when he sat down, the ankles showing above the winkle picker shoes were as thin and white as Dad's pipe-cleaners.

After a 'damn good rest', plenty of scouse, bacon butties, and regular capsules (our vitamins came in the form of cod liver oil capsules, swallowed daily after our main meal) . . . the damage was repaired and Paul and the Beatles (Be*A*tles it was quickly pointed out) got a residency at Pete Best's Casbah.

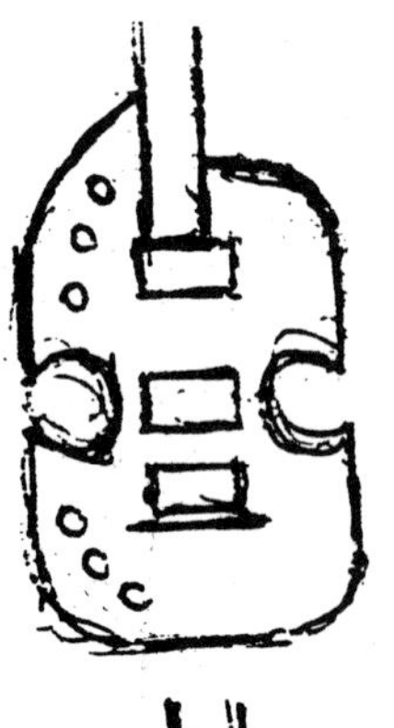

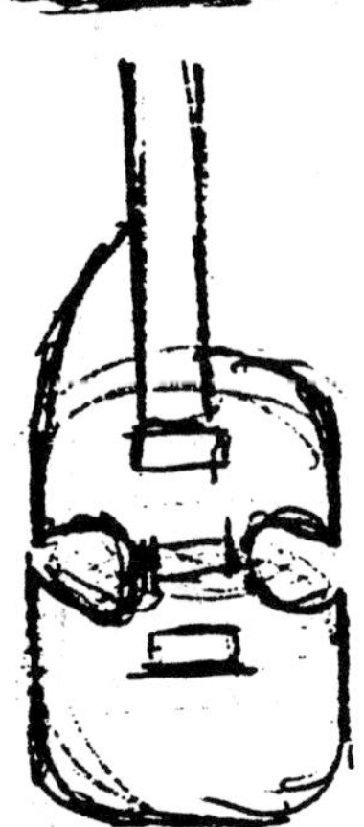

Paul's design ideas for early Beatles' guitars.

* Having entertained audiences in the theatre for two hours every night . . . *that's* a LONG time.

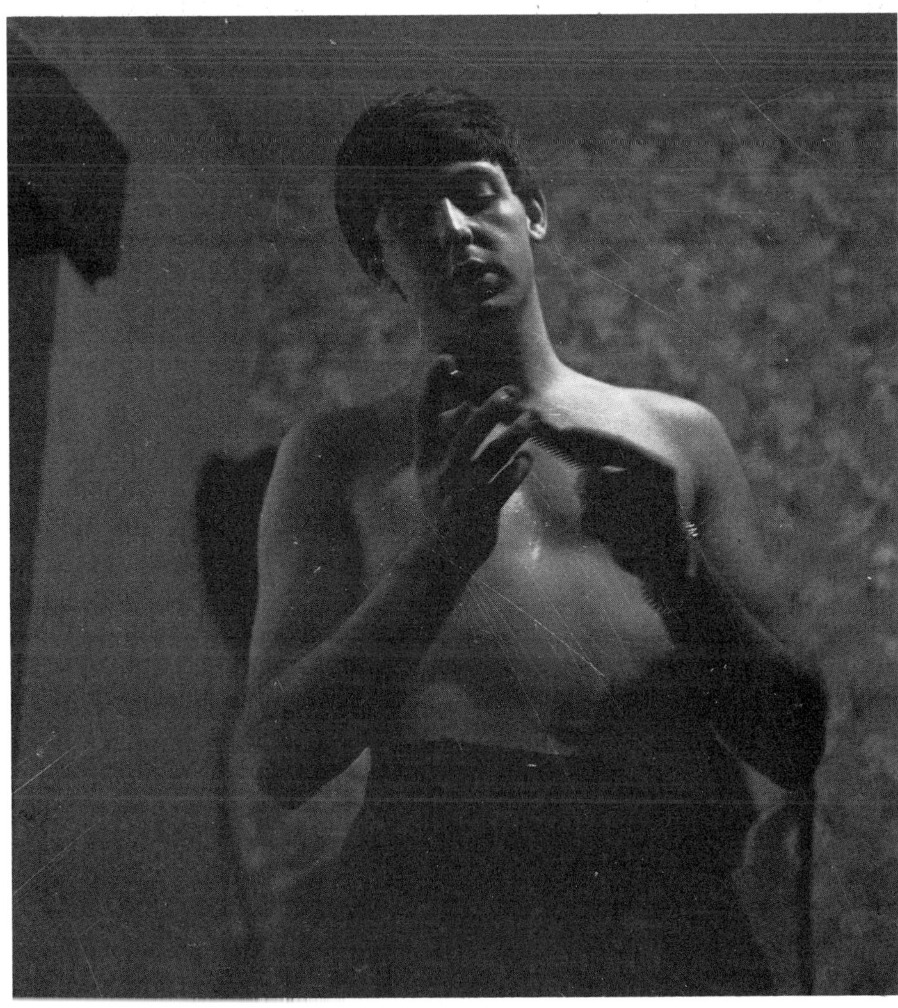

Brother recovering from four months hard labour in Hamburg, knocks the biddies from his biddy rake in our Forthlin bedroom.

RORY 'MR SHOWMANSHIP' STORM

One evening I was having a few illegal ales with George's brother Pete Harrison before joining Paul and 'the lads' at the Casbah where they were playing that night. When the pints of numbness had reached the cheeks or fingertips (I can never remember which) I decided to leave the West Derby pub and head up to the club on my own.

Being even friendlier than usual I struck up a conversation with two fellow leather-jacketed rockers obviously *en route* to the Best club. Our chat was unusual in that one of my new found chums had a pronounced stammer but still insisted on monopolising the conversation. Never having been to the Casbah they asked my opinion of the new club.

'Oh it's great,' I obliged.

'Any g-g-g-good groups on?'

'There's a fantastic new group on tonight, actually.'

'Oh aye?'

'Yeah—they've just come back from Germany.'

'What are they c-c-called?'

'The Beatles.'

'The B-B-Beatles?'

'Yeah—I know it's a funny name but they're gear.'

'Have you ever heard of a group called Rory St-St-Storm and the Hurricanes?'

'Yeah our kid played with them in Hamburg and he says . . .'
'Whose your k-k-k-kid?'
'Paul McCartney, one of the Beatles and he told me *personally* that Rory Storm's last.'
'Oh aye, but I heard that St-St-Storm's a bit of an athlete and jumps around the stage and all that.'
'Yeah, but they're just gimmicks, he's not a patch on the Beatles.'
'Really!'
'Well judge for yourself. This is the Casbah now.'
'So this is the C-C-C-Casbah.'
'Yeah, but it'll cost you to get in . . . a bob (5p) . . . see you later.'
'O.K., b-b-by the way what's *your* name?'
'Mike McCartney . . . what's yours?'
'Rory St-St-Storm.'

Rory & girlfriend, Johnny Guitar's girlfriend and JG in the centre, then Mrs. Caldwell. Dot has her arms around brother's neck.

THE 'STORMS'

Rory wasn't the only comedian in the family; there were also his parents Mr. and Mrs. Caldwell. As Paul dated Rory's sister Iris for a while, he and I gained entrance to the Caldwell house and to the antics of Mr. and Mrs. 'Storm'.

On one occasion, Mr. Caldwell, a man not afraid of a pint or two, had watered the garden as usual from the upstairs bedroom window before retiring, and was now in dreamland with his wife. Suddenly screaming 'Look out!', he jumped out of bed, grabbed hold of the mattress and tilted it, and the contents (Mrs. Caldwell) onto the floor.

'What the 'ell do you think you're doing?' enquired his wife (not unnaturally).

'You should be thanking me,' said Mr. C. 'I just saved you from that *express train*.'

Another time, Rory, who loved his parents, had saved up his pop wages to take them to a slap-up meal at a post rezy (restaurant). Everything went A1, OK, tickety-boo until the end of the meal when Rory ordered crêpe suzettes ('they're just posh pancakes, Mum,' he confided). When the *maître d'hotel* flamed the crêpes, and the flames leapt high in the air, Mrs. Storm sprang to her feet, grabbed a nearby soda syphon and with cries of 'Don't worry, luv, I'll save ya,' proceeded to put the fire out.

Sadly, some years ago, after the death of Mr. Caldwell, Rory and his Mum committed suicide together.

ART COLLEGE, I.O.W., JACKSONS, THE CAVERN AND GOD LOVES A TRYER

After nearly drowning in Woolton Baths (I knocked myself unconscious on the bottom and Paul saved *me* . . . for a change!), Mum dying, and breaking my paralytic arm, my next traumatic experience was to be Art College.

Not relishing the thought of being kicked out into the big wild world from the card-playing womb of school life, I decided to delay the process a little by joining the art fraternity next door. As John Lennon was already there doing lettering, and as I fancied myself as a better artist than him, plus the fact that I had passed my art GCE, I thought there'd be no problem gaining entrance to the 'arty set' and delaying the world for a couple of years. Whilst on tenderhooks waiting to see if they would accept me, I asked John how many GCE's he'd passed. 'I didn't get *any*.' 'How did you get in then?' 'Like this,' he said and drew me this lightning cartoon.

A Lennon original explaining to me how he got into art college.

Not only that, there were the birds, hundreds of them. Lennon even got his girlfriend Cyn to sub for most of his work whilst he sat in coffee bars with Geoff Muhammad Ali, or practised his guitar through his glasses. As I was a normal, healthy cripple, needing a little warmth and affection, I saw no harm in joining him. Before entering the art col I decided to earn me some big money by doing a summer job. Big John L. had dug roads in his hols and big brother Paul had been given pound notes for working as a second man on a Lewis's store van, so I wrote to my cousin Bett in the Isle of Wight (or as the locals call it the Oil of Woit) and asked if there were any jobs going in her husband's new Ryde pub. Mike Robbins wrote back the letter overleaf . . .

THE OIL OF WOIT

Not knowing if Mike was serious I agreed to the conditions and set off down to sunny R (I.O.W.) (Rio de jeget it?), passing my first hovercraft on the way! On arrival I found that Mike was deadly serious and either I 'wear a chef's hat . . . you're dealing with food' or 'get your hair cut . . . short'. Not wanting to blow my cool for all those college women but not fancying the idea of looking like the end of a lamb cutlet, I chose the haircut. (If I remember correctly a small inducement of five pounds was included in the deal.) Mike came with me to make sure I kept to my side of the bargain and with constant suggestions to the

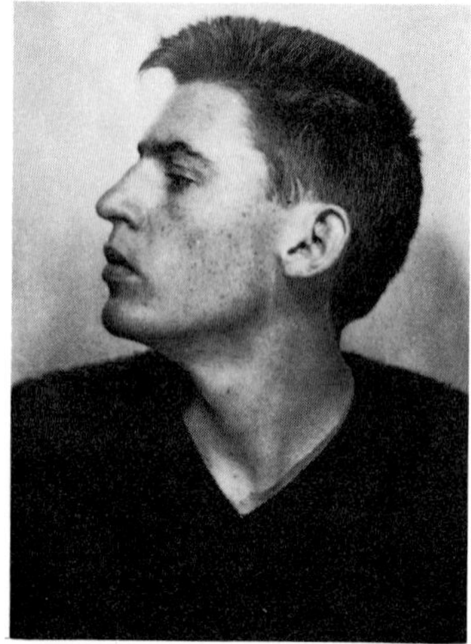

Blowing my cool, with a very crewl crew cut, (plus a £5 inducement, you understand).

The Bow Bars

RESIDENT MANAGERS MR. & MRS. D. M. ROBBINS

A COURAGE - BARCLAY - SIMONDS HOUSE

UNION STREET, RYDE
ISLE OF WIGHT
TELEPHONE : RYDE 2084

Thursday. 6th. July.1961.

Dear Mr. Muckheartnea,

We were pleased to receive your letter of the 94th. ints,
(or something like that.) When we received it, we were a little ~~nonplees nowluss~~
~~noonplowed~~ ., we did'nt know what to do! As we could'nt think of a situation that was
going in our ~~establushmint~~, place., but at last we have thought of something, here
it is, take it, or stick it on the wall, (No offence meant!)

You will be working for us, not Simonds Ltd. We require a bloke
to cook and serve Hamburgers only , on that Hotplate in the window of the Snack Bar,
(We have now had a large window with a serving ledge put in just above the Hotplate
for outside sales.)

SNAG No.1:- You will be required to wear a Chefs' Outfit complete with Chefs' Hat.(Supplied by us of course) THIS IS SERIOUS? NO KIDDING.

SNAG No.2:- You will be required to wear Reasonably short hair. (Reasonably short meaning able to see.) Also reasonably short nails on hands.(Toes do not matter.)

SNAG No.3:- You will be required to work from approx. 12.00pm. to 2.00pm. and 8.00pm. to 12.Midnight.

Things on the more pleasant side:-

No.1:- You will have a day off per week.

No.2:- You will be supplied with free "Food and Kip."

No.3:- You will be paid a basic ~~renumur reenoemurrat~~ wage of £3 per week. (To hell with N/Health and I/Tax this is on the side.)

Plus a commission of 1d. on every Hamburger you sell.
We are at the moment selling approx. 400 Hamburgers per week, this should at
least double during the peak season which is to come, if it does'nt, you will
be FIRED INSTANTLY.

THIS IS SERIOUS
BY THE WAY
WE'RE NOT FOOLING

Also you will be responible for your own Hamburger Stock and will run your own till completely independant of the snack bar.

Well, What do you think? Please let us know by return. We dont know when you
are able to start, but if possible, we suggest that you come down sometime around the
back end of next week, approx. 14th or 15th. so as to start work about the Monday.

Hoping to hear from you as soon as possible,
We remain, (In case you should ever use this as evidence)
SNODGRASS. PEABODY & JONES. Ltd.
(Lame duck and Blind horse Manufacturers.)

J.H.T.

barber of 'shorter', ended up with what they called a crew cut.

I now needed a chef's cutlet hat to hide the haircut but no mind, the money was lovely (my first job), the ale was lovely (although seventeen and still under age I was every inch a man and could 'take my ale'), the weather was lovely (with Ryde beach and sunburning girls two seconds down the hill) and Carl and Tommy were lovely! My second holiday abroad and I am introduced to my first homosexuals! At first I was somewhat apprehensive but I soon grew to love Carl and Tommy (in the most brotherly way you understand), once I discovered the two lovely personalities behind all the camping round.

In turn they introduced me to the gay world of Ryde. After work, Carl and I would be in some queer old bar on the island when he'd say, 'Oh look, isn't she varda,' referring to the homosexual prowess of one of the most butch, muscle-bound sailors you'd ever seen. 'Bugger off,' I would reply, when sure enough the next minute his or her boyfriend would walk in and the two would waltz off to a little, nearby cottage.

I don't know if I was trying to assert my manhood but soon afterwards I picked up a bustiful young lady down on the beach. After a weekend of proving that I definitely hadn't gone gay, I arranged to meet her on the beach during Monday.

'Oi should be there 'bout five, OK?'

'Foive . . . five 'll be fine.' I replied, as the thought of being lost in those enormous warm breasts overcame me.

At the appointed hour she arrived with a giggling girl friend in full school uniform!

'Sorry Oim late, but we got loins in school'.

Suppressing my horror I asked, 'Darling, just how old are you?'

I didn't go down to the beach much after she told me . . .

After tending my hamburgers and hot dogs in the window of the Bowbars one day, I nipped upstairs for a break in Mike and Bett's lounge, and who should I bump into but Ruby Murray, a *big* Irish singing star of the day. She turned out to be a natural, warm, gravel-voiced lady who just happened to have a string of some four hundred-odd consecutive number one hit records under her belt. Her husband Bernie was one of the Jones Boys, another successful act at the time (I'd seen them on the telly so they *must* have been stars).

Mike and Bett had met them in Butlins before fame struck and they were all good friends. I couldn't believe my luck. What a story to tell Paul (and Dad) when I got downstairs to my writing paper in the bowels of the Bow. He'd be mad jealous! But hold on now, there's a thought . . . Bernie just so happened to manage Ruby, and if he could manage *one* successful star why not a *group* of successful stars . . . No, he'd never do it, not an unknown Liverpool group (Liverpool was still north of Watford to them thar Londoners). Just a minute though, Ruby was from Belfast, that's spud-throwing distance from Liverpool . . . I'll give it a try . . . nothing to lose . . . everything to gain.

I found the Beatles' first publicity pic (full leathers, the lot) and approached Bernie a little nervously. 'I've seen your group on the television, Bernie.'

'Have you son?'

'Yes, you're fabulous.'

'Thank you Mike.'

'My brother's in a group.'

'Really?'

'Yes, they're called the Beatles.'

'The what?'

The Jones Boys. Bernie turned the Beatles down and it's not hard to see why, when you compare this with the Beatles' first publicity photo . . .

Me (rather drunk), Pete Best and, as ever, super-cool, black leather gloved Bri. Dig that crazy bouffant!

ART COLLEGE

Imagine my horror when I returned from the Isle of Wight to find that a new educational system had been introduced from Switzerland which required at least five GCEs for admission to my art heaven. An interview was arranged with the boss of the college.

'Have you got five GCEs? I'm afraid it's compulsory.'

'Well, not exactly, Mr. Norman, but just look at my work, here's one . . .'

'Have you got *five* GCEs?'

'Well, not exactly, sir.'

'Four GCEs?'

'No.'

'Three?'

'Nope.'

'OUT.'

'But John Lennon hasn't even got . . .'

'Who's John Lennon . . . OUT!'

And out into the great vortex sailed I, portfolio under arm, thinking what a strange future art schools would have, full of mathematicians, scientists and so on. I did try for Laird School of Art in Birkenhead and they did accept me, but only on the condition that I got a grant from Liverpool, which the latter refused. As Dad couldn't afford to pay for me to go through college it was all over in a matter of days—a crushing blow because I'd have really liked to put my artistic capabilities to the professional test. No matter, someday it will out (if you'll excuse the expression).

But what to do here and now? A seventeen-year-old, working-class, ex-grammar, 'satisfactory, football playing' skewl lout with no passport to the outside world, no credentials, no rich daddy, no university degree, in fact nothing!

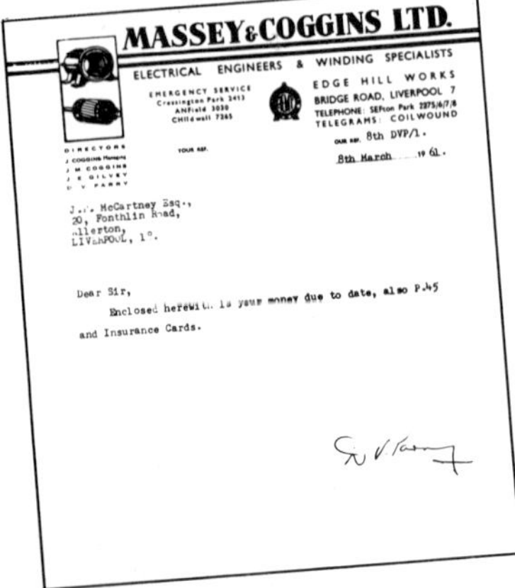

MASSEY & COGGINS LTD.
ELECTRICAL ENGINEERS & WINDING SPECIALISTS
EMERGENCY SERVICE
Cressington Park 2413
ANField 3030
Childwall 7265
EDGE HILL WORKS
BRIDGE ROAD, LIVERPOOL 7
TELEPHONE: SEFton Park 2275/6/7/8
TELEGRAMS: COILWOUND
DIRECTORS
J. COGGINS Managing
J. M. COGGINS
J. E. GILVEY
D. V. PARRY
YOUR REF.
OUR REF. 8th DVP/1.
8th March 1961.

J. M. McCartney Esq.,
20, Fonthlin Road,
Allerton,
LIVERPOOL, 18.

Dear Sir,
Enclosed herewith is your money due to date, also P.45 and Insurance Cards.

JACKSONS THE TAILORS

Paul had already tried 'working for a living' at Massey & Coggins as an armature winder, which didn't go down too well with either brother *or* Massey & Coggins at the time (although in later life, he insisted that it had done him 'a lot of good'). He went to sweep the yard out, but as he was obviously 'officer material' with those magic GCEs, they promoted him indoors winding cogs.

So it was with no great relish that I stood in the dole queue for the first time. There followed a series of uneventful but 'educational' jobs, in the sense that they involved working with people in the same position as me . . . broke.

An old Liobian school friend at the dole office couldn't help but get me my first job at Jacksons the Tailors in Ranelagh Street in the city centre where I became a proper little Mr. Polly with starched, razor-edged collars (which were obtained from Collars Ltd. in a brown cardboard box), and in which you had to be careful not to turn your head too quickly.

'Mr. McCartney.'

'Yes Mr. Bra . . .agh!' and your head's off, blood all over the terylene and worsted, dog-tooth, pin-striped bunch.

But Jacksons had one advantage, it was back streets away from Collars Ltd. and Collars Ltd. had the added advantage of being just behind Matthew Street, where brother and chums were doing lunch time sessions at the Cavern.

Memorabeatlia, 1961 . . . Working at the Cavern

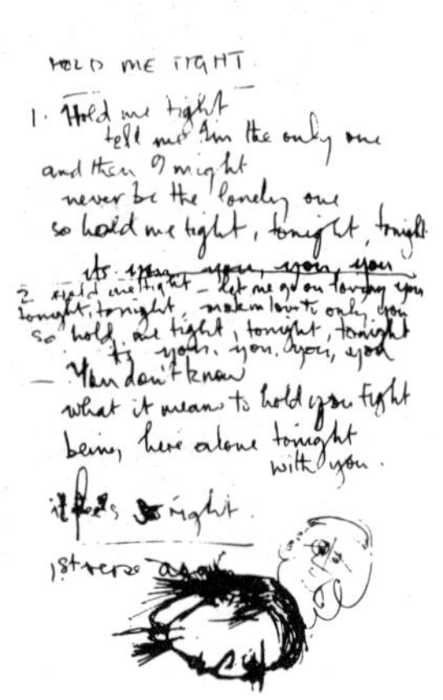

HOLD ME TIGHT
1. Hold me tight
tell me I'm the only one
and then I might
never be the lonely one
so hold me tight, tonight, tonight
its you, you, you, you
2. Hold me tight – let me go on loving you
tonight, tonight, making love to only you
so hold me tight, tonight, tonight
its you, you, you, you
— You don't know
what it means to hold you tight
being here alone tonight
with you.
it feels so right.
1st verse again

In January 1979 I was driving my children through Liverpool pointing out where we'd been to school, Ma Gees, The Art College, the Cathedral, Jacksons, and asked them if they'd like to see the Cavern?

'What's the Cavern?' they replied. I couldn't believe it . . . a life steeped in modern history and my three children didn't even know what, never mind where, the Cavern was.

'It's where your Uncle Paul played when he was a Beatle.'

'Oh . . .' (at least they'd heard of the Beatles!)

We tried to get to it, but the one way systems beat us and we had to get home because, 'We're hungry daddy'. Anyway, I could have only shown them a concrete car park . . . The original Cavern was pulled down and filled in back in 1973 to make an underground railway ventilation shaft. Bulldozer driver Terry Palmer remarked, 'It's just another job,' as he ripped through the historical remains. It must have been like pushing down the leaning tower of Pisa with your finger.

The Cavern had been opened twenty-two years previously in January 1957 as a jazz club by one Alan Sytner (a doctor's son) and was an attempt to emulate the Bohemian jazz caves of the Parisienne left bank. In 1959, Ray McFall (the Sytner accountant) took over the club, opening with Acker Bilk's Paramount Jazz Band, and 'direct from the US of A' Sonny Terry and Brownie McGhee, blues artists.

Other kids had bowls of fruit and the budgie's cage to practise on. I chose Paul's first amplifier, geet and banjo case for my school still-life.

Ray first introduced the more infra dig 'beat groups' as interval attractions between the big jazz names and the going rate for brother and fellow rockers was three pounds ten shillings for half an hour.

Paul and the Beatles first played the Cave, as it was known locally, in

The 'Rodgers & Amersmif' of Pop rehearsing at Forthlin Road. No flash, natural lighting taken during a sagging off school afternoon and one of the many times that John came round when Dad just happened to be out. (He wasn't exactly loved by Dad who suspected he was a 'trouble-maker'). They're reading from our kid's schoolbook of songs (recorded in our heads, but few went down on tape—they didn't think them good enough, that's how professional they were). This particular song did make it—*I saw her standing there*.

Paul, John (doing one of his typical-of-the-era 'cripple' things), Ray McFall (ex-accountant turned Cavern owner, mimicking John) and Cynthia (John's first wife).

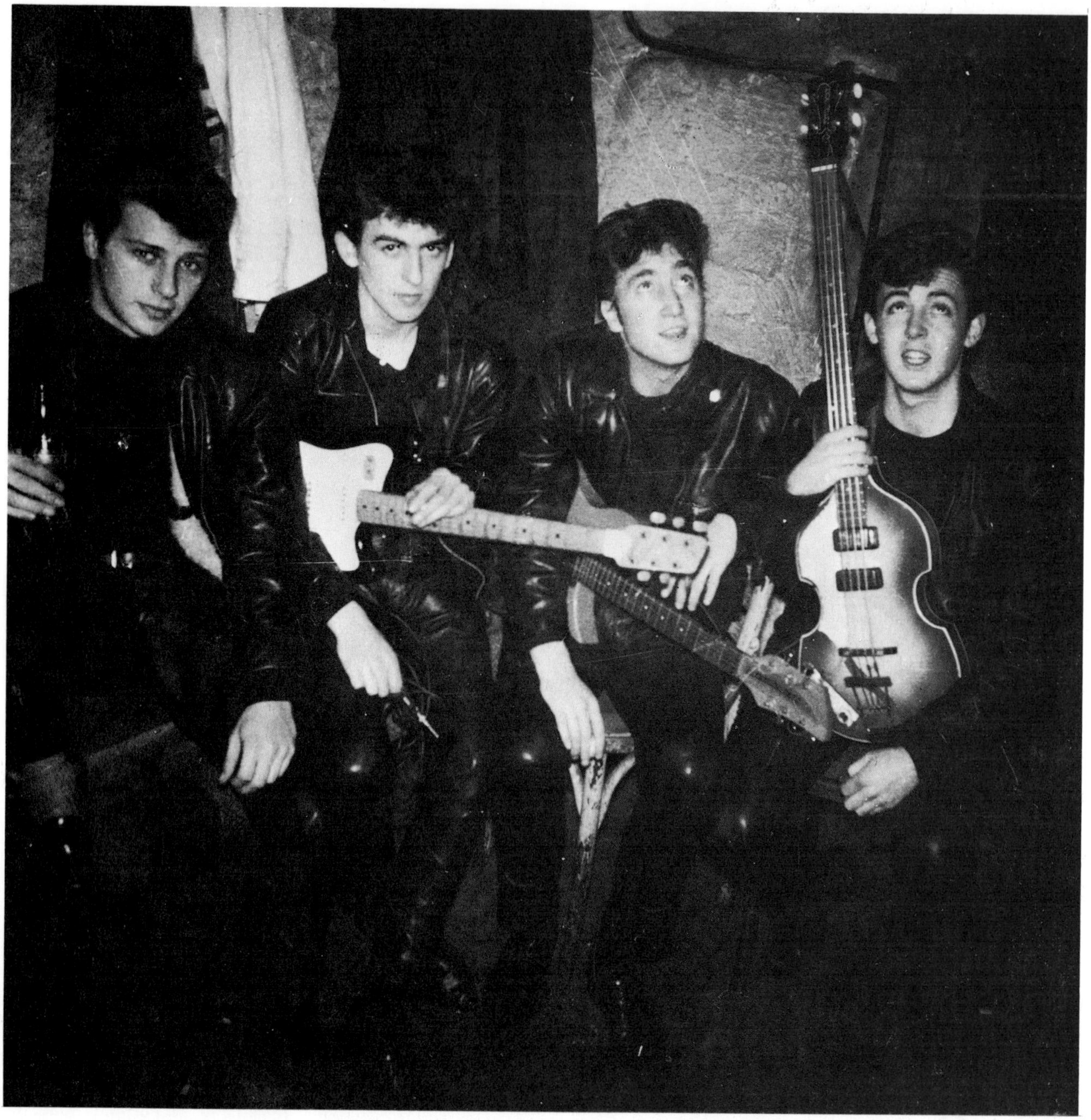

The tiny Cavern drezy showing the steps up onto the stage and my theory why Pete Best never made it . . . he wore grey socks! (Really, poor Pete just didn't fit in. Although good-looking, moody *and* magnificent, he didn't have their sense of humour.)

81a. Renshaw Street,
Editor: Bill Harry.
MERSEY BEAT
A FORTNIGHTLY GUIDE
TO ENTERTAINMENT
ON MERSEYSIDE
Phone: ROYal 0033.
Liverpool 1.

THE CAVERN
BOB WOOLER
THE CAVERN DEE-JAY
HOME ADDRESS:
23 CANNING STREET
LIVERPOOL 8
TEL: ROYAL 8029
CLUB ADDRESS:
8/12 MATHEW STREET
LIVERPOOL 2
TEL: CENTRAL 2674/5/6

THE CAVERN
RAY McFALL
THE CAVERN CLUB
HOME ADDRESS:
52 WILLOWDALE ROAD
LIVERPOOL 9
TEL: AINTREE 3860
CLUB ADDRESS:
8/12 MATHEW STREET
LIVERPOOL 2
TEL: CENTRAL 2674/5/6

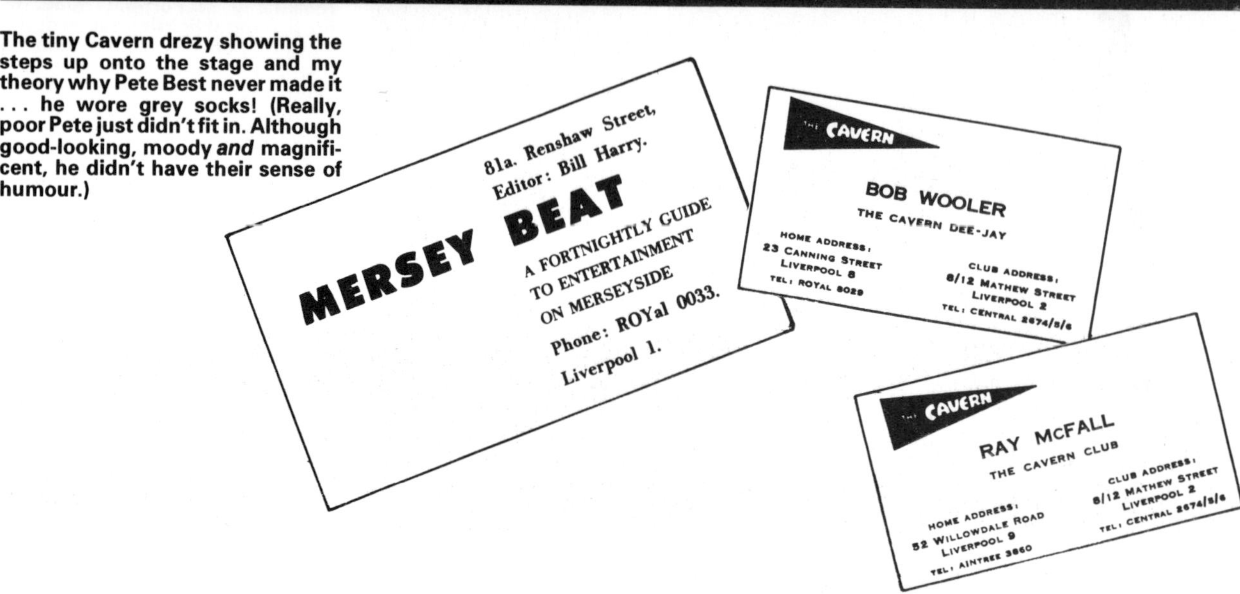

March 1961 as guests of the Blue Jeans, and they went down a bomb,* creating a large 'underground' following.

THE CAVERN CONGA

Working at the Cavern was a Jekyll and Hyde affair. Jekyll was the tedium of boring rehearsal after boring rehearsal, first at our Forthlin home, when Dad was out at work and I was sagging school or work, then on to the 86 town bus carrying guitars, amplifiers and my Köln camera, past the unloading fruit lorries in Matthew Street, and down the steep stone staircase into the dark. Opening the heavy door to the dimly light, cold, dark arched catacombe, we'd pass the cleaning ladies, get our Cokes, and head for the stage, over and through the wooden chairs facing towards Mecca (or is it Macca, I can never remember?).

Plugging in, turning on, sitting down and tuning up would follow, and then the slow belt into the numbers, till everybody knew their bits and harmonies were worked out to perfection. Our small Grundig tape recorder helped to expose the mistakes on playback, and it's great fun two decades later listening to 'the Beatles first recordings'. This went on all afternoon with me just listening, reading the New Musical Express or taking relaxed pics.

* In 'English':—a big hit.

HIPPY
SHIMMY
~~SHEIK~~ RED HOT
BESAME
RHYTHM & BLUES
OPEN
LOVE ME DO
POSTMAN
PICTURE
FEETS TOO BIG
SWINGIN' THING
FOOL OF SOMEBODY
DARKTOWN
BABY IT'S YOU
DREAM
P.S.
MONEY
ROLL OVER BEETHOVEN
LONG TALL SALLY

From behind-the-stage picture of Paul and first-cum-first-seated fans, or vice versa.

Then we'd go to the Grapes pub just down the street to get a bit of energy juice down for the coming all-night session. The various other artists on the all-nighter would pass in (and out) till it was time for the lads to 'mach schau'* back at the Cavern.

Their black leathers started to shine and rise till, as one, the Beatles rose to the occasion. Out of the Grapes into the cobbled streets of Matthew, moonlight glinting on the round black stones . . . up the narrow warehouse street . . . past the queuing customers (with the odd girl-gasp of . . . 'it's them!') . . . through Paddy and the other heavy bouncers: 'It's all right Pad,' Paul used to explain. 'He's our Kid,' and the Bluto arm was lifted like a heavy drawbridge.

We'd left Jekyll back at the pub, now it was down into the HYDE.

The cool, fruit-smelling cellar of the afternoon is now transformed into an oven-hot blast of air as the door is opened, coupled with a loud blast of good old rock 'n' roll (Derry, Rory, Gerry, The Mersey Beats, or my favourite, King Size Taylor and the Dominoes) and then the crazy walk through the audience, all holding on to the Beatle in front of you, as the girls sense their presence and close in, until the Beatles, roadies and relatives conga reaches the dressing-room door by the left-hand side of the stage.

The door opens to Aladdin's Cave only after three or four heavy 'open sesame' kicks with the bottom of the boot (soul, brother) and into the 'drezy'. This consists of a small brick cellar room with a bench and wooden chairs round the walls, coats on hangers, and Bob Wooller on the Oxbridge microphone. His record player is a part of him. They'd sit in the right-hand corner, next to the open curved arch which leads up the steps and onto the flaky ceilinged Cave stage.

I sit down, stand up, take some slightly less relaxed pics, then say, 'I'll get the Cokes in,' and exit with my camera.

'Let Mike out, Mal,' was the order of the eve, and I promised to give the magic three, four, or 8½ Fellini bangs on my return.

In the middle of my 'Cokes for the band please' order, the Beatles go on, no messin' . . . straight into strong, heavy rock 'n' roll which lifts the back of your neck off. The whole place breathes in. There's no air left, but they all breathe in, the sweat just drips from the ceiling, the body, the nose, and the soul.

'Sitting on pillar boxes with the wind whipping up from the Mersey.'

As the bogs are next to the Coke counter, the smell of urine, sweat and rotting fruit fills the nose with each hot breath.

Gathering the band's cold (thank God) Cokes in my hands and arms, I head for the Lad-in's cave door. Bang, bang, bang—nothing! Bang! Bang! Bang!—nothing—they're all watching the Beatles. In the end you give in and stand on tiptoe to watch *your* favourite act . . . the lads.

I mainly watch Lennon. He's like a caged animal, never mind a Beatle. Not that I've got anything against my brother, but he's just a brother (you know, the one who picks his nose and won't come off the toilet 'cos he's playing his guitar or reading those nudy books). Lennon just stands there, legs apart, defying you to come up an' hit him, with the odd, razor sharp intro and mongol movement, but Paul gets the girls (and some of the musical lads) going with *Till there was you*. It's a most unusual, Dad orientated, melodic song in the middle of all the

* 'mach schau' (make show) was the German encouragement shouted by their Hamburg fans.

rock 'n' roll screamers. Then he finishes 'em off with a more than passable *Long Tall Sally*.

When it's all over and the magic Sesame Street door to the drezy finally opens and SLAMS behind me (to keep out the fans), the inevitable 'the Coke's warm' follows . . . usually from George. After stripping off the dripping black T-shirts and leathers and towelling down their sweat saturated bodies, they dress in blue jeans and black polos. Then the 'Cavern Conga' snakes back through the girls once more and down to the pints of bitter. This procedure continues *ad infinitum* till the pubs close and then we all sit it out in the drezy till morning.

At daybreak Paul and I climb our weary legs out of the all night cave and headed, tireder but somehow wiser (and certainly happier) for the number 86 bus stop, where we look at the latest winkle pickers in shoe shop windows or sit on pillar-boxes with the wind whipping up from the Mersey, and wait for the first bus home . . . magic days.

Winkle picker browsing after all-night session at the Cavern.

BEAT NOTE

Out of the millions of pounds eventually made from quick-thinking promoters, manufacturers, record, film, TV and radio people and assorted hangers on, Bob Wooller was one of the ones who got the least for all the early work and devotion he put into the Beatles. I'm not saying this should be in any way changed, but the thirty-year-old (then) quiet-spoken, posh-accented, resident compere, with his outrageous, corny, music-hall puns, had a genuine love of the Beatles and has a corner in my heart.

Anyone who wrote, 'The Beatles are truly a phenomenon. I don't think anything like them will happen again' in *Mersey Beat* back in 1961, two years *before* Beatlemania, can't be all that bad.

A much-used, but never credited-to-me pic of Gene Vincent with arms round John & Paul. Sounds Incorporated are on stage at the Cave, and this is the arched dressing room doorway to the stage. On the right-hand side is Bob Wooller's corner.

THE CATHOLIC BIBLE REP

In between jobs, whilst 'resting' on the dole, various jobs were written for. One reply from the City of Liverpool Children's Committee, applying for a training course to look after little kids, went as follows: *'Dear Sir, I acknowledge receipt of your letter dated 7th March 1962, but would inform you that the training course administered by this Committee is for women only. Yours faithfully. Children's Officer OBE.'*

When I spotted another ad in the *Liverpool Echo* (Echo Echo): 'AMBITIOUS MAN required to train as an assistant to Sales Manager, must be well spoken and of good education, previous experience not essential, but must be free to start immediately,' I thought . . . It's me!

On arrival at the deserted St. John's Buildings in the town centre on Saturday 7 April 'between ten and one', I found a rather RADA* trained, smarmy man in his early thirties who implied that the job 'we' were about to embark on (he would assist until I got to know the ropes) was important, exciting and what's more, remunerative.

'That's nice, but what do we *do* Mr. Kerr?'

'Sell Catholic bibles Mr. McCartney.'

'Oh my God.'

Having been christened a Catholic, the initial idea of flogging bibles to Catholic brothers and sisters was not over joyful, but not having been indoctrinated by my religion and being broke, I took the job.

'What about the money, Mr. Kerr?'

'A percentage situation on each Bible sold.'

'Fine, so let's go.'

'Have you ever sold books before Mr. McCartney?'

'No.'

'Then I suggest we cover ourselves.'

* Royal Academy of Dramatic Art.

'Covering ourselves' meant me learning off pat (sorry, off Kerr) a carefully constructed paragraph: 'Good afternoon, I am the Catholic bible representative for this area, dealing particularly with the Catholic Faith. Do you happen to be of the Faith by any chance?' (Of course they bloody were, RADA Kerrful had checked the Church Register) and would continue, 'Father Mahoney has instructed me as the official Catholic rep. . . . etc. etc. . . .' (Oh no, he'll have a personally signed letter from God next, thought I).

With the kerrfully rehearsed text properly learned, we set off in his car for the first sucker . . . sorry customer . . . sorry parishioner.

'*This* man is very important. He's a retired headmaster and if we get his sale the whole district will be ours.'

'A headmaster!' (I'd only been out of school a few months and the last one was terrifying enough.)

'Don't worry, if you get in any trouble I'll be right behind you.'

So off we set, more bibles than brains, to my first customer, rehearsing all the way 'Good afternoon, I am the Catholic bible rep. of this area dealing particularly . . . etc. etc.'

When we arrived at the house, RADA stayed in the car and I presented myself to 'The head's door.

Knock! Knock!

'Yes?' answered a Professional, Tough, looking Nut.

'Good afternoon . . . erm . . .'

'Well!' (Hard to crack nut.)

'Yes . . . erm . . . well, I'm the Catholic of this Representative . . . good afternoon area, dealing particularly . . . erm . . .' I stopped.

'What *are* you trying to say boy?'

RADA was by my side quicker than either Tom or Jerry, 'What my colleague is trying to say sir, is that we are Catholic . . .'

'No you're not, you're nothing of the sort, you're cheap salesmen and if I see you round this district again, I'll call the police d'you hear?'

'Thank you sir, good day.'

Because I needed the money this soul-destroying job went on for about a week, but in the end even money couldn't save me. I had just sold my only bible of the week to next door's understanding Catholic saviours, when God caught up with me. I went upstairs feeling rather queer, drew myself in the mirror and then went down for Dad's tea. Just before retiring for the night I caught sight of what I'd drawn . . . I looked like the Devil.

The next morning I returned all the bibles and went back on the dole.

5-day week. Write. Fleet
phone: Studio Manager,
Illustrating Limited, 16 John Dalton
Street, Manchester 2.

AMBITIOUS Man required to train as an Assistant to Sales manager, must be well spoken and of good education, previous experience not essential, must be free to start immediately, call and see Mr. Kerr, Room 19, 12 St. John's Lane, Liverpool 1, on Saturday, April 7, between 10 and 1.

AMERICA
Excellent positions available for Mothers' Helps, Maids, Couples. Fare Bonus ... experience needed. Brochure.

The day God caught up with his Catholic bible representative.

'After all I've been good to you Michael'

First Beatles poster rough.

There aren't many occasions in this often predictable, sometimes boring, day-to-day life when something presents itself above and beyond the call of duty and causes you to see through all the bull-shit, and have a bloody good belly laf.

A few of the times it's happened to me are witnessing Marcel Duchamp's *R. Mutt 1917* Piss (oire) Pot, hanging from the Tate Gallery ceiling in the middle of an otherwise sedate surrealist London exhibition (smile); watching Marlon Brando soaked to the snakeskin in the opening of *The Fugitive Kind* at an empty Liverpool cinema (chuckle); and opening the following Hamburg letter from Paul (with a little help from his John) on the early morning, zombie, top deck of a number 86 bus going on to my new place of work. Addressed to 'Michael and his Dad'; it read:

dated 9.5.62

Dear Me and his Dad,

Thanks for the letter and the papers—gear, ta!
I'll try to make this letter a decent length, and informative.

Roy Young (who's playing with us, as you know) went to Eng., and he's signed Gene Vincent for here in August and Johnny Kidd for a bit earlier. Roy's convinced that he can get Jerry Lee Lewisses out here too, and Chuck Berry. I doubt it, but if he CAN get them we've already put in a claim to back *him*.* Its gear about Andre Bernards† cos you can start earning good money if you like it. I don't know why I said that, maybe it's because I used to fancy doing it too.

† Guess who they'd rather back . . . and he wasn't white.
‡ My next job as Ladies Liverpool hairdresser.

Cowboy-booted Beatles on the roof of the Bambi kino in Hamburg, taken by . . .? (It wasn't me this time. I was back home doing my homework.)

Self-portrait with Paul's present of a Rollei magic.

Oh yes!!! the best bit of news. It's no use me keeping it as a surprise. I've ordered a *Rollei*, (camera). Exactly the same as Astrids!* Its dear, but it's a fab one, but . . . you'll give me a go of it, won't you? Mind you, all my presents (i.e. the blue mac for instance) turn out like that.

I had a look at Astrid's photos, they're fab gear (so that's who started it all). I think that's the trick, most photos look gear *enlarged* to about the size of this paper.

We'll be playing in a few minutes, so I'll carry on later . . . yes . . . mmm . . . see you later then . . . yes . . . OK man . . . its a knockout . . . its a gas man . . .

This Bit is Later . . .

Gerry, the Pacemakers and Bernie arrived tonight, laughing and bringing us ten Players ciggies, which taste horrible when you've been smoking German ciggies, but he's not to know, kind simple Bernie.*

John says 'Winston Atlee'. I'll ask John if he has any news. He says: 'However black the clouds may be, Michael, in time they'll pass away, Michael. Have faith and trust and you will see, Michael. God's light make bright your day, Michael.' He says, 'remember that, Michael.'

St. John v. 23 ch. 8 page 45. Platform 9 and various other . . .

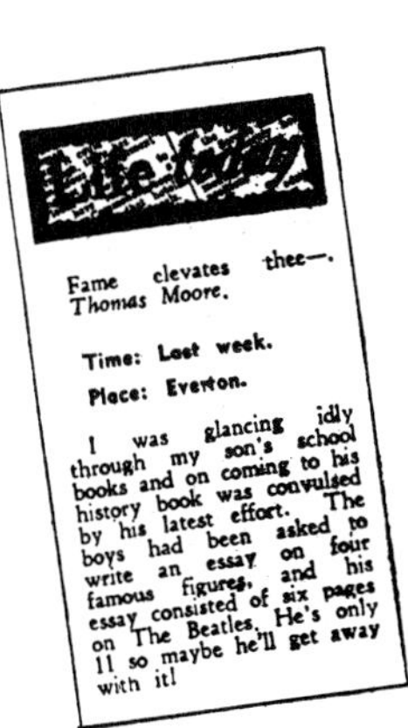

Fame elevates thee—. *Thomas Moore.*

Time: Last week.

Place: Everton.

I was glancing idly through my son's school books and on coming to his history book was convulsed by his latest effort. The boys had been asked to write an essay on four famous figures, and his essay consisted of six pages on The Beatles. He's only 11 so maybe he'll get away with it!

* Astrid Kirchner—Stu Sutcliffe's German girlfriend (later fiancee).

* Bernie 'Nems' who later became roadie to the stars (including John Mayall etc.)

Astrid, John and Stu taken outside the Cavern. Astrid—a waif-like, Mia Farrowish figure—came over to Liverpool just prior to Stu's death in Hamburg. I sent this one to John and Yoko in New York, just for the memory.

Dear Michael,

Seriously now, to hit a serious note , with regard to your hairdrying application, I'm happy to inform you, you've lost the job, remember that Michael. 'However black the "Believe me, Michael". Believe me when I say it's true after all I've been good to you. However black the man may be, good old Michael, a friend from us. Platform 9.

Yours simply

Rod Lennon

P.S. A big Hi from Rod (dictated to me by Rod) There's a cripple in the air, it's a flying cripple, says Rod.

Dear Michael,

Arrived safely after a hasty voyage. The club is great, Michael. Everyone is so good to us, after all, we've been good to them . . . Gee thanks Michael. As she slipped the hot silk from her charlies, Michael. Ogden social club welcomes white men. 'Marijuana make those eyes at me for,' Boy. Remember that Michael, after all I've been good to you Michael. Me and my charlies. Russ Conrad cooks Jock Flannery for breakfo. Quote were just good friends to you, says Stirling Moss, who is still lying uncultured in Whaltham la-Thames hospital. Emergency Platform 10. Emergency Ward Bond, and various other activities. Emergency make those eyes at me for boy.

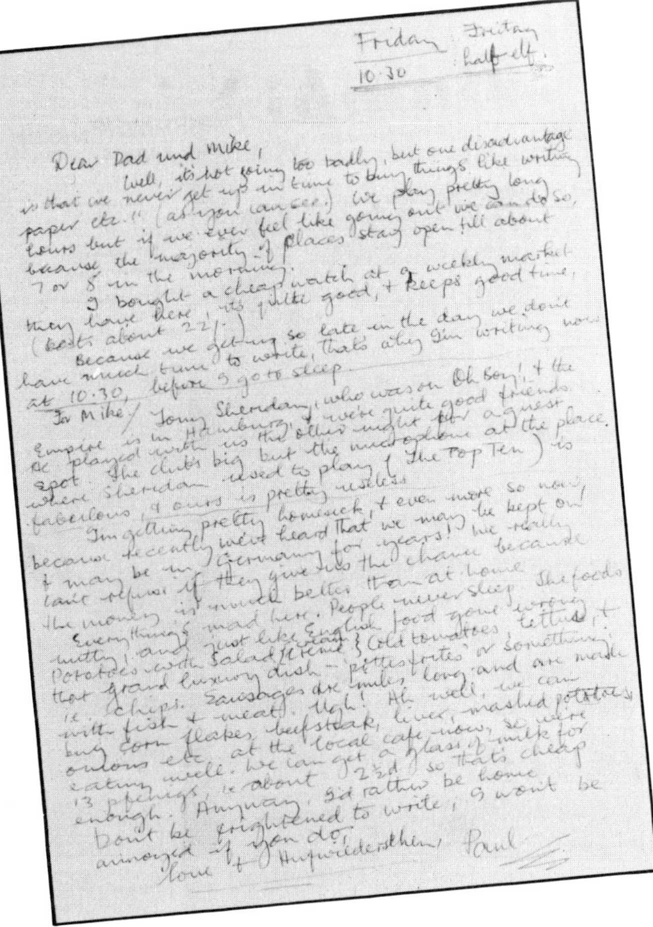

Friday : Freitag
10.30 : half elf.

Dear Dad und Mike,
Well, it's not going too badly, but one disadvantage
is that we never get up in time to buy things like writing
paper etc.!! (as you can see.) We play pretty long
hours but if we ever feel like going out we can do so,
because the majority of places stay open till about
7 or 8 in the morning.
I bought a cheap watch at a weekly market
they have here, it's quite good, + keeps good time,
(costs about 22/-)
Because we getting so late in the day we don't
have much time to write, that's why I'm writing now
at 10.30, before I go to sleep.
To Mike / Tony Sheridan, who was on Oh Boy!, + the
Empire is in Hamburg, + we're quite good friends.
He played with us the other night for a guest
spot. The club's big but the microphone at the place
where Sheridan used to play (The Top Ten) is
fabulous, + ours is pretty useless.
I'm getting pretty homesick, + even more so now,
because recently we've heard that we may be kept on
+ may be in Germany for years! We really
can't refuse if they give us the chance because
the money is much better than at home.
Everything's mad here. People never sleep. The food's
just like English food gone wrong
witty! and just like English { Cold tomatoes, lettuce, +
Potatoes with salad cream } or something;
that grand luxury dish - pottesfrites or something; made
ie. chips. Sausages are miles long and are made
with fish + meat! Ugh! Ah well, we can
buy corn flakes, beefsteak, liver, mashed potatoes
onions etc at the local cafe now, so we're
eating well. We can get a glass of milk for
13 pfenigs, ie about $2\frac{1}{2}$d so that's cheap
enough. Anyway, I'd rather be home.
Don't be frightened to write, I won't be
annoyed if you do,
love + Aufwiedersehen, Paul

The place where they slept.

Dear Michael,

Gee there's a swell looking coloured woman, gee, there's Mal Perry too, Mersey Beat editor. Woopee, Ma, the circus has come to town, she cried in a voice that bode no ill. Hes Dick Turpin so fast I can't get it down. Gee, ma, there's a Hebrew elephants. You can tell it's Hebrew by the Sunny Side of the Street

Dear Michael,

Arrived quickly after a hasty Fields. However Stirling Moses may be, In time he'll pass away, Michael (dear reader) are you sitting comfortably, then I'll beguine, then I'll be damned, then albino.

Dear Stirling,

Derived softly after a hairy voyage. The club is wonderful, they're very good to us here after all, I've been good to you . . .

Dear God,

Depraved safely as I lift you, arthur all I've been good to youston, platform 9. Stop. Stirling, he say.

'Dear Michael—cheap seat with dining car attacked' After all, I'll be goofy too. Stop. I'll Hitler. Sheridan sings songs of the good old regime. Beatles back Hitler—'It's a gas, man.'

Dear Kelly,

Arrived after a safe abortion, After all, 'gone fishing' Ba-biddi, boop boop-bip, bip boopee doop doop boop, bopitty boop.

Jingle Bells, jingle bells riding through the glen, Jingle Bells, jingle bells, with his band of hope and various veins, says Stirling. Enter Sir Hilbert, larfing. 'Where's her ladyship, Jenkins?' The boot (for Jenkins, the boot they call he).

'Her ladyship has sailed, Sir Philip.'

'Where has she sailed' he quoth

'She's sailed the bloody furniture, Sir Stirling.

Dear Jesus,

Arrived safely after a rough *cross*ing, missed the boat, walked all the way. Got a gear coat (camel hair) off Joseph.

Enter the 35th His Royal Majesty Queen Stirlings Dragoons, brandishing the 34th His Royal Majesty Queen Stirling's dragoons.

'Rabbi Burns for Pope,' he said in a voice that bode no diddley.

'Aha,' said Sir Philbert 'a-sailing is she?'

'Gee, m'lud, you're lookin swell.'

'Swelling is she?' answered Sir Pilfering politely.

'Sure,' said Jenkins the boot, with a twinkle in his eye, (for they called him twinkle boot).

'Twinkling is she?' said Michael, which just goes to show, I've been good to you, Stirring.

Yours furiously

Paul, George, Rod the bass
(after all, Ivan good to you)

LADIES BARBER TO THE STARS

On the advice of Auntie Jin, 'hairdressing is an art son', my new job (after the bibles) took me up Ranelagh Street from Jacksons to Andre Bernard's, ladies hairdressers, as an apprentice ladies barber at the princely sum of £1.10.9d a week for three years! Not *big* money even in those days (our kid earned £7.0.0. a week at Massey & Coggins), but as I was learning 'a trade' this made all the difference (so they said). No wonder Jimmy Tarbuck was leaving to become a comedian!

The normal apprentice usually begins when he leaves school at fifteen or sixteen, but having dilly dallied at school and the Art College plus taking assorted dead-end jobs I now found myself at the grand old age of eighteen required to empty bins, brush floors, wipe dust from razor sharp blinds, store towels, pass pins, and if I was lucky shampoo hair till my hands bled. Not only that, I had to change my name. As there was already a 'Michael' I was now required to choose a new Christian name. All manner of manly names shot to mind, Hunk, Clunt, Bulk, but eventually I settled on my first name, and a badge was ordered for 'Peter'.

Cockney coiffeured 'eavy 'airdressers with their Bill Haley - jackets in Bernard's staff room, Liverpool.

Until we were passed as fit to wear the Andre Bernard green tartan half-sleeve 'Junior' jacket (not unlike Bill Haley's), us apprenticeship lads had to wear white shirts with rolled, up sleeves, and dark blue AB Ties (ABy, ABy, ABY my boy).

The sleeves could be rolled up (*a*) very high, which was considered rather working class, (*b*) just on the elbow . . . fine, or (*c*) below the elbow which got them wet when you shampooed Mrs. Goldsteinburg.

Bernard's was owned by Bernard and Richard Mizelas, two London relatives. Richard was my boss (or should I say *Mr.* Richard as all hairdressers were referred to as 'Mr.', particularly the boss.)

From the shampoo basin window you could gaze down on Brian (Epstein's) new NEMS record store (as you washed madam's itchy scalp), and as Bri had just signed up my brother and group, I now had a vested interest in how much business his shop did. (Oyvey! Already a business man.)

Whilst pretending to wash containers, mirrors etc. by the dispensary window you could watch young couples meet under the infamous nude male statue (you know, the one called Nicholas*).

Bernard's was also next to Blackler's store where George (Harrison) worked for a while as an apprentice electrician, which came in handy when you fancied a chat and a nice cup of tea in the cold winter months, and finally my new work place was just as near the Cavern as Jacksons the Tailors.

But it wasn't all roses. As I pointed out, I was eighteen at the time, in contrast to the younger juniors, and being made to do such menial jobs round the shop was at first humiliating, so I approached the work with great 'distance'. My aloofness was immediately interpreted as superiority by some of the hairdressers and for a while it was touch and go whether I would be accepted by them. In fact Mr. Richard gave me an ultimatum; either I 'pulled my socks up' and came down in the world, or I'd be out!

As this was the first job that I could see had any future, this placed me in quite a predicament. Either I rebel against the system, or eat some shit and join it. I chose the latter . . . there was no alternative.

MY FIRST LOVE AND BOB 'FOLK RUBBISH' DYLAN

One day my first real love, after mum, walked into the salon; she was one of a group of models posing for the *Daily Post and Echo*. I was brushing up the hair as it cascaded endlessly down on to the floor. It wasn't exactly the brushing up which excited her, it was the *way* I did it (isn't it always?). The brush was balanced, she later recalled, on the end of my index finger, the furthest point from my body and, with absolute disdain, I followed it across the shop floor.

Not being a *Post and Echo* model at all, but in truth a hungry student plying her body for money, she returned for the free evening classes where she became my model, and I discovered that her name was Celia. From a model customer she became a model model, and from a model model we became a model couple.

She was the first woman I gave myself to, and she gave herself in return. In her Husky Street flat we got lost in each other's body and mind; we swam together through many Liverpool 8 late nights and often into the morning, when she would get up to cook breakfast and put on records. I would just lie there, male chauv-like. One morning she kept playing a particular album which didn't impress me.

'Who's *that* Ceel?'

'Someone they keep playing at college . . . Bob Dylan.'

'Never heard of him.'

'Neither had I, but after a while he's quite good.'

* 'Knock! knock! . . . 'Who's there?' . . . 'NICHOLAS' . . . 'Nicholas who?' . . . 'Nickerless boys shouldn't climb trees.'

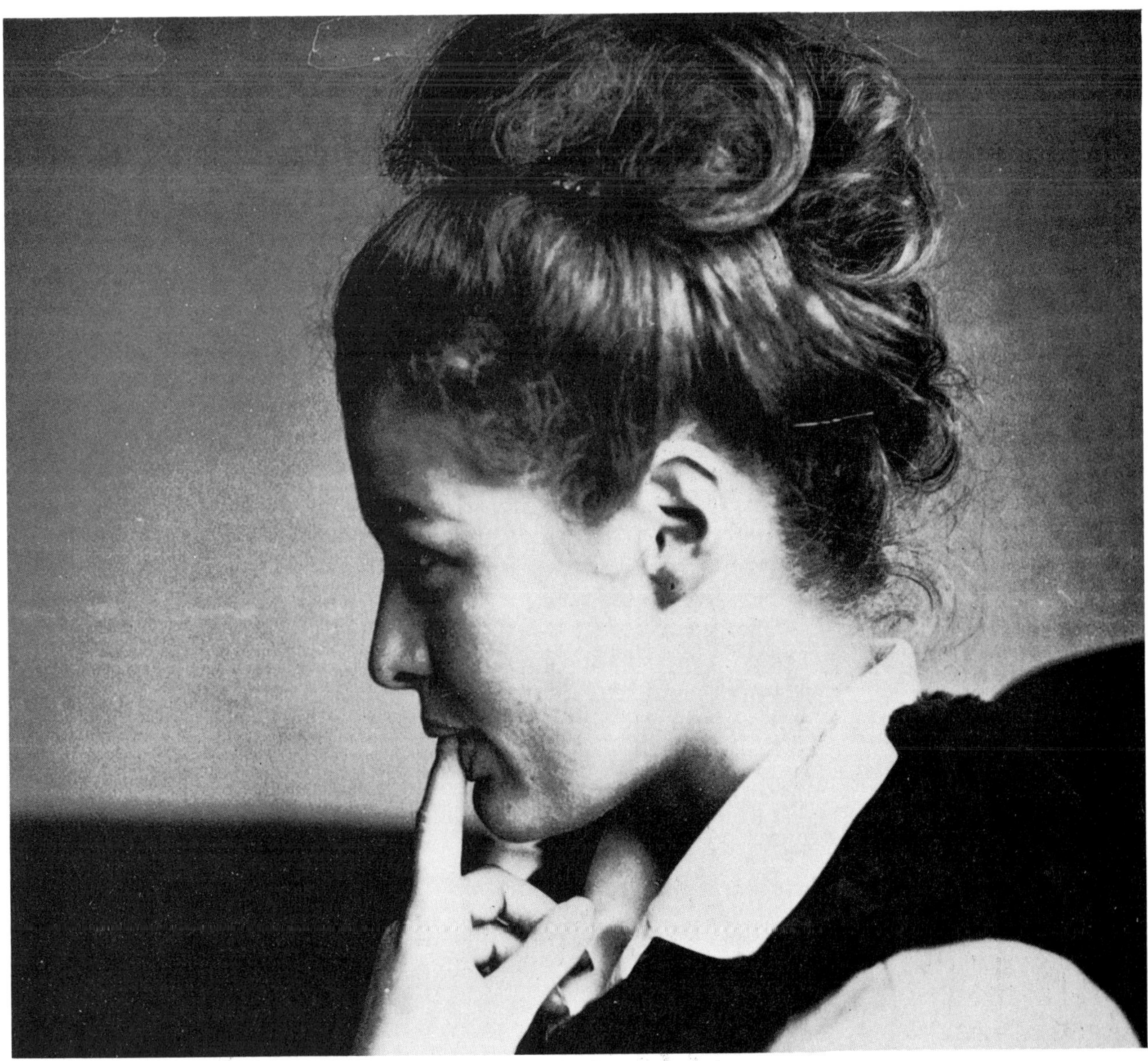

Ceel—my first real love (after Mum).

'Folk rubbish.'

The next few heavenly-bodied weekends, however, saw me sold on Bob Dylan with songs about New Orleans brothels, 'Pretty pretty pretty pretty, Peggy Oh', and 'If you'll just let me follow you down . . .' He *must* be all right.

Celia let me borrow the album for a while and one evening brother Paul came home early from a Beatle gig (at one o'clockish) to find me playing it quietly to myself (the record that is).

'What's that crap?'

'That's what I thought when *I* first heard it.'

'Who is it?'

'A bloke called Bob Dylan.'

'Never 'eard of him. Folk crap. See yer, is Dad in bed?'

'Yeah. It'll grow on you ya know.'

'Rubbish.'

'There's a note from Dad to remember to take your capsules. Good night.'

'Good night.'

'The Beatles, spelt BeAtles, and they're doing very well, they've just made their first record in Germany.'

'Really, what's it called?'

'*My Bonnie* . . . It's an uptempo version of that old Scottish folk song. But what they really need is a manager. Would you like to . . . erm . . . see their picture?'

'Certainly.'

I produced the fab pic and watched his face closely. To a seasoned 'pro' the sight of four, dirty, long-haired yobs in head-to-toe leather with not even a showbiz smile on their faces, must have been an extraordinary sight, but I must say he handled it rather well.

'I have to admit to you Mike, what with Ruby *and* the Jones Boys, I've got my hands rather full at the moment.'

'Just thought I'd ask, they're going to make it big some day you know.'

'I hope they do Mike . . . I hope they do.'

Later that night, it was the 7th August 1961, I got drunk for the first time. In December of that year Brian Epstein wasn't so backward coming forward and signed the Beatles up at 25%.

Black leathers ... 'I've got my hands rather full at the moment,' said Bernie.

'The Beaties', a group of Liverpool boys who have started recording for Parlophone. They had a wonderful reception when they appeared in the recent Star Show presented by Brian Epstein (Nems Enterprises Ltd., Liverpool) at the Tower Ballroom, New Brighton. The group includes John Lennom, Paul McCarthey, George Harrison and Peter Best.

It wasn't long before they listened to Bri . . .

THEM AND US

Meanwhile, back in the Saloon as we called it, I would chat to the customers about 'my' and 'their' lives.

The customers came in two types: the upper-middle-class, over-the-water (or Southport), nail-and-foot-manicure-at-the-same-time snots, or you and I.

With the snots the conversation usually went something like:

'Good day, madam.'

Silence.

'What shampoo are we going to try today?'

'Normal.'

'Normal, madam? Are we sure? It's looking a teeny bit greasy. Would you like to try a medicated this time?'

'Normal.'

'Certainly, madam.'

Shampoo ordered at the dispensary, carbon under new page, slip written out . . . 'Shampoo and set, twelve shillings and sixpence.

'Would you like a conditioner, madam?'

'No.'

'Thank you.'

Rip off top slip and push onto spike, collect towel and test-tube of shampoo, and return to 'madam.'

'Head up, please' . . . towel round neck . . . 'head back in the basin please' . . . water on, cold and hot over your left hand, till temp just right, water over hair careful not to spill over face (but dying to).

'Lovely day, madam.'

Silence . . . (battle on!)

'It's frustrating in here on days like this.'

Silence.

'I saw a very exciting "up and coming" new group last night madam.'

'Group?'

'Yes madam.' (got ya)

'What sort of *group*?'

'A musical group madam, called the Beatles.'

'The WHAT?'

'The Beatles, Be*A*tles.'

'What a horrible name!'

'Perhaps (you old cow) madam, but I think you'll be hearing more about them soon . . . (and they'll knock you and your bloody phoney kind right through next week's wet *Echo*) . . . Madam.'

With *you* the conversation went more like this:

'Good morning madam.'

'Good morning Peter.'

'And what can we get you today?'

'I think I'll try normal shampoo please.'

'Are you sure? It's looking a bit greasy, how about medicated?'

'Are you sure, Peter?'

'Yeah. It's all right, I won't charge you.'

'Well OK then.'

'Conditioner?'

'Yes please, and *I'll* pay for that.'

'Thanks.'

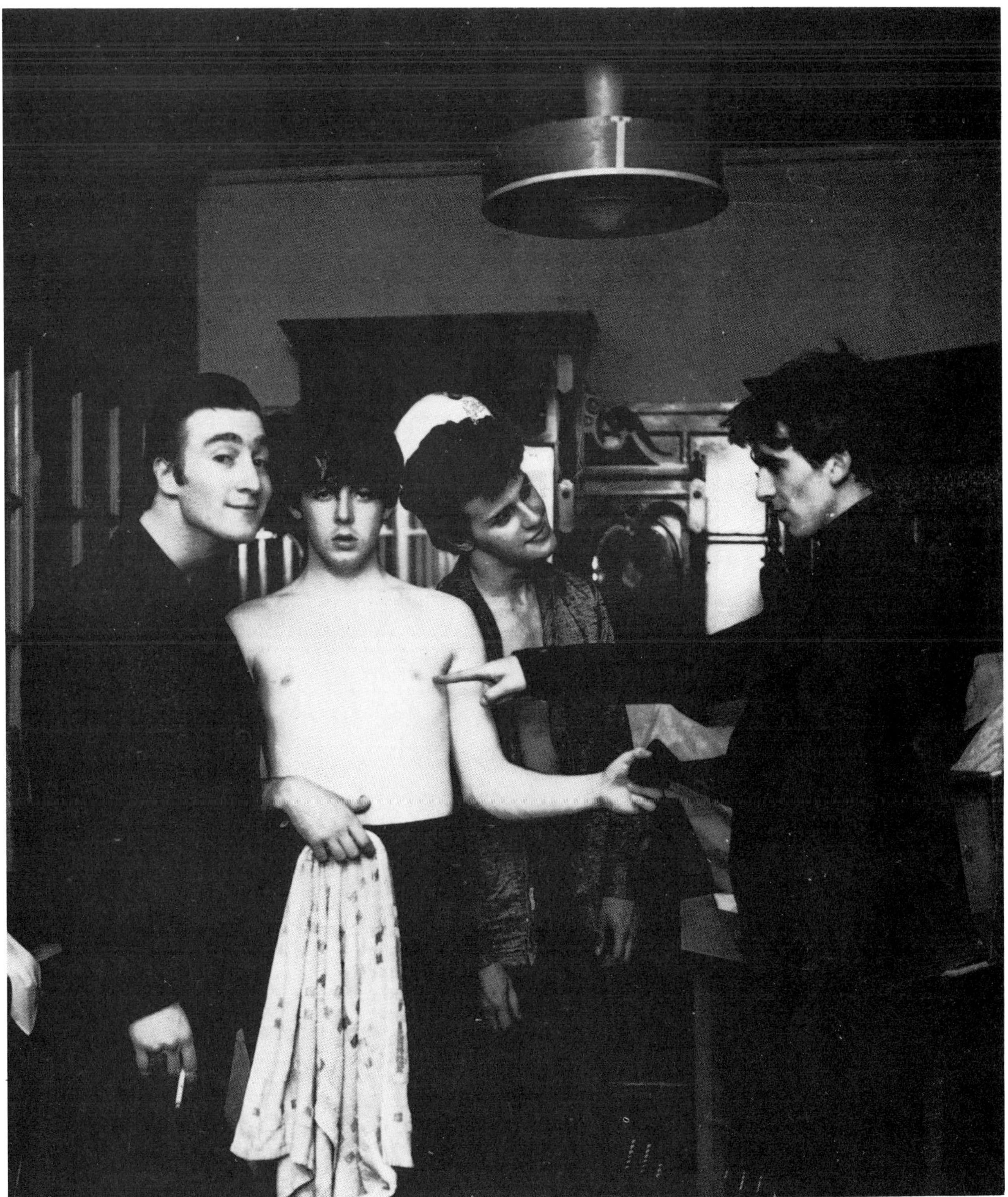

A very exciting 'up and coming' new group.

To dispensary, two towels (ask for warm ones this time), two shampoos, and into the washing, and I *was* a good shampooer (even if I say it myself, with my soft velvet fingers on their scalps reaching down to parts that madam wouldn't ever dream about in the daylight.)

'Fabulous day.'

'Is it? I've been busy shopping.'

'Yeah, blue sky, white clouds, what more could you ask?'

'It must bc frustrating for you locked in here on days like this.'

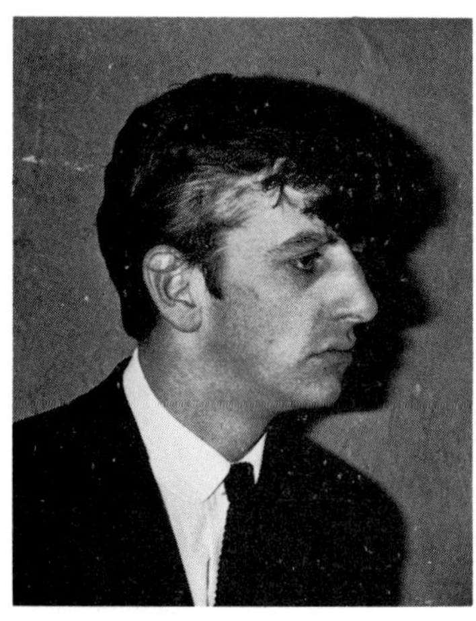

'They've just rehearsed a new drummer called Ringo . . .'

'Quite . . . it's our kid's birthday today.'
'Your brother's, is it? . . . what day is it today Peter?'
'June 18th.'
'And how old is he?'
'Twenty.'
'Is he really? Now what's that group he's in again?'
'The Beatles madam.'
'That's right, what a funny name . . . a skiffle group isn't it?'
'*Beat* group madam. Well actually, a rock 'n' roll group.'
'Really.'
'Yeah, they're doing very well. In fact you may have heard them on the Radio, in *Teenagers Turn* on Whit Monday.'
'I don't think so Peter, I was at my Mother's that day.'
'They've just rehearsed a new drummer called Ringo, and . . .'
'Ringo?'

MERSEY BEAT

PAGE 4

OPERATION BIG BEAT

PHOTOGRAPHS IN MERSEY BEAT CAN BE OBTAINED TO ORDER FROM THE OFFICE

THE HURRICANES RIP IT UP ! . . .
. . . Gold lame shirts included. Johnny Guitar, Rory, Ringo and Lu at New Brighton Tower.

Photo by Dick Matthews

THE BEATLES IN ACTION . . .
George, Paul, Pete and John, appearing at the highly successful "Operation Big Beat" at the Tower Ballroom. Fans of this popular group will be pleased to hear that copies of their record will be available soon at Nems.

LIFEL

Listen does not mean by have bee Liverpool lifeless time. H get? W any fi think that going group Raven Torna the R scene ingoe T.T.'s Steve others Cyclo drum and Barc

Ha ne m . a grc .. of . ti w p

'Well, he wears all these rings all over his hands you see, but he's a fabulous drummer . . . Now this is a secret . . . 'cos the other drummer doesn't know, but they went down to London to record their first single a couple of weeks ago.' (Well, you couldn't plug the *Bonny* flop could you?)

'Really?'

'Yes, for EMI records.'

'What's it called?'

Love Me Do, and *P.S. I Love You*, but it's not certain which is the top side yet.'

'That's marvellous.'

'It is, isn't it?'

'Well, I hope it's a *big* success Peter.'

'Thank you madam—it will be.'

(At least Brian and I knew.)

'Who's drum kit is this?' asks Pete looking at Ringo's equipment just prior to a Royal Iris boat cruise (with Acker Bilk).

PEOPLE AND PLACES AND PASS OUT WILL YOU PETER

A couple of months later, in October 1962, EMI released *Love Me Do* and the Beatles were available for exploitation . . . sorry promotion. This came sooner than anticipated when Granada Television in Manchester wanted the boys for their local news and magazine programme, *People and Places.*

Now, one of my many chores as a ladies' barber junior included leaving the salon spotless at the end of each gruelling day, and with 'chatty' customers (or randy hairdressers *and* chatty customers) this meant me leaving Bernard's at half-past six, seven o'clock and sometimes even half-past eight at night (still two pounds a week though).

The TV programme started at half-past six. So the night 'the lads' were on, I broke my back trying to make the place spotless so that I could get the hell out of there and watch them on Auntie Dill's telly at her and Uncle Bill's Eagle Hotel.

'Peter, take madam out, will you.'

'—Yes Miss Greta.'

'Peter, pass up will you . . .'

'Yes Mr. Richard.'

'Peter, put madam under the dryer will you . . .'

'Yes Miss Arlett.'

'Peter, shampoo Mrs. Goldamayer please . . .'

'Yes Miss Helen.'

'Peter, pass up will you . . .'

'Yes Mr. Richard.'

'Peter, get me a beer shampoo . . .'

'Yes! Mr. Martin.'

Now, this was more like it. Under the counter, into the dispensary, with the beer bottle opened in three seconds flat, and whilst fellow junior, Lew 'Cuckoo' Collins* pours the beer into the impossibly small bottle, I open my mouth underneath to catch any drops.

* Lew is Lewis (no less) Collins, a fine (h)-Actor on our British TV screens, now known for his work in *The Professionals* but will be world renowned when he takes over the 007 Bond role in future years (fab prediction?).

Andre Bernard's star factory. Will Lew Collins be the next James Bond?

'Oh dear Mike. Seems like more's gone in your mouth than in the container.'

'You mean you've spilt it Lew.'

''Fraid so, it's only half full . . . this means another bottle I'm afraid.' 'Dear oh dear,' I murmur, as another pale ale is opened and we repeat the procedure, but this time we reverse positions. 'Oh dear Lew. Seems like more's gone in your mouth . . . etc. etc.'

By the time madam gets her beer shampoo, both the tiny bottle and the two juniors are tanked up to the top.

'Peter, pass up will you . . .' (*'Piss up?'*)

'Er, certainly Mr. Richard.'

'Peter, take Mrs. Goldermayer out will you . . .' (*'Where to? The Wimpey bar, Lime Street? . . .'*)

'Certainly Miss Helen.'

'Peter, put madam under please . . .' (*'Yeah, for good!*)

'Certainly Miss Arlett.'

'Peter, pass out will you . . .' (*Certainly Mr. Lewis's* . . . but I didn't.)

Instead I got Lew to do my chores, changed jackets, and belted down the back stairs out of the shop, past the fruit and veg barrow. I was legging it down Ranelagh Street to Auntie Dill's when I noticed the time—dead on half-past six! I realised I would never make it to the Eagle on time, so looked round desperately for a passing telly. (It's not like these days when *everybody's* on television. In those days it was a *big deal* if you got your face on the box . . . not only that, it was *my brother's* face.)

I spied a television in the pub opposite Jacksons' window and it was on the right channel. I could see Gay Byrne miming an announcement through the glass. Panting into the pub, I ordered a pint just as he finished the announcement.

'. . . so here they are, from Liverpool . . . the Beatles!'

1962 and Love Me Do

And there they *were* in living black and white . . . on the TELLY. But something's wrong! That's not John Lennon singing! It's *his* mop top, *his* guitar, *his* new mohair suit, *his* open legs, *his* open mouth, but the mouth is singing *You Ain't Nothin' but a Hound Dog*, and I realise that the pub juke box is on . . . full blast!

Thank God, Elvis fades and the Beatles cross-fade into the bar (is this a message for Elvis I ask myself) . . . 'Shake it up baby now . . . Twist and shout . . . Come on cum on cum on cum on, baby now ow ow . . . Twist and shout . . . ah . . . ah . . . ah . . . Ah . . . yeah . . . blap blap . . . end.'

'Fabulous . . . Gear . . . Fabtastic', I shout to myself in the indifferent bar.

After a short interview in which they sound like they're putting on Liverpool accents (particularly Paul and John), 'and now their new single *Love Me Do*'.

'FANTASTIC . . . turn it UP!' (I shouted in my head). That's my brother . . . my bloody brother! . . . My head's exploding . . . 'so ple-e-e-se love me do'.

That's our kid! . . . I can't take any more! And suddenly it's all over. They've gone, and so has my pint.

'Dya want that fillin' up son, or wa? You look like ya need it.'

'No thank you, my man,' says I, puffin' up like a peacock. Cocking my snook at the indifferent members of the public bar, with its RU18 sign, and realising for the first time that I *was*, I strutted out of that Puke Box Brewery.

CAN I HAVE YOUR AUTOGRAPH?

I dashed back to Forthlin to tell Dad I'd seen our Paul on the TELLY and then waited for Paul to come home to see if he'd changed at all. By the time he eventually got in, Dad and I were in bed but I was still awake. The conversation probably went like this:

'Psst . . . here you.'

'Is Dad asleep?'

'Of course he is, it's past two o'clock.'

'We were celebrating. Did you see it?'

'Yeah it was gear, it really was. I had to watch it in a bar down from Bernard's, but it was fabulous.'

'Could you see the velvet collar?'

'Sure, you could see everything.'

(When the decision to 'go commercial' and buy suits instead of the cool Hamburg leathers was reached, mainly by Brian, Paul had smoothed over the shock by saying, 'But ours are different from anybody else's . . . *ours* have got velvet collars . . . look.' As the cardboard box lid was lifted and the white tissue paper unfolded to disclose the dark blue 'Dougy Millins' tailor-made suit, sure enough, the highly polished, trouser creased, mohair suit was topped with a black velvet collar.)

Paul's rough designs for the first, decision-to-go-commercial Beatle suits.

'But why did you *talk* like that on the TV? It sounded like George gone wrong . . . *you* don't talk like that.'

'I know that, *you* know that, but *they* don't know that . . .

John sporting the new Dougy Millin's tailor-made version at a Liverpool gig.

It's part of the image . . .'

'Monkey suit and phoney accents? . . . anyway it worked, it was fantastic.'

'Gear, I'll be off then, ny nyte.'

'Nigh-night . . . psst can I have your autograph?'

'Sod off.'

The Merseyside Arts Festival

Whilst all this was going on, fate now decided to deal *me* a few cards on the gambling table of life; whether I picked them up or not was my problem.

I was 'passing up' pins to a tall, thin, very Jewish-looking friend, Mr. Vincent, whose speciality was long hair.

'Are you watching closely Peter?'

'Naturally Mr. Vincent.'

'Well why do you keep falling asleep?'

'Sorry Mr. Vincent.'

'You're on the artistic side aren't you?'

'More the autistic side, but yes, so they tell me.'

'Would you be interested in the Merseyside Arts Festival?'

'What's that?'

'An artistic festival run by some friends of mine. Would you like to meet them?'

'Certainly Mr. Vincent.'

'My pleasure Mr. Peter. You can go back to sleep now.'

Mike (Mr. Vincent) Weinblatt, a good Catholic boy at heart, took me up to the Hope Hall, a cellar underneath the Everyman Theatre where 'arty things' were going on. These consisted of American style 'events', poetry readings, art exhibitions, folk singing etc. They had a rhythm 'n' blues/rock 'n' roll group, the Road Runners (featuring Mike Hart), who even commissioned me to take their picture.

The organiser of all this mayhem seemed to be one John Gorman (a seriously funny man), who was assisted by a studious, curly-headed bloke with glasses (or 'horn rimmed testicles' as Dad would say) called Roger McGough. He, with fellow poet Adrian Henri, seemed to be the writer.

The start of the Merseyside Arts Festival with John Gorman holding the flag, me on the left and Mike Wineblatt sitting down outside the Jacaranda (Stu's murals—giant faces in half shadows—covered the walls downstairs).

wimdane,

Dear Michael, I'm sorry but I feel,
creeping with negative sluggish hands
across these arms of mine –
pardon, I'll very distinctly move
it – nay but that was a
truly heartening effort – my
other hand you know! There
across a 'vortex' of ebullition
these hands – both of them fail
will built, God concerned things
of travail.
Your letter of course – questions
murals!! of course I'm quite
incompetent to answer your
queries, murals!!(??!). Yes!
first, the emotional sacrifice
will weaken you so inconsid-
erately as to leave you totally
unprepared for the quite
inadequate emolument which
you will receive.'

6. to conscription, a new game of hand
licking – to be wiped carefully
under the skirt.
But I'm there when you get it,
then I can tell you, soon after
you receive me I will be in
Liverpool, tell not my little
[illegible] who sistered me while
I was brothering my mothers other
daughter – a surprise you
see!!
I'll then goodbye.
greetings from ASTRID and me to
brother PAUL, and father.
Stuart:

I wrote to Stu Sutcliffe asking him how to do a mural. This came back in reply . . . sonambulism creeping over him.

At an early age I had succumbed to anything 'different'. (Witness levitating bricks, the kamikaze turnip attacks on trains, the crucifixion of innocent Bluebell frogs on barbed wire, the love of oblique black and blues artists, Muddy Waters, Ray Charles, MJQ, Bo Diddley, the great interest in surrealist painters like Magritte, Dali and Ernst and film maker Luis Bunuel who influenced me so greatly that I went upstairs to my bedroom and drew giant mushrooms on the door, after seeing a TV documentary of his work). So I was easy prey for the quick-thinking-speaking McGough whose machine-gun word-imagery soon splattered my mind against the Hope Hall Wall. From then on I had found an alternative to my big hero . . . the Beatles.

So, in 1962, I became part of the Merseyside Arts Festival, even though nothing could have been further from my mind (one show-off in the family was quite enough). In fact when Gorman–McGough asked me to take the part of an old man in a comedy sketch, I answered, 'Sorry, but I don't do that sort of thing.'

'Why not?'

'I don't know how to.'

'Neither do we. We just read the script.'

'Well I'll have a go, but no promises.'

The 'old man' took hold of me and turned me inside out. On the first night in front of my first audience (second if you count the Butlins Don and Phil McCartney show) I not only found that I could do it, but more important that I *enjoyed* doing it.

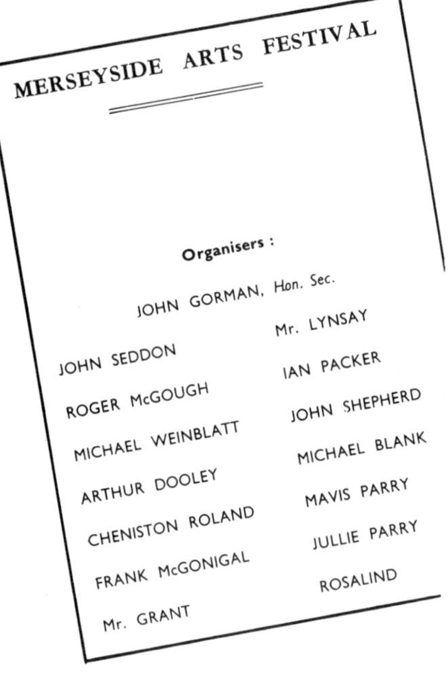

MERSEYSIDE ARTS FESTIVAL

Organisers :

JOHN GORMAN, Hon. Sec.

JOHN SEDDON
ROGER McGOUGH
MICHAEL WEINBLATT
ARTHUR DOOLEY
CHENISTON ROLAND
FRANK McGONIGAL
Mr. GRANT

Mr. LYNSAY
IAN PACKER
JOHN SHEPHERD
MICHAEL BLANK
MAVIS PARRY
JULLIE PARRY
ROSALIND

There were now *two* show-offs in the family.

Social commentary and satire were the order of the day (*That Was The Week That Was* was the only TV show that could get you out of the pub to watch it), and this, coupled with poetic word-play, Liverpool docker humour, and ideas nicked from *American Happenings*, soon brought us a steady following.

I was now devoting all my spare time to the Merseyside Arts Festival and when John Gorman asked me how I wanted my name to appear in the official programme I asked him to 'put it blank' as Paul was becoming quite a local celebrity and I didn't want to cash in on him. He scribbled something down and we went back to our Jackaranda bacon butties. (Downstairs in the 'Jack', Stu Sutcliffe's giant, black-faced murals stared at you as you chatted up the birds to the sweating music of the Caribbean Steel Drum Band.)

Weeks later Mike Vincent gave me the festival's printed programme, and I flicked through it on top of the 86 going home to Allerton. Then I flicked through it again a little slower. By the end of the journey I had scrutinised every bleedin' page of the official Merseyside Arts Festival Programme and my bleedin' name wasn't in it, not even on the back page, of 'ackbleedinnowledgements!'

I was mad. After *all* the free time I'd given those b.....ds, and Gorman hadn't even given me the smallest credit.

And then I saw it, there on the inside of the front cover, as an 'official organiser' in big print: Michael BLANK.

Rehearsing and reading scripts.

SPOT CHECK

Yes, Gorman was our Lennon. He confirmed this one day when he and best friend Bernie Start bought pin-stripe suits, bowler hats and umbrellas, and changed into them in their small Falkner Street, Liverpool 8 flat. The fact that they were both broke at the time didn't seem to bother them, and when they were all togged up, clean-shaven and immaculate, they headed down to Lewis's, one of the city's biggest stores.

Striding military style across the large emporium they marched through the 'No Entrance' doors into the kitchens.

'Good day. May we speak with your employer, please?'

The chef was sent for and came running, obviously in the middle of his daily toils, but even more obviously worried by the sight of two city gents in his kitchen.

'Good day. I take it you are the chef, Mr. .....?'

'Paolozzi, sir.'

'Mr. Paolozzi . . . my colleague and I are from the Ministry of Hygiene and find ourselves in the confines of your fine city. I think this is what they refer to as a "spot check". If it's not too much trouble we'd simply like to sample an average Lewis's meal.'

'I know nothing abouta this.'

'No prior warning allowed, I'm afraid . . . catch you on your toes . . . all that sort of thing.'

'Oh I asee sir . . . confeeadential, I a understand. If you'd like to come a with me, I'll escort you through to my restaurant.'

'If you don't mind we'd rather sample your morsels here in the kitchen, but if you *insist* . . .'

'Certainly anot sir, Tony bring amee a table and your best linen.'

There then followed the most extraordinary meal that my colleagues had ever experienced—lobster bisque with brandy, caviar, roast pheasant with chestnut purée plus game chips, and crêpes suzettes to follow, all served with the very best wines, the finest cutlery and the most attentive waiter service.

'Brandy to follow sirs?'

'Just a double my man.'

'Certainly sir . . . cigar?'

'Thank you my man. Bring me the chef.'

'Certainly sir.'

Whoosh!—the chef.

'Now you are certain this is an ordinary average meal which you would serve to your average daily customer?'

'Oh *yes* sir.'

'Well we have no hesitation in giving this establishment our highest recommendation (hic). Good day.'

'Good aday sir. And thank you.'

'Thank *you* my man,' and, umbrellas under arms (giving their *true* ranks away) they swerved back the few miles to their Liverpool 8 garrett on foot, as they didn't have enough money for the bus fare.

THE LIVERPOOL ONE FAT LADY SHOW

The 'end (Mersey Arts) product' of Gorman, McGough, McCartney, girlfriend Celia, her best friend Jenny Beattie and Adrian Henri was collectively called *The Liverpool One Fat Lady All Electric Show*. *Monty*

Yes, we had a John too! Picture of Gorman was taken in his Rodney Street flat—the Harley Street of Liverpool.

Beyond the Fringe Satire

"ON THE SCAFFOLD"

Currently appearing at the "Blue Angel Club"

FRIDAY, 19th APRIL, 1963

at 7-30 p.m.

— AT THE —

ALEXANDRA HALL, CROSBY

Entertainment in the Modern Manner

Price 7/6 Double Ticket **10/-**

Come and Bring your Friends

Python's Flying Circus was palin comparison (get it, Eric?)

We were booked, never paid, but booked, into the Blue Angel,* Hope Hall, a Liberal Party Conference, and once we even played the Cavern (not exactly the perfect venue for witty verbal exchanges).

By this time the beat boom was at its height and the Beatles had exploded out of Liverpool and were spending most of their time in London, leaving somewhat of a vacuum which resulted in the sucking in of several vacuum cleaner salesmen to our fair city, all ready to clean up.

JANE ACTRESS

Back in 1963 one of the highlights of BBC TV's weekly *Juke Box Jury* was the presence on the panel of a London actress called Jane Asher. She was young, beautiful, black and white haired (well on our telly she was), had a well-cultured, Dad-admired accent, and when she smiled, the set lit up . . . in fact it can now be disclosed that Paul and I both 'fancied her'.

You can imagine, then, how knocked out I was when Paul broke the news that he was 'going out with Jane Asher'! I couldn't believe it. But not only that—he was bringing her up from London *that night*!

It was all too much for a young teenager and a working class Liverpool cotton salesman to take in at once. So we went to bed in our holes in the carpet, flaky bathroom ceiling, terraced Forthlin home.

When they eventually arrived in the very early hours of the morning, Dad was asleep and I was tucked in but wide awake . . . like Christmas.

Paul brought 'my present' upstairs and whispered, 'Mike, are you awake?'

* Alan (man who gave the Beatles away) Williams's night club.

'No,' I answered.

'I've got someone to meet you.' And there in the half-light of my tiny back bedroom was Jane Asher!

I felt such a fool. Well, wouldn't you, lying there snuggled down in a hot water-bottled bed in your pyjamas, with an international film star kissing your hand. But there was no need for first-night nerves. Jinny was calm, natural, fun-loving, fab-looking and her black and white hair had turned red. (It must have been the excitement of meeting me.) She whispered something about . . . 'It's you I really love Michael, but I've got to go along with your brother and all this Beatle business for the moment . . . Can we get together later on in life?' and was gone, just like that.

It can now be disclosed that Paul and I *both* fancied Jane Asher.

I went to sleep wondering what *else* Father Christmas had for me in the morning, if *that* was the aperitif. (Mind you, what do you expect, she was, after all, a fellow Thespian.)

In later years I got to know Jane, brother Peter (of Gordon fame) sister Claire, Mrs. and Dr. Asher rather well, and look forward to meeting them again someday. One part of this wish has been granted as Pete and I met in Los Angeles in 1974 over roast beef and Yorkshire pud in his Beverly Hills home, but sadly Dr. Asher, a lovely, eccentric, Mensa of a million (like Peter) and joke teller extraordinaire, is now dead.

The joke he once wrote down for Dad to show me (as I was in the 'humour' business) goes as follows: (2B read in broad Dick van Dyke cockney).

Cockney customs official:	'Excuse me sir, is that your case?'
Gent traveller:	'It certainly is.'
Cockney:	'I'm sorry sir, but you left a pie on that case.'
Gent:	'I beg your pardon?'
Cockney:	'You left a pie on that case.'
Gent:	'I did not.'
Cockney:	'You did not what sir?'
Gent:	'. . . leave a pie on that case.'
Cockney:	'I didn't say you left a pie on that case sir, I said . . . you left a pie on that case.'
	(P.S. you'll have to pay on that case . . . ger it?)

GAY PAREE

In January 1964 Dad and I were invited to Paris where the Beatles were playing the Olympia for three weeks (at the same time, their first American number one was slowly but surely climbing the US charts . . . whoopee!)

After being given the secret number of the lads' suite, Dad and I walked along the overheated corridors of the posh George V Hotel and presented ourselves outside the door.

Paul opened it and showed us into the room. The latest Bob Dylan album was blaring from the speakers. 'But you said Dylan was folk rubbish!' I whispered heavily aside, rather glad to have caught him out.

'Oh! . . . that's John's, honest,' ad libbed Paul, without batting an eyelid.

Later that evening after the show. we were all taken to a delicious left bank rezy (restaurant) by Brian Epstein, with original surrealist drawings on the walls and for the first and last time . . . ice cream with HOT chocolate sauce. I swear the chocolate remained hot until the end of the ice cold cream. I have never since experienced this unique dish without the chocolate going cold, although I've ordered it in some of the world's top restaurants (Rezys).

To round off the evening we were taken by Bri to a traditional Paris nightclub, given the table with the best view of the coming cabaret, and generally made a great Le Fab Four fuss of. The talent was in abundance, and I had my charms set on a beautiful blonde, who obviously fancied me too. The Beatles, Brian and Dad were furtively whispering to each other and every now and then broke out into giggles. I took this to be a sign of the ale, plenty of which had been consumed by now. My beautiful blonde circled dangerously near when Ringo grinned and said, 'Ask her for a dance Mike.'

'But I can't speak French.'

'It's O.K. she can't speak English.'

The logic escaped me but I didn't have to be asked twice and leapt onto the dance floor with my 'squiffy beef'. For some strange reason everyone found this hysterically funny and as the beautiful blonde and I glided around the floor even the waiters gathered around to witness the event. Being twenty years young, from Liverpool, and pleasantly loaded, the comedy completely escaped me and anyway my bird was by now kissing me, so who cared?

At the end of the dance I strutted cockily back to our, by now tear-drenched, rib-clutching-with-laughter table, just in time for the cabaret announcement. 'Mesdames et messieurs, et maintenant nous presentons notre cabaret magnifique!' After the long opening music I suddenly found out the reason for the mirth . . . First out on the stage was my beautiful blonde, only she was . . . a man!

No wonder they call it Gay Paree.

Superpuff, Peedlemania and name game change

In the middle of Mersey Mania, ABC, a commercial television company, saw the possibility of contemporary humour (a little, but not *too* late) for a new magazine programme they were planning along the lines of Johnny Carson's Chat Show in America, and they dangled a seven-week comedy carrot slot in front of the *Liverpool One Fat Lady All Electric Show*.

Being studious teachers . . . (Roger McGough), hard-working post office engineers . . . (John Gorman) and eager hairdressing apprentices . . . (Mike McCartney), we all threw in our jobs immediately.

The fact that 'a Beatle brother' might be in the deal was a pure coincidence, but let's just say that when it was whittled down to five of us (Jenny Beattie, Ada Henri, John G, Roge McG, and Mike Mac) the latter three got the job. The 'one fat lady' disappeared and Scaffold tumbled out of Roget's Thesaurus to become part of our lives for the next fifteen years.

a new revue by

The Scaffold

Birds, Marriages & Deaths

Traverse Theatre Club

Programme Sept 19 to Oct 4 1964

CROSBY DIVISION LIBERAL ASSOCIATION

Beyond the Fringe Satire

"ON THE SCAFFOLD"

Currently appearing at the "Blue Angel Club"

FRIDAY, 19th APRIL, 1963, at 7-30 p.m.

At THE ALEXANDRA HALL, CROSBY

Refreshments

Price - 7/6

Licensed Bar

My only problem was that my contract with Andre Bernard's hadn't expired. This could have proved very tricky, but Richard Mizelas, one of nature's gentlebusinessmen, realised that I was no great Sassoon of the saloon, and besides it could be good for business if I was a TV star, even a five-minute one, before I returned to the barber business.

In later years, I kept telling journalists how grateful I was to Richard and would they please 'put it in print', but none of them ever did . . . till now.

In retrospect it was quite a gamble to risk my career on a seven-week telly show, but following Owen Mohin and Jim McCartney's instinct I took the gamble and luckily beat the bookies by 10–1 (or was it quarter past?) when the series raced off to a thirty-two-week success.

SUPERPUFF

Back in 1963–4 it wasn't particularly *what* you did on television, it was the fact that you were on at all, so it was with great anticipation that I attended a Scaffold group rehearsal the day after our first dose of mass exposure.

My first fan! Outside the ABC TV studio, Didsbury, Manchester.

In the middle of rehearsals we decided to take a break and head for Church Street, the busiest part of town, just in case anybody recognised us. Sure enough, TV being the instant media it is, we were immediately asked for our autographs both outside and in the Kardomah coffee house. Just like the coffee . . . instant fame, but where's the catch?

The catch, of course, is number 22 . . . yourself, but not knowing this I was only too eager to get home, tell Dad *I'd* been mobbed for my autograph, and get tarted up for the night-time recognition. Normally I dressed down if anything, but that night I decided to dress up for a change, and who knows I might have gone a little bit 'over the top', but after all I *was* a superstar.

I'm not saying that I rushed things, but when I walked into O'Connors bar that evening, let's just say . . . it was virtually empty!

Anywhere else in the world, people naturally divide up into their 'own kind' when it comes to drinking. Artists to 'arty' bars, city gents to 'gentle' bars, pop people to popular bars etc . . . but not in Liverpool. In Liverpool, it being the capital of Ireland, we are all MICKS together.

So it was no great surprise that just as I was about to order my drink I noticed two enormous dockers next to me at the bar. One had his back to me, the other was eyeing me coldly through the bar mirror (having obviously missed my TV debut the night before!).

The order for 'Pernod with ice' suddenly changed to 'A PINT of Guinness' in my deepest voice.

Sensing the desired panic, the docker with his back to me rose from the slouching bar position to his full eight-foot height, turned round ever so slowly, faced me, pint in hand, looked me down . . . and up, and demanded simply 'Are yous a puff?' (Did I have homosexual tendencies?) The silence in the empty bar was infinite.

Having seen this Liverpool *modus operandi* many times in my short life, I now realised that *my* time had arrived. If I said no . . . he was going to smash my face in, if I said yes . . . he was going to smash my face in.

I decided to take a risk 'Yeah,' I answered, straight to his navel.

There was another longer silence . . . with God in attendance.

'All right then,' said the giant, containing a smirk, 'Just testin,' as he slowly turned back to his fellow stevedore.

All was at peace with the world. My Irish cheek had worked.

Lucky Mick, thought I . . . lucky Mick!

PEEDLEMANIA

But now, as well as being a Liverpool Superstar, I had another slight problem . . . the Beatles! Don't get me wrong, I still loved them and hopefully they still love me but they were getting too big. No-one could have foreseen what was about to happen, but we had a glimpse when, in March 1963, they had their first fab number one (for six weeks!) with the single *Please Please Me* and replaced the American stars Chris Montez and Tommy Roe at the top of the bill on a tour of Britain. They released their first LP, with the same title, in May, and their next number one and first silver disc, *From Me to You*, in June, this time topping Roy Orbison!

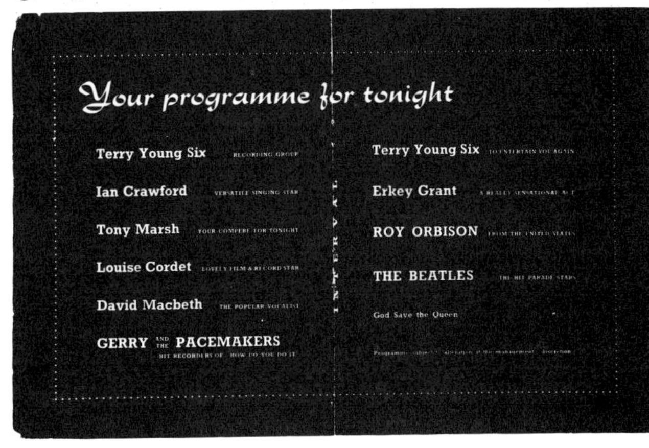

Your programme for tonight

Terry Young Six RECORDING GROUP
Ian Crawford VERSATILE SINGING STAR
Tony Marsh YOUR COMPERE FOR TONIGHT
Louise Cordet LOVELY FILM & RECORD STAR
David Macbeth THE POPULAR VOCALIST
GERRY AND THE PACEMAKERS HIT RECORDERS OF 'HOW DO YOU DO IT'

INTERVAL

Terry Young Six TO ENTERTAIN YOU AGAIN
Erkey Grant A REALLY SENSATIONAL ACT
ROY ORBISON FROM THE UNITED STATES
THE BEATLES THE HIT PARADE STARS
God Save the Queen

Programme subject to alteration at the management's discretion

Paul's rough for the first Beatles album cover.

Paul had his twenty-first birthday party at Auntie Jin's and the Shadows came. The Beatles had their next number one (*She Loves You*) in August, topped the bill at the London Palladium and became hard mass-media news in October. They had Beatlemania-size crowds at London Airport on their return from Sweden, had their own Beatles tour (plus Austin Princess!) in November and released their *With the Beatles* LP, which in December received the biggest advance orders anywhere in the world—250,000, (and this was *before* the States). In the New Musical Express Poll contest they were voted Top World Group, with Elvis second (I did warn you Elvis!), and by December they had seven singles in the top twenty with all four 'mop tops' taking over the nation's number one TV record programme *Juke Box Jury*.

Nobody could have foreseen all that, not even the lads.

Wasn't I proud *and* wasn't I put in an intolerable position? Unless you were part of it, you'll never know the feeling, but believe me it was ELECTRIC! Beatlemania . . . impossible, unprecedented, euphoric, dangerous, knickerwetting, irresponsible, arrogant, fab, gear, but most of all what the hell do *I* do . . . Paul McCartney Beatle brother! (It was like being the Queen's daughter's husband.)

To protect the innocent and retain a little dignity amongst the absolute chaos I decided to change my more than ample, historically proud family name (I can assure you it was *that* crazy). And it wasn't only the desire not to cash in on brother's new Beatle fame that made me do it. You see, my parents and family had taught me certain ethics, standards, pride, whatever you call it, which were impossible to go against, even if I wanted to. But Liverpool nouse also argued that with a change of name you got twice the coverage!

But what to?

The Scaffold, our producer Clive Goodwin, and ABC TV executives Tom Brennand and Roy Bottomley (now responsible for the Eamon Andrews *This is Your Life* programmes) met above Uncle Bill-Dill's oldest dockside pub in England—The Eagle Hotel, Paradise Street (the nearest any of us got to heaven).

The close contenders for the name of the year were Mike Dangerfield (from J. P. Donleavy's *The Ginger Man*) and can you believe, McFab. But the one that was synonymous with Liverpool, sounded Irish and rolled off the tongue, was Mike McGear ('gear' being Liverpool slang for 'great').

So there was I with two name changes in the space of a year. I should have gone the whole hog and called myself Peter McFab.

Naturally, 'McGear' didn't fool anybody but at least it gave me the pleasure of hearing tired, unimaginative journalists repeating 'Which one is it again?' to the three of us, over and over again.

MIKE MCGEAR

Not that we delighted in tampering with the press, but when (for just *one* instance) Scaffold arrived at the Edinburgh Festival for the first time in 1964 with our *Birds, Marriages and Deaths* theatrical revue, the Scottish *Express* arrived for a 'What's on the Festival Fringe' interview and pic. Being used to the English Beatle overkill, we were amazed when the interviewer didn't ask the usual banal Beatle questions (Celtic cool we thought . . . nice change), and at the end of the session he asked for our names. Being fun loving 'lively whacker wits'* we

* A tag given us by the media.

Paul's 21st after cutting the cake in Auntie Jin's back garden, hastily erected marquee. Top act of the day, the Shadows, turned up. The Beatles *must* have been famous.

answered 'John MacGorman, Roger MacGough, and Mike MacGear'.

The old interviewer looked slightly puzzled.

'You're not all Scots, are you boys?'

'Scottish ancestry,' we answered in all innocence.

'Oh that'll be it . . . cheerio the now.'

'Bye bye.'

Half an hour later, he was back like a scalded Celtic cat . . . half angry, half apologetic.

'Now you boys didnay tell me that one of you is a Beatle brother!'

'You didn't ask,' (lively Beatle answer).

'I nearly got the sack! But boys would you be doing me a great big favour—I know you're opening in the wee Traverse Theatre here tonight, but my editor has asked me if you'd possibly do some pictures for the feature page tomorrow?'

Not wishing the kindly old Scot to get the boot for our feeble jokes and certainly not afraid of the publicity . . . we agreed.

edinburgh festival 1965

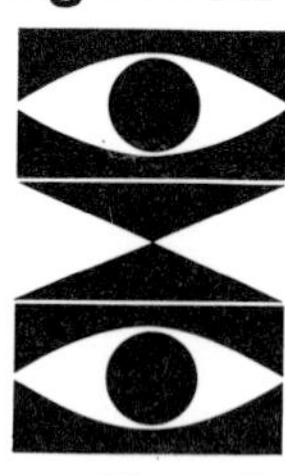

traverse theatre club

poetry readings 3.00 pm		in club bar
Hugh Macdiarmid, Anselm Hollo, John Esam, Pete Brown, Alan Jackson, Roger McGough, Pablo Fernandez, Robert Shure, Alex Trocchi		24 Aug till 5 Sep NOT Mondays
plays—afternoon		**club theatre**
Green Julia the premiere	by Paul Ableman director George Mully	till 29 Aug 3 pm NOT Mondays
Oh, Gloria the premiere	by Robert Shure director Max Stafford-Clark	31 Aug-5 Sep 4.45 pm
Report to an Academy and **Dialogues**	by Franz Kafka director George Mully by Paul Ableman	7-12 Sep only 4.45 pm
plays 7.30 pm		**club theatre**
Happy Days are here again	by Cecil Taylor director Charles Marowitz the premiere	opens 24 Aug nightly till 12 Sep NOT Mondays
late-night 10.30 pm		**club theatre**
a programme of **dance and mime**	Lindsay Kemp and Jack Birkett	
from the works of **Samuel Beckett**	compiled by John Calder	31 Aug-12 Sep NOT Mondays
late-night 12 midnight		**club theatre**
Dublin Fare	a new revue director Max Stafford-Clark	2[illegible] Aug-5 Sep NOT Mondays
The Scaffold	Liverpool group in a new revue	7-12 Sep only
Edinburgh String Quartet	two concerts in club theatre	29 Aug 8.00 pm 30 Aug 10.45 pm

Performances Tuesday to Sunday inclusive. Seats, all bookable, available to Members and Guests only: *Happy Days are Here Again* 7/6; all other performances 5/-. (Telephone bookings must be collected an hour before the start of the performance.) Membership £2.2.0 annually (joint husband and wife membership £3.3.0, student membership £1.1.0). SPECIAL FESTIVAL TEMPORARY MEMBERSHIP £1 (students 10/-). THEATRE DAY MEMBERSHIP ONLY 1/- per ticket. Club open seven days a week 10.00 a.m.-2.00 a.m. Licensed restaurant and bar (open until 1.00 a.m.) CAL 7563. Ask at Box Office (CAL 6895) for additional Monday activities. This programme is subject to alteration. Further details in daily Press.

public performances		
Macbeth by William Shakespeare director Michael Geliot	produced by Traverse Festival Productions Ltd. for the Edinburgh Festival Society Ltd. as part of the official Festival programme. Tickets from Festival Booking Office.	Assembly Hall 23 Aug - 11 Sep 7.15 pm
There was a Man Traverse Festival Productions Ltd. director Gerard Slevin	John Cairney in a new play about Burns by Tom Wright	Morton House 20 Aug - 11 Sep 8.00 pm NOT Suns
Larry Adler	in his one-man show director George Mully	as above 11.[illegible] pm
Group One Ballet	devised and directed by Geoff Moore	23 Aug-11 Sep 10.30 pm Cathedral Ho. Albany St.

art exhibitions		sponsored by the Traverse Gallery
Patrick Heron Bryan Wynter presented jointly with Department of Fine Art, University of Edinburgh	paintings at Hume Tower George Square	30 Aug - 11 Sep daily 10 am - 6 pm Suns 2 - 6 pm
Jasper Johns on loan from U.S. Information Service also exhibition of Rick Ulman prints and circum-stances by Tam	lithographs at Morton House Blackfriars Street	24 Aug - 11 Sep daily (NOT Suns) 11 am till 11.30 pm
Richard Demarco	paintings and drawings at Traverse Club Gallery	24 Aug - 11 Sep daily 10 am till 8 pm
William Featherstone sponsored jointly with Keith Ingram Ltd.	sculptures at Keith Ingram 124 Rose Street	24 Aug - 11 Sep 9.30 am - 6.30 pm Sats till 1.00 pm
Barton Lidice Benes sponsored jointly with The World Council of Christian Education	drawings 1st floor 24 York Place	24 Aug - 11 Sep daily (NOT Suns) 11 am till 6 pm

james ct lawnmarket cal 6895

The show opened in the tiny sixty seater Traverse (Paul was playing 20,000-seater baseball stadiums in the States) to good reaction and good reviews, so when Old Jock came for us the following morning we were in good mood.

'Right, where to?' one of us asked.

'To Holy*rude* Palace, just below Arthur's Seat.'

'There's no answer to that!'

When we arrived in the courtyard of the Palace, there was a small white sports car at attention, and a lady with a bad tempered hamper.

'Ah *there* you are Hamish,' said the kept-waiting lady. 'Now, which one's the brother?'

'Him.'

'Him.'

'Him,' we answered, pointing to each other.

'Now let's not fool aroond, gentlemen,' said Frosty Face. 'We haven't got all day.'

When I volunteered the information she opened the hamper to expose a tartan tweed cape and tartan Sherlock Holmes hat, and what *appeared* to be dozens of aftershave bottles. The former were draped round my personage, the latter were placed all over the top and bonnet of the white sports car.

'Now could we have a shot with . . . what's your name?' asked Jock.

'Mike.'

'One with just Mike, and the car.'

Having sussed this one out long ago, I answered, 'Sorry we're a group, we don't have leaders.'

'Of course ye are, of course ye are. Well how about one with all *three* of you boys in front of the car? That's it!' Click!

'Now one with . . . sorry, what's your name?'

'Mike.'

'Mike . . . standing here, and the other two boys sitting on the bonnet.'

'Mind the aftershave gentlemen,' added Frozen Features.

'What's the perfume for?' we asked.

'It's a fashion article, son.'

'Oh, we see.' Click!

'Now one with erm . . . Mike Laddy here on the bonnet and the other two behind the car . . . a little lower boys . . . lower . . . *lower* . . .' (till they disappeared). Click!

'*That's* the one, thank you gentlemen. As Flora said it's a wee bit busy today what with the Festival an' all, so we'll away. Nice to have met you . . . erm . . . Mike, cheerio.'

'Cheerio.'

This was just one of the many variations. The usual fab foto session around this period was: 'Right, lads, this way.' Click!

'How about a nice big smile then Mike?'

'Don't feel like smiling.'

'Why not?'

'Got cracked lips.'

'Fabulous, have you heard the one about . . .'

Click!

'Look this way would you, Paul . . . sorry Mike.'

Click!

Before *She Loves You* became number one in August 1963 Dad thought that Paul's mock scouse accent was bad enough, but when he heard the blatantly Americanised 'She loves you . . . yeh, yeh, yeh' this was the last straw.

'All these phoney accents won't get you anywhere son, why don't you sing "she loves you . . . yes, yes, yes", that's *much* nicer.'

Don McCullin and Jonathan Miller (merging into John Gorman's flat).

THE 'REAL' LIVERPOOL

At the height of Beatlemania, Jonathan Miller (author-playwright of *Beyond the Fringe* fame) and Don McCullin (famous cockney war photographer) were commissioned to write and illustrate an article for a big US magazine about the 'real' Liverpool.

They bumped into me and my two Scaffold colleagues on our weekly Manchester TV magazine programme *Gazette** with other guest star Willy Rushton ('That Was the Celebrity Square Week That Was' satirical cartoonist). On completion of our fifteen minute, carefully rehearsed 'improvisation' spot, we learned of their mission and were only too happy to offer ourselves as the key to 'Beat City'.

After the pilgrimage to Liverpool from Manchester we were deposited by the coach (which contained our faithful fans) outside our first port of call . . . the Blue Angel.

'It all happens at the Blue,' we said smugly leading Jonathan, Willy and Don into a somewhat dead nightclub.

'Er—it's only twelve . . . too early,' we ad libbed, sending a minion to find out where the Saturday night parties were at.

With a few swinging addresses under our belts we downed our whisky and cokes (fab drink of the day), jumped into our limos (Morris 1100 and Ford Classic, actually) and headed for the first party . . . 'Now we'll show you some REAL action!'

* Fab original title for a magazine programme, ney?

The first joint didn't seem to be jumping, but we rang the door bell anyway. From the distant murmurings and putting on of lights, it slowly dawned on us that we'd woken someone up!

'Terribly sorry,' we apologised to the lady in her rollers. 'But we thought there was a party etc . . . etc.'

'Ooh look Dad, it's them Scaffolds off the telly . . . Come on in love.'

'No it's all right . . . really, it's just that we were told . . .'

'Don't just stand there, lads,' said Dad, fastening his nightgown. 'Bring your friends in and we'll have a nice cup of char . . . Mother, put the kettle on.'

'But . . . but . . .'

'We saw you all on the telly tonight,' said Mum, making us at home, 'and yous was luvly.'

When we'd all had tea and biscuits (it could only happen in Liverpool), we thanked and bade farewell to Mum and Dad, and hotfooted to the next address.

'Sorry about that, but *this* one's a CERT.'

At the second house, more lively sounds greeted our somewhat dampened enthusiasm. We parked the cars and walked up to the brightly lit, noisy semi.

John Gorman, the most recognisable of the Scaffold, knocked on the door: Knock! Knock!

Door opens . . . female giggles of recognition are heard.

Door shuts.

Knock! Knock!

Door opens . . . large Liverpool lad looms.

'What d'you want?'

'Hello, is this the party?'

'Who are you?'

'John Gorman of the Scaffold.' (More girly giggles.)

'I don't care if you're John fuckin' Lennon, you're not coming in 'ere!'

Door shuts . . . Bang!

'This doesn't seem to be our night,' one of our guests wryly observed.

'Nonsense,' we argued. 'There's a country club on the outskirts of town that's ALWAYS open,' said we, ushering our entourage into the transport. Trumpets blow . . . horses follow hounds . . . hounds follow foxes . . . Tally HO HO.

We eventually reached The Gorsey Kop Country Club, and, happy to see that it was indeed open, begged for entrance.

'Sorry squire, but you've got to have a tie,' came the reply. This was the last straw—totally dejected we decided to call it a day and head home.

As we floated soberly back to Liverpool our flotilla was forced to a halt by an accident and in the flashing blue police light we could make out an upturned Mini squashed flat in the middle of the road.

Being a fully qualified doctor, Jonathan Miller offered his services to the police, and he and I were guided to a young couple who'd been flung from the somersaulting mini before it pancaked onto the road.

By some freak of nature they were both still alive and the girl was cradling her lover's head in her lap. They were bleeding pretty badly, but on looking up through her tears, the girl suddenly recognised me and, shaking her loved one violently, said, 'Wake up, Johnnie, (read: 'don't die Johnny'). Wake up . . . it's Paul McCartney's brother!'

THE POPPIES

After the Liverpool explosion, Roger McGough, together with Clive Goodwin, decided the world was now ready for an all black girl singing group called The Poppies. Roger knew three sisters who fitted the bill perfectly. They were beautiful, not quite black and rather sexy. There was only one slight drawback . . . they couldn't sing!

Now, being from Liverpool, the girls thought this was the least of their problems and were preparing themselves for the coming world onslaught.

That week Bob Dylan was due to appear in Liverpool and with a warning from Paul (who'd caught his first concert in London) that Bob might be 'slower' in the second half (soft drugs were intimated) Roge and I were pleased to witness an excellent solo performance at Liverpool's Odeon (*both* halves and not at all 'folk crap').

After the show and a meal, Roge and I bombed down to the Blue Angel, and were highly delighted to bump into our new hero Bob Dylan coming out, draped with two of the Poppies.*

'Bob, this is Mick and this is Roge from the Scaffold, and Bob, Roge is our new manager.' After hellos were echanged, Bob and the girls invited us 'on up' to the posh Adelphi Hotel for drinks.

True to his word we were made welcome in his hotel room, and soon Roger and Bob were deep in poetic discussion (being one to the other, as it were). In fact at one stage I swear Roge was losing Mr. Zimmerman with his poetic prowess.

Suddenly the calm was shattered by an announcement by the Poppies (who'd now found their other sister with manager Clive) that they were about to sing!

The fact that there was no accompaniment didn't seem to deter the girls and after a quick 'one, two, 1234' they launched into the Crystal's 'Da Doo Ron Ron Ron da doo ron ron.' This wasn't *quite* the launching that Roger and Clive had foreseen and even the most untuneful of the small party soon realised that 'dese goils woint no Supremes'. Undeterred and full of confidence, the girls finished the song, complete with Tamla routines . . . the lot.

What could have been an awkward silence was broken by Bob who, judging by his applause, loved it all,* but before the Poppies could launch into their *full* repertoire Roge and Clive held a quick business conference with the girls (references to the lack of backing facilities, adequate PA, lighting facilities, make-up etc.) and that was it for the night.

Soon after this, for some strange reason, Roger made the decision not to enter into the heady world of show-biz management, but decided instead to concentrate on being a poet once more.

* It's not hard to see why the Poppies were so popular with such superstars as Dylan (and later on Marlon Brando) they were young, beautiful, brown, quick witted, happy, *AND* had Liverpool accents!

* Not that I'm suggesting that Bob sings flat . . . his *Girl from the North Country* duo with Johnny Cash surely proves otherwise.

Clive Goodwin went on to launch *Black Dwarf* (the underground political magazine) and then became one of Britain's most respected stage and television agents, until 1977 when he was arrested after a stroke in the lobby of the Beverly Wiltshire Hotel, California, charged with drunkenness and later died mysteriously in an LA gaol, aged 45. Warren Beatty was only one of the people who had misgivings about Clive's death, and was last seen suing the city of Los Angeles on behalf of Clive's twelve-year-old daughter, Boty. Any help I can give, please contact Warren.

AS SNUG AS 2 BUGS IN A REMBRANDT RUG

In early 1964 Paul and the Beatles 'took the States' with ten thousand screaming kids at Kennedy Airport on their arrival, did the Ed Sullivan network television show to seventy-three million viewers, and received a telegram from Elvis. (This was well before the startling quote that he actually thought that 'the filthy unkempt appearances and suggestive music of the Beatles is responsible for many of the problems the USA is having with young people'.*) They goofed round with Muhammed Ali; fifty million dollars of Beatle goods were sold (of which the lads saw very little as everybody cleaned up except Brian and the Beatles) and then in March *Can't Buy Me Love* was number one here and in the States, with a world record three million advance, plus the top six discs in the US hit parade. When they returned from their US Tour of twenty-four major cities, which smashed records everywhere (including the hundred thousand dollars for half an hour Kansas City concert offer) Dad was asked if he'd like to retire from his ten pound a week job as cotton salesman back home in Liverpool.

Dad, strangely enough, agreed, and Paul suggested we both move from our somewhat dilapidated Forthlin Road home (no mother around the house for nine years didn't help) to somewhere across the water 'away from it all'.

Before we left, Aunties Jin and Mill (who came every Monday at 1 am to cook and iron for us) insisted on painting over our superb drawings on the toilet walls (a great favourite with Cyn Lennon) which had accumulated over the years, lest the fans got in before the next occupants and tore it apart brick by brick.

Dad was immediately magnetised by Heswall, Cheshire. He'd admired the district ever since he used to be a gardener for the cotton bosses in the 1920s, and we had visited Mum's nursing friend 'Ozzie' there a couple of times. But would Heswall have us? The idea of Beatle fans trampling round their posh gardens didn't exactly appeal to the 'hupper class' stockbroker belt Heswallites, and indeed the first house we bought fell through when they discovered who we were.

Our second retreat looked more sound and after lengthy but gentlemanly negotiations by Dad, we purchased 'Rembrandt' a fine detached eight thousand, seven hundred and fifty pound property in Baskervyle Road overlooking the river Dee and North Wales and, coincidentally, just up the road from 'Ozzie'. But before we could move in, extensive alterations had to be made. Roofs had to be reslated, painting done inside and out, extra plumbing by Uncle Joe, carpentry by Uncle Harry and Cousin Ian (who else my dears), full central heating (when we first visited, Dad and I had to keep our

* That's good, coming from 'the Pelvis'.

Rembrandt—Dad and I were like too little Lord Fauntleroys in our ivory Heswall castle.

overcoats on as it was so cold), and a 'BAXI' fireplace had to be installed. (Harry, Ian and Joe passed that on to each other as none of them knew how to fit it.)

This gave me time to organise the interior and, putting my 'arty' cap on, I set about scouring all the 'better emporiums' both up here and down in London. We could have hired an interior designer, but this would have been too impersonal and Dad was over-sensitive about 'outsiders'.

Eventually we moved from Forthlin in a van booked at midnight ('We don't want any fuss, son') and the extreme luxury (from comparative poverty, remember) was quite a contrast, to say the least . . .

At first it was unbelievable . . ., to run on the lounge-to-hall-to-stair-to-bedroom thick pile carpets with your shoes and socks *off*, to sleep in each of the five bedrooms (like Goldilocks) till you found the one that was *just right*, to bathe in the *long* (I'm six feet one inch) bath with softened water, to walk grandly round the extensive overlooked-by-no-one grounds, and to sit in the warm carpeted bog, (all *three* of them). But the most impressive feature (particularly for

Dad) was the enormous grand piano in the long, bay windowed lounge. Surrounded by all these rich trappings, we soon became accustomed to our new fairy bubble, and settled in with alarming ease. But like all bubblies it eventually burst, with something of a shock.

In retrospect, the sudden contrast was too much. Dad a man of action who'd been striving for something 'better' all his life had suddenly been given it . . . on a plate. From nothing to everything like Paul and the Beatles, life was sort of over before it had started, or as Auntie Mill would say . . . 'Here we are, where are we?'

One day, whilst lounging on my sumptuous double bed upstairs overlooking the Welsh coast with Dad pottering round the garden below, I had a sudden apparition of 'Rembrandt' burning down around me, and all that was left was . . . me! No home, no money, no future, but most of all, no parents, family or friends!

But that was all in the future; for 'here and now' Dad and I were like two little Lord Fauntleroys in our ivory Heswall castle, as snug as two bugs in a rug.

Hard Day's Night, afternoon boredom and fab première

One of my off-the-set photos of Dick Lester and George during the shooting of *A Hard Day's Night*.

After wiping out the *entire* United States in 1964, the Peedles (as they were known to their German fans) returned to England to start work on their first feature film, *A Hard Day's Night*, at Twickenham Studios.

As I was launching my showbiz career with the Scaffold, I thought I'd find out how the 'professionals' do it by visiting Paul and his chums on the set of their film. Dozens of fans were swarming round the entrance of the studio but when they spotted my car they soon dispersed* and when I got to the set I was made welcome by my fellow Liverpudlians. Paul cleared it with the director, Dick Lester (a charming man), for me to take some pictures of him and the lads and I roamed round the set happily snapping away with my Rollei-Magic F&H Hamburg present, being careful not to bump into Ed Sullivan who was finishing off an interview with the chaps.

The Beatles were remarkably relaxed and professional but in contrast to their whirlwind existence up to that point, filming (with take after take after take) had become quite boring. So the lads set up a diversion in their dressing room to stop them going crazy. The diversion was called blue movies.

The black and white, blue film rolled merrily along to its climax (sorry) and then was dutifully wound back 'to the top'. This produced an unexpected, hilarious explosion from the company—the various, gyrating, anatomical parts going *backwards* was a sight for sore eyes. I remember Johnny Moondog and me demanding a reverse nipple 'bloop' repeat more than once. (Oh the carefree naughtiness of it all).

The following day a photographer from *Woman* magazine turned up to take some pictures of Paul and me. I remember with acute embarrassment trying to get big brother to pose for the picture with me.

'Why *us*?' he eventually asked.

'It's for a *Woman* article.'

'About us? But who's writing it?'

* Such is the calming effect created by my inner peace and rational behaviour.

'Well *I* am sort of.'

'You're writing about *us* for *Woman* . . . why?'

'For money.'

'Well, that's all right then, where's the photographer?' and instead of returning to the set, he held up a *Hard Day's* filming till his picture had been taken with 'little brother'.

Sometimes my brother is rather slow in catching on but when eventually he does, he soon makes up for it. On seeing the impossible position I was in, being a Beatle brother with very little personal money (I had only just started my star-spangled showbiz career), he arranged for me to receive a weekly tax-free 'covenant' of ten pounds from his accountants till I was on my feet. Since then a Nikon camera, an Omega 'Geneve', wafer thin watch and even a Vauxhall Chevette, 'hunch back' car have all found their ways into my Christmas and birthday stockings (and, oh yeh, I nearly forgot a trip to LA for a party, but I was working with Scaffold).

LONDON PAVILION PICCADILLY CIRCUS

ROYAL WORLD PREMIERE

in the gracious presence of
HER ROYAL HIGHNESS THE PRINCESS MARGARET and THE EARL OF SNOWDON
to aid THE DOCKLAND SETTLEMENTS and THE VARIETY CLUB HEART FUND

on MONDAY, 6th JULY 1964 at 8.30 p.m. (DOORS OPEN 7.30. SEATS MUST BE TAKEN BY 8.20 p.m.)

THE BEATLES

IN "A Hard Day's Night"

DRESS CIRCLE ROW E SEAT No. 15 gns.

MAIN ENTRANCE PICCADILLY CIRCUS

The Royal World Premiere of *A Hard Day's Night* was at the London Pavilion, Piccadilly Circus, smack bang in the centre of the capital on the 6th July 1964 in the gracious presence of Her Royal Highness Princess Margaret and the Earl of Snowdon.

For some reason, apart from me, only the aunties made it down from Liverpool for the auspicious occasion, coupled with Dad and new wife Ange*. The aunties' outwardly cool, regal composure only thinly disguised their obvious joy and pride, bubbling under nervous excitement for the coming event ('and ROYALTY will be there too').

On the big day the girls had their pictures taken at a posh West End hairdressers by the *Daily Express* (a reliable paper) and in the evening we all dressed up to the nines in our evening dresses and suits before presenting ourselves at the main entrance to the Pavilion.

The crowds outside were phenomenal—thousands of young girls all at fever pitch with a constant line of stretchers carrying the wounded to the back (where they would come round, get back in the crowd, make their way to the front . . . and pass out again).

Battling through the sea of hard core media men we headed up the regally red carpeted staircase to the dress circle, where I was glad to see that our fifteen guinea seats were still screwed down. (Doors open

* We had acquired a new mother, sister (Ruth) and Grandmum (Edie) when Dad suddenly got married in North Wales . . . the young rascal.

The aunties' outwardly cool, regal composition only thinly disguised their joy, pride and excitement. Anticlockwise from Paul (with a halo round his head) is Dad, me, Auntie Joan (uncle Joe's wife) and Auntie Dill (me mum's brother Bill's wife). Clockwise from Paul is Auntie Jin (the McCartney matriarch), Auntie Edie (the eldest McCartney sister) and just out of the picture is poor old Auntie Mill. In the mirror you can just see George Harrison's Mum.

7.30—seats 'must be taken' by 8.20 pm.) Sitting in number twenty-four, row E, we waited for the filum to start. The Beatles were already ensonced just next to us and as the lights went down, ribald Liverpool cinema jokes shot into the night air ('Arreh mam, purra nuther shillin' in the meter' etc.), mainly from John but with a little help from his nervous friends.

In the transcendental blackness, lightning flashes of the past two years tumbled through my mind: this time two years ago the Beatles had been turned down by Decca . . . I was on the dole at St. Mary's unemployment exchange, Garston . . . Stu had died in Hamburg . . . and CHANG! the opening guitar and piano chord of *A Hard Day's Night* split my head in two (it still sends a shiver down my back). Straight into double-tracked Lennon threatening that 'he's been working like a d-o-o-o-g', followed by a gloriously out of tempo cowbell and a beautifully constructed song.

Any first-night misgivings we might have had were shattered by the response at the end of the film . . . There was a standing ovation, and tears came to the eyes (I told you us McCartneys had their bladders too near their eyes).

After 'the pics' we all headed for the Dorchester Hotel (where else) for a supper party to follow the success or failure of the film.

Dad and I were circulating when Paul introduced Princess Margaret to Dad.

'How do you do, your Majesty.'

'Fine thanks Jim, how's the cotton business up in the Pool?' they *didn't* really say.

At the midnight hour Paul produced a painting out of thin air and, presenting it to Father, said 'Happy birthday Dad, all the best.' It was the 7th July and Dad was sixty-two.

'Thank you, son. It's very nice,' said Dad, a little bewildered.

'It's a horse,' added Paul.

'I can see that son,' Dad was still confused, 'It looks lovely.'

'It's not just a painting . . . it's a horse. I've bought you a bloody horse.'

My father, a lifelong racing man and inveterate small stakes gambler, just stood there with a one thousand pound horse in his hands

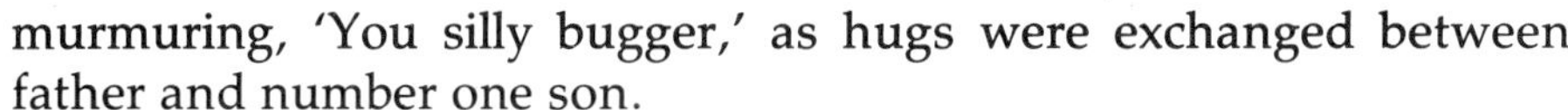

murmuring, 'You silly bugger,' as hugs were exchanged between father and number one son.

This was the beautiful climax of a never-to-be-forgotten day for the McCartney clan.

Two years later Drake's Drum came first in the race before the Grand National at Aintree Racecourse*; nowhere near the iron, but within horse-shoe throwing distance of Dad's brother Joe's house. In all, it won over three thousand pounds for us . . . not bad for a painting.

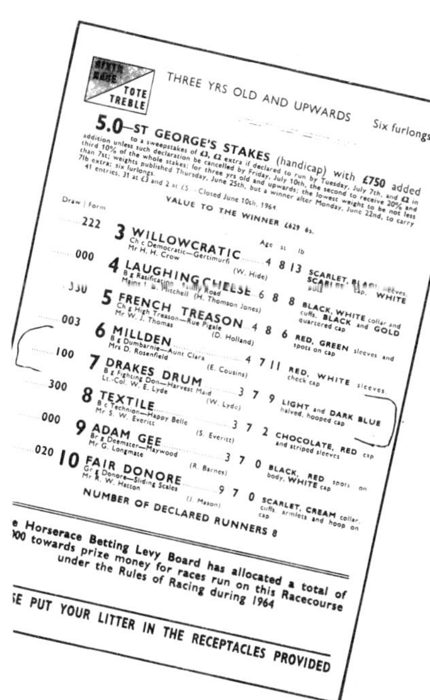

TOTE TREBLE

THREE YRS OLD AND UPWARDS Six furlongs

5.0—ST GEORGE'S STAKES (handicap) with £750 added to a sweepstakes of £3, £2 extra if declared to run by Tuesday, July 7th, and £2 in addition unless such declaration be cancelled by Friday, July 10th, the second to receive 20% and third 10% of the whole stakes; for three yrs old and upwards; the lowest weight to be not less than 7st; weights published Thursday, June 25th, but a winner after Monday, June 22nd, to carry 7lb extra; six furlongs.
41 entries, 31 at £3 and 2 at £5 - Closed June 10th, 1964.

VALUE TO THE WINNER £629 6s.

Draw / Form	No.	Horse	Age	st	lb	Colours
222	3	WILLOWCRATIC, Ch c Democratic—Gertimurfi, Mr H. H. Crow (W. Hide)	4	8	13	SCARLET, BLACK sleeves, SCARLET cap, WHITE
000	4	LAUGHING CHEESE, B g Ratification—Family Road, Maine ... Mitchell (H. Thomson Jones)	6	8	8	BLACK, WHITE collar and cuffs, BLACK and GOLD quartered cap
330	5	FRENCH TREASON, Ch g High Treason—Rue Pigale, Mr W. J. Thomas (D. Holland)	4	8	6	RED, GREEN sleeves and spots on cap
003	6	MILLDEN, B g Dumbarnie—Aunt Clara, Mrs D. Rosenfield (E. Cousins)	4	7	11	RED, WHITE sleeves, check cap
100	7	DRAKES DRUM, B g Fighting Don—Harvest Maid, Lt.-Col. W. E. Lyde (W. Lyde)	3	7	9	LIGHT and DARK BLUE halved, hooped cap
300	8	TEXTILE, B c Technion—Happy Belle, Mr S. W. Everitt (S. Everitt)	3	7	2	CHOCOLATE, RED cap and striped sleeves
000	9	ADAM GEE, Br g Deemster—Maywood, Mr G. Longmate (R. Barnes)	3	7	0	BLACK, RED spots on body, WHITE cap
020	10	FAIR DONORE, Gr g Donore—Sliding Scales, Mr R. W. Hatton (J. Mason)	9	7	0	SCARLET, CREAM collar, cuffs, armlets and hoop on cap

NUMBER OF DECLARED RUNNERS 8

...e Horserace Betting Levy Board has allocated a total of ...000 towards prize money for races run on this Racecourse under the Rules of Racing during 1964

...SE PUT YOUR LITTER IN THE RECEPTACLES PROVIDED

THE KEYS TO THE CITY

A couple of days after the London premiere of *A Hard Day's Night* we were all flying up to Liverpool, where the Corporation had at long last conceded that the Beatles deserved the 'keys to the city' . . . any city! Sadly some of our city fathers are sometimes lacking in vision—take for instance the filling-in of the Cavern, which lost them forever the opportunity of turning one of Liverpool's world renowned landmarks into a Presley Graceland for tourists.

GILDED COFFINS

Just imagine if they hadn't knocked it down, I can just see it now . . . Over the Cavern a twenty-feet high, neon-winking sign, 'Welcome to the Cavern . . . The Home of the Beatles' (blink, blink), and above the door, 'They played here 292½ times' (blink, blink), and as you step down the red carpeted staircase, the electronic hidden eye beams open the silver, Beatle crusted door, labelled, 'Step inside luv' . . . You step into the suitably subdued lighting cave with taped 'muzak' versions of the Beatles' greatest hits, playing gently through the gold-disc, fur-lined walls . . . Past roped-off areas signposted 'the Coke Counter', with smaller labels saying 'the screwed up straws which the Beatles threw away before drinking their Cokes' . . . Past 'the bogs which used to smell of urine and decayed vegetables', plus small cans of the odour which can be bought and opened if you nostalgia will take you back the far . . . Past a broken chair labelled, 'The chair which killed Freda in the third row after she'd asked Beatle Paul to play *Searchin* for

* Paul and I had a £1 each way on 'Drakie' and when he came in at 20 to 1 (the field) we collected our winnings like two little kids on Christmas morning.

the 282nd time, thrown by John Beatle Lennon (he was aiming at Paul, but didn't have his glasses on *again*)' . . . Up onto the highly polished wooden stage labelled, 'This is the fourth Cavern stage where the Beatles stood'; the rest are in various parts, in various parts of America!' . . . Past the small jar labelled 'Plecys', containing broken guitar plectrum pics used by 'the Beatles' own hands' . . . Past a pile of mouldy sandwiches labelled, 'The sarnies which Lennon mistakenly played instead of his mouth organ on *Love me Do* lunchtime sessions' . . . Through an archway consisting of 'Identical replicas of the Beatles' guitars' . . . Down the tasteful black carpet into the tiny dressing room, and there in four gilded coffins with glass tops . . . the Fab Four waxwork Beatles, lying in (a) State.

Beatles 'shrine' comes down...

...for a railway

Bricks crumble and timbers crash in Liverpool's city centre as demolition boss Terry Balmer makes history, for he has the task of demolishing the world famous Cavern Club in Mathew Street.

But as the giant caterpillar vehicle clawed at the warehouse, Terry, aged 32, said: "It's just another job."

The cellar that saw the birth of the Beatles will vanish to make way for an underground railway ventilation shaft.

And Terry, a director of the firm given the job of flattening the site, will be carrying bits of the one-time Mecca of pop music home to Parliament Street, Toxeth, Liverpool.

He said: "My 11-year-old daughter, Donna, has asked me to get her whatever I can as a souvenir."

Another director, Sid Fishgold, aged 44, of Carkington Road, Woolton, has had orders from his daughter, Jeanette, aged 15.

"She wants a brick from the back of the stage because it was nearest to the Beatles," he said.

EPPYS OFFER

But back to the plane flying high above England heading in the general direction of Liverpool. Brian Epstein sat down beside me and after sharing a wee dram, asked, 'Have *you* ever thought about a singing career, Michael?'

'Get your hand off my knee and say that,' came the razor sharp reply.

'No, I'm serious. I think with a little training you could make it in this business.'

'No way Bri, one singer in the family's quite enough and anyway I've just finished a telly series with the Scaffold and we're rehearsing to take a theatre show to Edinburgh and hopefully London's West End.'

'Well, let me know how you get on. And if you ever change your mind, just call me.'

'Sure Bri, thanks for asking.'

'You're welcome Michael'

When the plane landed at Speke Airport, having flown over our childhood homes, crowds of fans had already gathered, but that was nothing compared to what was about to happen. The lads got in their Beatle-wagon and Dad and I into the Austin Princess behind. The *whole* route from Speke Airport to the centre of town (a distance of some five or six miles) was lined with happy, waving people!

As we passed our old Forthlin Road home, there were a lot of extra neighbourly smiles (did I spot our piano teacher near the bus stop?) and I flashed back a few more years to the occasion when Queen

Elizabeth II took the same route to Speke Airport . . . in the opposite direction.

I had sagged off school (being a fervent Royalist you understand) and rushed out from No. 20 with my Köln camera. Just as her entourage was rolling down Mather Avenue, not able to get across the dual carriageway in time, I hid in the central reservation bushes till Her Majesty was level and popped up with my camera. Her Highness looked somewhat taken aback, as it must have looked as though I was either going to assassinate her or, even worse, flash myself. Neither was true of course and as my flash didn't go off anyway, all that came out of my back-bed-darkroom was a Royal blur.

When we finally got into the city centre it was absolute chaos . . . the City Fathers might have been a little slow on the uptake but the fans certainly weren't. It was the biggest turnout our home town had ever seen (over one hundred and fifty thousand people) and one of our proudest days, not because the lads had been accepted by Liverpool, but because they'd been accepted by the ones who really mattered . . . the *people* of Liverpool.

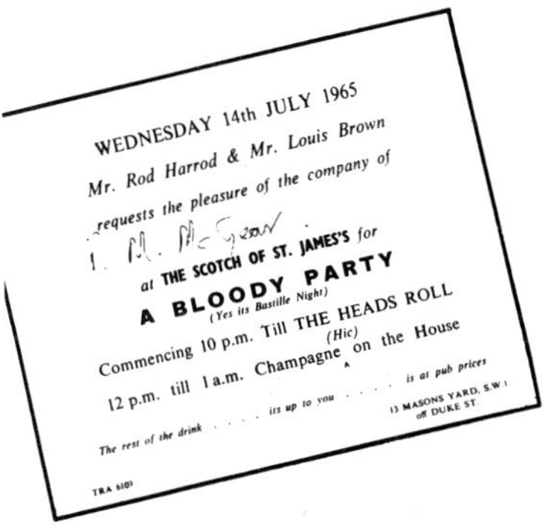

WEDNESDAY 14th JULY 1965
Mr. Rod Harrod & Mr. Louis Brown
requests the pleasure of the company of

at THE SCOTCH OF ST. JAMES'S for
A BLOODY PARTY
(Yes its Bastille Night)
Commencing 10 p.m. Till THE HEADS ROLL
12 p.m. till 1 a.m. Champagne (Hic) on the House
The rest of the drink . . . . . its up to you . . . . . is at pub prices
13 MASONS YARD, S.W.1
off DUKE ST.
TRA 6107

LE FRENCH LETTER

At the height of 'Swinging London'—Carnaby Street, mini skirts, flower power, peace, love, pot and the like (yes, it actually *did* exist)—it wasn't unusual for me to wake in the afternoon in either brother's forty pound grand mansion in St. John's Wood, or his 'secret' bachelor pad near Claridges, lounge around until dusk listening to the latest Beatle demos dress in borrowed brother clothes, slide into sports car, and brooooom down to the latest 'in' club, the Scotch of St. James, where a then unknown singer/guitarist called Jimi Hendrix could be seen performing on the tiny, tartan stage.

This particular evening, before I could order my next hangover, Louis Brown, owner of the Scotch, invited me to a party.

At his apartment the ale flowed healthily with American singers Ben E. King and Barry *Eve of Destruction* McGuire in attendance, and healthy young ladies who kept taking their clothes off. Now I've nothing against this sort of thing but after the first four hundred and thirty-two, you get a little bored with the sameness of it (or should I say them) all, and looking around for something else to do I noticed a man with a French accent doing the same. He spoke little English and I spoke no French, but the language barrier was immediately overcome when we became drinking partners.

All through the night little signs of friendship passed between us like 'Sheers' . . . 'Ger it down you' . . . 'Citroen presse' . . . 'In goes yer eye out' . . . 'Bottoms up', etc . . ., and just before I got *really* tired and emotional, the Frenchman scribbled something down and thrust it in my departing pocket.

On surfacing next afternoon I looked at the letter on which a naked woman with a fish's head had been drawn! It was signed 'VADIM' (Roger, husband of Brigitte Bardot*, that is).

'Funny idea of women,' thought I. 'Must have been all those strapping, stripping ladies.' Only months later when I saw Lady Oranmore and Browne's paintings in (of all places) Paris did I realise that Monsieur Vadim was trying to turn me on to Magritte (de Chirico's lad).

* And the rest.

1965, from frying pans to fires

1965 was yet *another* good year for brother and chums: they had their second film, *Help*, the top album of the same name, Paul's world-wide hit *Yesterday* and three big tours here, abroad and in America with a record three hundred and four thousand dollars paid for the Shea Stadium appearance . . . the biggest in show business history!

Until this time, the Scaffold had been managed by a small literary agency off Kings Road in London but now decided to broaden its appeal, and who else to approach but Brian and his NEMS Agency (he *seemed* to be doing all right with our kid). So just before the Beatles got their MBE's we signed up, not in a singing capacity as Brian had suggested on the plane but on the theatre side of the NEMS stable.

Before we left, our small literary agent suggested a small recompense (for our loss to Brian). I don't think Bri picked it up, but it just shows that even someone as remote and untouched by the pop business, as the book world, was aware of the phenomenon.

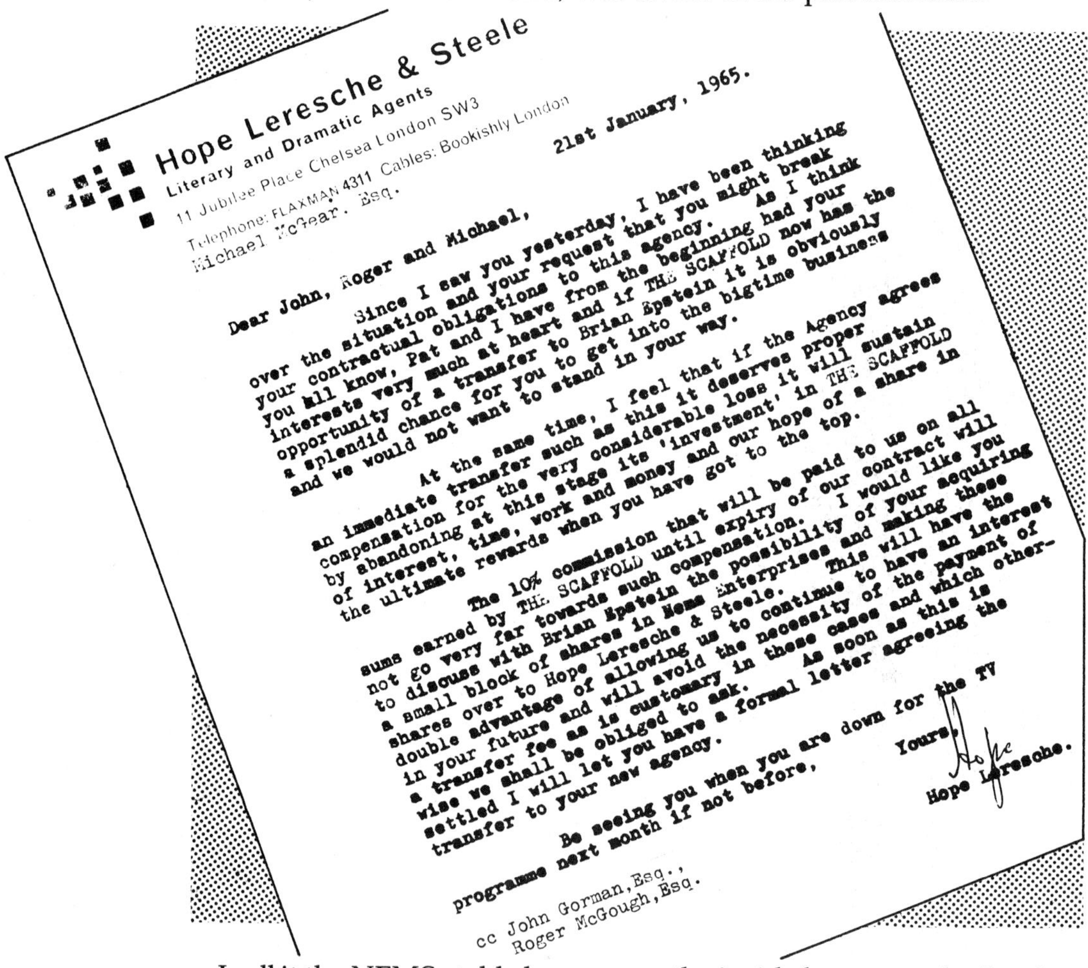

Hope Leresche & Steele
Literary and Dramatic Agents
11 Jubilee Place Chelsea London SW3
Telephone: FLAXMAN 4311 Cables: Bookishly London

21st January, 1965.

Michael McGear. Esq.

Dear John, Roger and Michael,

Since I saw you yesterday, I have been thinking over the situation and your request that you might break your contractual obligations to this agency. As I think you all know, Pat and I have from the beginning had your interests very much at heart and if THE SCAFFOLD now has the opportunity of a transfer to Brian Epstein it is obviously a splendid chance for you to get into the bigtime business and we would not want to stand in your way.

At the same time, I feel that if the Agency agrees an immediate transfer such as this it deserves proper compensation for the very considerable loss it will sustain by abandoning at this stage its 'investment' in THE SCAFFOLD of interest, time, work and money and our hope of a share in the ultimate rewards when you have got to the top.

The 10% commission that will be paid to us on all sums earned by THE SCAFFOLD until expiry of our contract will not go very far towards such compensation. I would like you to discuss with Brian Epstein the possibility of your acquiring a small block of shares in Nems Enterprises and making these shares over to Hope Leresche & Steele. This will have the double advantage of allowing us to continue to have an interest in your future and will avoid the necessity of the payment of a transfer fee as is customary in these cases and which otherwise we shall be obliged to ask. As soon as this is settled I will let you have a formal letter agreeing the transfer to your new agency.

Be seeing you when you are down for the TV programme next month if not before,

Yours,
Hope
Hope Leresche.

cc John Gorman, Esq.,
Roger McGough, Esq.

A letter of Hope!

I call it the NEMS stable because on the inside lane were the Beatles, followed by Cilla Black, Gerry and the Pacemakers, the Four-most, and so on; then of course there were the US acts they were starting to handle, the Supremes, Johnny Mathis and Herb Alpert among them; and last of all, on the outside lane, Scaffold. From the frying pan it seemed we had jumped into the fire. We withstood the heat for a while but in the end we nearly melted away.

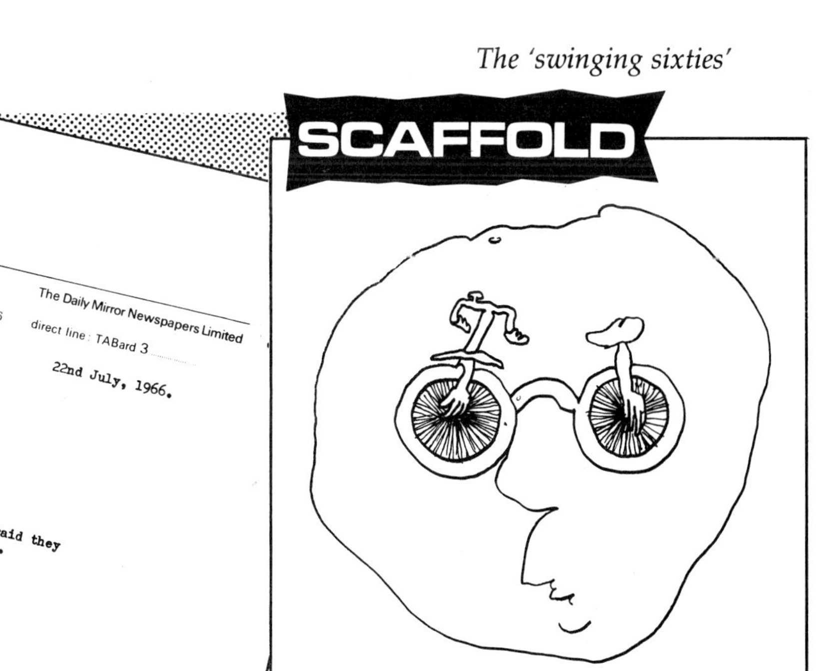

Daily Mirror

33 Holborn London EC1
telegrams: Mirror London EC1
telex: 21165
switchboard: FLEet Street 0246
The Daily Mirror Newspapers Limited
direct line: TABard 3

MW.

M. McGear, Esq.,
"Rembrandt",
HESWALL,
Cheshire.

22nd July, 1966.

Dear Mr. McGear,

Thanks for letting me see your drawings. I am afraid they are way, way too far-out for us, so I am returning them.

Yours sincerely,

E.F. Herbert
Cartoon Editor

Enc:

Stepping through the burning embers we finally gave in to Bri's singing advice and recorded a nice little cockney dirge called 2 *Day's Monday* coupled with *Three Blind Jellyfish* (what else?), produced by big George Martin, not, strange as it may seem, for his Beatle connections but for his Goon work, in particular Peter Sellers' *Songs for Swingin Sellers* LP which Paul and I used to roll around the floor to at home 2 *Day's Monday* didn't exactly smash any chart records but as ex-Goon and humanitarian Spike Milligan said on *Juke Box Jury* just after Dylan's *Everybody Must Get Stoned* single 'This is a very funny record by a group called the Scaffold . . . Mcgear, McGOCK! and Gorman. There ought to be a hit parade for funnies, symphonies, pops and popular murderers . . . this would top it'.

Marianne Faithful added . . . 'I like it and I'd buy it, but then I don't know if I'm a hit!' Although it was voted a (DING!) hit and got us a small cult following, it missed with the mass buying public.

We tried 2 *Day's Monday* out (or 'Two dies Mondie' in Cockney) in an extravaganza organised by the giant Russian Bear, Georgio Gomelski. It was to be a new musical theatre concept involving us in comedy sketches with such pop luminaries as Manfred Mann, The Yardbirds, Paul and Barry Ryan, Goldie and the Gingerbreads, Garry Farr (boxer Tommy Farr's lad), Jimmy James and the Vagabonds, and the Mark Leemonade Five . . . to name but many.

The only drawbacks to our grand esoteric package were . . . the girls—thousands of them, screaming and being held back from lead singers Paul 'Mann' Jones and Keith 'Yardy' Relf. So when we set off on the Marquee Tour with theatre sets, well-rehearsed sketches and very honourable intentions, we soon discovered that not only did 2 *Day's Monday* and the sketches need rethinking but we also found ourselves standing between x thousand screaming teenage girls and their idols. That was when I wondered if it mightn't have been wiser to take Brian's offer and become a simple pop singer?

But no; not for me . . . off next to finish the Establishment (London's

"Aren't there times when other English groups seem to outsell them in England?"

"The Beatles," Epstein replied coolly, "can't be compared with other groups. The other groups aren't sort of in the same field as the Beatles."

"Why is it that American groups haven't made the same impact in England, when actually your sound is American folk music with a special treatment?"

"I don't know. The Americans seem to have forgotten how to do it. By the way, I've got a group called 'The Scaffold' — singers who decided to talk rather than sing."

"Why did you call them 'The Scaffold'? Has it anything to do with hanging?"

"No — just because it's a good name." FEB. 6, 1965

famous Greek Street satirical club) where Ivan Vaughan (the man who introduced himself to John Lennon's brother) had been the bouncer when Lennie Bruce was on. We not only appeared at the Establishment with Texan guest guitarist Shaun Phillips ('now, a little old number apropos the current day musical trends . . . friends'), but with the help of a few notorious Soho gangsters, we also closed it!

Before we bade farewell to Brian and NEMS we tiptoed through smouldering charcoals to host one of the final *Ready Steady Go* TV shows instead of resident hostess Cathy ('super') McGowan. Shortly after, this too folded. These weren't exactly milestones in our new 'go ahead, young man' showbiz careers, so I thought it best that Bri and I had a little chat, man-to-man like.

Mr. Brian Epstein
At Home
on Wednesday, August 12th 1964
at 15 Whaddon House, William Mews, London, S.W.1.

R.S.V.P.
15 Whaddon House
William Mews
London S.W.1

Buffet Supper
9.30 p.m.
Informal Dress

He took me round the corner from his busy Albermarle Street office to Wheelers restaurant and over a quiet sea-food pancake we discussed Scaffold's future.

Before I could get a word out, Brian said, 'I think I know what you're going to say, Michael. And quite honestly I agree with you . . . NEMS is not the organisation for you.'

And that was that . . . we were out of the fire.

Before our departure, we had put out feelers to see what interest, if any, there was in a unique, non-profit-making organisation like the Scaffold, and got reaction from two managerial firms, one of which was a 'well-established Tin Pan Alley co-operative'.

After being shown into the boss man's office, I explained that we'd been with a well-known agency for the last couple of years, but we were swamped by all the other acts on the same bill. Now we needed some *personal* management and *not* at an exorbitant percentage.

The boss man listened attentively (feet on desk, cigar in mouth) and answered, 'quite honestly', that he was the man for us; not only could he give us 'personal' management, but his agency was just the right size . . . and expanding, so that he could look after us on both managerial and agency level . . . *all* at a reasonable percentage.

After a few further meetings we agreed that this was indeed an honourable man and bartered businesslike over time periods and percentages.

'So we're all agreed then, gentlemen—three years at fifteen per cent, said our new boss.

'Yes,' (times three).

The contracts were sent upstairs for typing and as we were in the usual hurry to get back to Liverpool, we thanked the boss for the celebration drink and asked if we could have the contracts to take home with us. After a long delay (*just* as we were about to leave for the train), the contracts arrived back from the typist.

'Why not just sign them now, boys, so that we can forge ahead with your new careers,' suggested the boss.

'We haven't really got time, can we take them with us?'

'It won't take a minute.'

'But we might miss the train.'

'Here, take my pen.

'Well OK, but can we read them first?'

'Of course.'

We scrambled through them quickly and the businessman amongst us noticed two slight errors.

'We *did* agree three years at fifteen per cent didn't we?'

'Yes.'

'Well it says here five years at twenty per cent!'

'Never! Let me see . . .' said Bosscat. 'My goodness me, a typist's error. Wait till I get hold of that girl.'

Out of the fire into the frying pan?

GLENDA SHAW AND SANDY JACKSON

All those years ago, like many other hot-blooded lads, I fell in love with a bare-footed, short-sighted, Dagenham girl singer on *Ready Steady Go* called Sandie Shaw!

She had the same glazed charm that Lennon had—i.e. they were both blind as bats! But this was of no consequence (even if I'd known) because I was in love with this thin, awkward, cocky cockney sounding girl.

I'd come into lens contact with her through mutual *RSG* dancing friends of ours . . . Patrick and Theresa Kerr. Pat and Terry lived next door to Joan 'Loves' Maitland, our first lady producer, who was wonderfully theatrical and had collaborated with Lionel Bart on the Musical *Oliver*, so we kept bumping into each other in their Hampstead homes, and one thing led to a Sandie.

At that time, Sandie was gloriously inconsistent . . . one minute up, the next minute right down, and like a love-sick fool I allowed myself to be jerked up and down with her moods like a puppet on and off a string.

In fact I got *so* involved that at one stage I was nearly cited as co-respondent (whatever that meant) in a divorce which had nothing to do with me, and everything to do with Her Majesty. But it didn't bother me, as a young man's love knows no bounds.

Sometime later when I was still a gay young batchelor living with Dad at Rembrandt there was a phone call for me.

'It's a Sandie Shaw,' Dad shouted upstairs.

'Bloody hell,' thought I . . . 'Hello,' I said, on one of the many extensions.

''Ello, Mike?'

'Yes.'

'It's Sandie, I'm in the Cavern.'

'The Cavern!'

'Yes, come and get me.'

Naturally, being a gentleman (and a full blooded one at that), I left immediately. She had played the Cavern and was feeling less than elated, and was next performing at the Garrick Cabaret Club, Leigh, Clive . . . sorry, Georgie Fame's home town.

I went with her to the 'doubling up' clubs, and what we did later on has nothing to do with you. But it was here that I first realised what a formidable, lonely task a girl solo singer has on her hands, or feet. At least a member of a group has the other members to talk to, and get nervous or drunk with, but for a girl singer performing to mostly male, stoned, randy audiences, it must be a frightening occupation.

Many years later, when we were all married and 'settled down', my wife Angi received a call at our Sunset home . . . 'It's Sandie Shaw for you,' she said suspiciously. Mrs. Banks, as she'd now become, wanted the pleasure of our company at a charity 'do' in London, and as we were foot-loose and fancy free, we agreed (after me reassuring the wife that any love there might have been had long since gone with the wind).

The dinner-dance was held in an army tent in the middle of a London barracks. At our table were Sandie and hubby Geoff 'The Dress' Banks (a beautiful man), Angi next to me, and opposite, who else but . . . Glenda Jackson (so *that* was why I came down all the way from Liverpool)!

There was something I'd long wanted to sort out with Glenda Jackson (the more than adequate Merseyside actress) so I thought this might as well be the time and the place. 'Excuse me,' I said over the pâté, 'but I never went out with you, did I?'

'I beg your pardon,' she replied with faint amusement, particularly seeing that her elder statesman husband was listening to our conversation.

'It's just that I used to go out with a girl the spitting image of you in Liverpool . . . you never lived above a greengrocers in West Derby Village did you?'

'No, we came from over the water in Hoylake actually, and my Dad was a bricklayer.'

'Thank God for that then . . . the thought of turning down Brigitte Bardot* *and* you would have been too much to live with for the rest of my life.'

PARIS II

The second time I went to Paris was at the request of young Tara Browne. Tara was a Guinness heir (and a right honourable one at that). I was a Beatle brother . . . so we had mop and hop tops in common (or should I say commons, as Tara's Dad was in the House of Lords).

Being two gay young blades, one with too much money, the other with not a lot of sense, we believed in living life to the swingin' London full, but when Tara suggested we go to Paris for a week or so, I had to admit to him that I wasn't *that* well off.

'Oh, don't worry Mike . . . I'll pay the difference.'

Being of stubborn, Liverpool working-class stock, with great Northern pride, I readily agreed (*vive la difference*), and as my passport was in the Pool and I was in Tara's Eaton Row Mews house, a provisional passport was arranged and we were on the next flight to gay Paree.

At the airport to meet us was a chauffeur with the most extraordinary Mercedes I'd ever seen. It was so long it looked as if a bit had been stuck in the middle. This magnificent creature (and the Merc) floated us to Boulevard Suchet in the posh Trocadero part of Paris, where we disembarked into the wrought iron lift which zoomed us slowly to the roof garden apartment.

Tara's mum, the Lady Oranmore and Browne was in the south of France, so Tara showed me round the Magritte-littered lounge (this was the first time I'd seen a Magritte 'live'—so that's what Vadim was on about . . . not at all fishy, but very tasty) and up to the bedrooms.

'Shall we share bedrooms?' he asked.

'Oops!' I thought. We didn't know each other *that* well, and here is a gay young titled gentleman asking me to go to bed with him.

* Because I was a contrary child, there were two things I never took up at school . . . smoking, and a crush on B.B.

'D'you mind if we have separate bedrooms . . . I snore.'

'Not at all, see you downstairs in half an hour.'

I needn't have bothered. Tara was as straight as a dye; he was just being courteous.

After a shower, I dried off in head-to-toe towels, had a lie down, (the cham*pagne* on the *plane* was mainly to *blame*), and we met downstairs in the more than comfortable lounge (with a telly in the bookcase . . . disguised as books!).

'Right! Show me Paris . . . I missed it last time as I was feeling a little gay.'

Tara showed me Paree all right; the chauffeur-driven Merc took us to La Coupole for a drink and a bump into Vidal Sassoon, then to a beautiful little restaurant called La Petite Bedon where I had my first sparrow in red wine (I think *they* called it quail but whatever it was, it was excellent). The pot-bellied chef even came to our table, he didn't *do* anything . . . just came to our table. And then on to the gay Paris nightclubs, where some ale was supped, eventually ending up at Castell's . . . the club of the day.

Here we were checked in by a beautiful, cool Paris lady, who spoke not a soupspoon of English.

'I fancy that,' I overstated to Tara.

'That's our Letty, it's good to know her.'

'Letty,' *dictated I as a mental note*, as we descended the Castellian stairs to debauchery. We were posing in the middle of our whisky and Cokes when through the dark, staggered the Yardbirds. As soon as they saw me they chirped in perfect unison 'Today's Monday, today's Monday, Monday's washing day, is everybody 'appy? You betcha life we are' (Scaffold's first resounding, but popular flop).

It's lovely being loved, but Tara and I were there for the serious purpose of enjoying ourselves, so we opened the Castell cage door, sent them flying, and continued with our night-time revelry alongside beautiful, black and white, pencil thin models, and me popping upstairs to let Letty in on the fact that my intentions were entirely honourable.

Just as dawn was breaking (or was it Françoise) we swayed gently out of the 'in' club and across to the restaurant opposite, where we nearly got in a fight over our chilli con carne (because I hadn't clicked with Letty at the nightclub . . . if the truth were known).

As we emerged to the even chillier French morning, as if by magic the limo drew up and we fell in. He'd been waiting all night! Being working class *and* drunk (what could be worse!), I gave the chauffeur hell for not joining us in the night club.

All at once, in the early Parisian morning light, we were faced with a strange predicament. The limousine was suddenly surrounded by thousands of French cyclists on their way to work . . . all facing *us*. Either we were in a one-way street or they were cycling backwards. Whatever, it was a stalemate, and we all stopped.

The gruff garlic comments from yer actual working-class Frenchies could be felt through the Mercedes skin. I put myself in their position: I've been up all night after drinking pastis, with the petite monstre-baby . . . shouting above the Pierre Douglas Show, the wife nags at me over coffee and *France Soir* . . . I climb on me cold velo bike . . . cycle through the freezing five o'clock rain . . . join my thousands of

Parisian rat-pack colleagues . . . and there in the middle of the narrow City rue is a long black car going the wrong way, containing two young, drunk, mop-top goldfish (not only that . . . it's a *bosch* car). Let's just say that if we were in the middle of a revolution and there was a Bastille nearby, they would have simply said 'Off wiz les cochons 'eads,' before carrying on to work.

Luckily, one of my many disguises is as the Scarlet Pimpernel and indicating a secret side-street escape route to the chauffeur, we avoided the hoard of Robespierrean Rats and headed for the safety of our Magrittien mansion (zey seek us here, zey seek us zere, zose damp froggies seek us everywhere).

More power-packed Parisian nights followed with the inevitable falling in love with me by Letty and many torrid nights of 'love' were enjoyed by all. In contrast to 'being in love' with Celia, here was a woman who taught me how to make love with more positions than an Indian Yoga teacher would dare to attempt, and all in French!

Tara's mum, Lady Oranmore and Browne, paid us a visit in the middle of these 'sumestas' and after my customary Butler-served fresh orange juice I felt slightly apprehensive about my first meeting with the upper crust lady matriarch (particularly with a bit of French fluff in the bedroom)!

Once again, I needn't have worried . . . 'Oonagh' turned out to be one of the warmest, coolest, quick-witted, most subtle women I'd ever met, and she made us both most welcome. She was a lady, but not just the 'lady' in the title . . . a *real* lady. I call her 'Mum', she calls me 'Dad', and we shall remain friends till the end.

FREDDIE (SUPER) STARR

One sunburnt night in 1965 with Dad safely packed off to Mexico for cousin Keith McCartney's wedding, I invited some friends back to Rembrandt for drinks. They comprised Freddie Starr (ex-Midnighter), Brian Auger (ex-Trinity), Julie 'Jools' Driscoll (ex-Yardbirds fan club secretary), Long John Baldry (ex-Hoochie Coochie Man), and a lad called Rod Stewart (ex-actly). The latter three were collectively called Steampacket.

Thanks to the angle that I took the photograph, here's a not-so-long John Baldry and brother Paul soliciting outside Lime Street Station in Liverpool. Note the price to Nottingham – 14/9 in those days.

The only proviso was that when we reached Rembrandt we must all keep absolutely quiet, as new stepmother Ange and baby step sister Ruth were fast asleep upstairs with grandmother Edie and must not be disturbed.

We crept into the long lounge, and on seeing the grand piano, the even longer John Baldry immediately commandeered it. On seeing the long, full length velvet curtains at the end of the lounge, Freddie Starr immediately declared them to be the 'Stage Tabs' and headed towards them. On seeing the long black leather settee, the rest of us spread gently out. (This being before Rod's superstar period he was unusually quiet).

When everyone's drink requirements had been quietly met, Freddie (who doesn't drink) whispered that the velvet curtains demanded a sexy striptease and offered to fill the bill, before anyone could object. After ordering some silent symphonies from Long John Pianerist, he slipped behind the red velvet and proceeded to disrobe, (as only Freddie can . . . better, more outrageous and definitely funnier than any stripper *you've* ever seen).

I don't remember how long he kept it up (the striptease that is) but let it suffice to say that in the end, just before the undies were due off, with ribs aching and tears flowing, Bri, Jools, Rod, John and I, burst from silent giggles to raucous belly laughter and applause . . . waking the whole house. Luckily my new relatives took to being woken in the middle of the night very well, and proceeded to make us all bacon butties.

Freddie Starr took his place as one of showbiz's nicest heavenly bodies . . . but look out VEGAS, he's heading in your direction next.

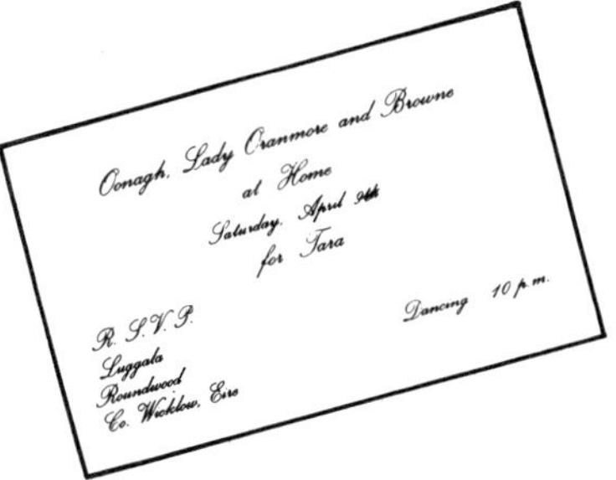
Oonagh, Lady Oranmore and Browne
at Home
Saturday, April 9th
for Tara

R.S.V.P.
Luggala
Roundwood
Co. Wicklow, Eire

Dancing 10 p.m.

TARAR TARA

In early 1966 Tara asked me if I would like to drive his AC Cobra two-seater sports car outside his Eaton Mews previously Eaton Row Belgravia home (round the corner from Buckingham Palace and Brian Epstein's Chapel Street* house). I put the beast into first gear and VROOMSHKA! it nearly took off without me, such was its power. After reaching 140 mph in second gear, I also reached the conclusion that small cars with big engines were too powerful for me. I stopped it and got out.

Later that year I accompanied Tara and his wife Nicky (MacSherry) to a Liverpool court, where he was fined for speeding on his entry to our fair (cop) city. When Nicky took off for more private parts, young Tara came to stay at 'Rembrandt' for a couple of days and as my brother was up from London, they smoked one of them silly ciggies together and insisted on going to cousin Bett's home on our two small motorbikes.

A couple of hundred yards from Bett's, Paul took the bend too closely and flew the rest of the way . . . causing severe facial injuries to one half of his baby face. On his return to 'Rembrandt' he insisted on me taking a memento of the occasion with my birthday Nikon camera.

'Are you sure, it looks pretty "bloody" awful.'

'Yes, because it's the truth,' (it was the way, the truth, the light up another one period).

'OK, be it on your own face,' . . . click.†

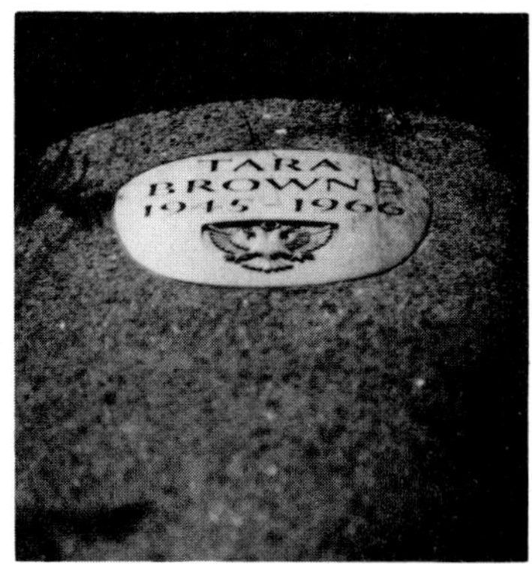

Tara Browne's tombstone at the foot of the Wicklow mountains, Ireland. The streams cascade close by—brown water against white froth rather like Guinness.

Soon afterwards (when the stitches were sewn by Pip the family doctor, with his maternity bag suture needle, and whose hand started to shake when he realised his artwork would be judged from then on with every photo taken of Paul) Tara broomed across the sea to Ireland.

In January 1966 I was twenty-two, in April Tara was twenty-one, and in June Paul was twenty-four. Tara was to inherit one million pounds on his twenty-fifth birthday, but on 18th December 1966 he went through red lights in his 110 mph Lotus Elan into the back of a parked van in South Kensington and was dead. A witness said: 'I saw the driver pinned like a doll in the wreck . . . the steering wheel was bent like a flower stem.' On hearing the news of Tara's death, Brian 'Stone' Jones wept and said 'I'm numbed . . . Tara was so full of life'.

THE 1ST SUPERSTAR ALBUM

In February 1967 the Beatles had embarked on what could arguably be

* Chapel Street houses the Irish Embassy where Tara was born!
† The fab pic was eventually stolen from Cave Avenue by a 'butler' and sold to an Italian mag to illustrate 'wild Beatle drug parties in swinging London'.

called their most important album. In contrast to their first LP which took a day to record and cost four hundred pounds, the new album was to take four months and cost twenty-five thousand pounds.

1967, Sergeant Pepper and LSD

The album was *Sergeant Pepper's Lonely Hearts Club Band* and the closing track, *'A Day in the Life'* arguably one of the most hard-hitting, moving songs for many years, included words by John, Paul and perhaps even me. Part of it was about a young son of a lord who didn't know the lights had changed, with the occasional reference to silly cigarettes . . . Tara was a friend of John's too.

When the Beatles completed this album, a milestone in popular music, Paul and I decided to work on a few silly songs that Roger McGough and I had knocked out together. We chose the day that Paul was accused of taking the 'heaven and hell' drug LSD by the nation's media, to start recording.

He had simply admitted to a paper man that he had indeed experimented with the mind expanding drug with brother John. But the Beatles had had *so* much success in such a short time that for the less scrupulous media people here at last was the chance to say 'I told you so' and prove that the fab four were human after all, by simply crucifying one of them.

The day Paul chose to be hung and quartered was the day he chose to be born twenty-five years previously, his birthday, June 18th.

Jane, who was usually domiciled in Paul's London home, was away in America on a theatre tour, so it was just brother and I who lowered ourselves into his dark blue Aston Martin DB6 at high noon on that fateful day.

The drawbridge to the Paul's castle was lowered and there, true to form, were the media vultures, already clicking and rolling their cameras away. We (and the Aston) advanced slowly into battle ready for the slaughter, when suddenly God stepped into the movie of life in the form of dozens of young girls with birthday presents for Paul.

Not being ones to lose a God given opportunity ('the wise man taketh the passing golden custard pie, the foolish man letteth it slip by' MIKIAH, chapter 86, platform 9), Paul and I buzzed down our electric windows and the gifts, chocolates and red roses, poured inside, with an odd caress of the cheek thrown in for good measure.

Fans reach out with birthday presents for the Beatle in a drugs storm

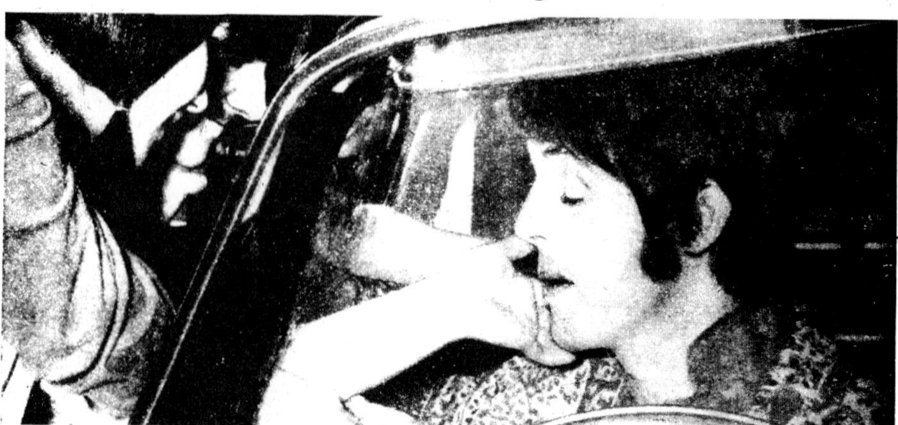

The enemy was almost annihilated, The 'Beatle drug addict' being inundated with happy birthday presents was *not* going to make good copy (but they printed it anyway). Paul and I continued to Dick James Music in New Oxford Street where we launched into the very first superstar album.

It certainly didn't start out as such but when our kid rings round for some musical help, more than a few people turn up for love . . . not money. It began with Brian Jones' pal Prince Stanislaus Klossowiski de Rowla, Baron de Wattevill ('Stash' to you and me) playing the red roses, (literally), Zoot Money being a drum, *Abbey Road* engineer Geoff 'Freaky Freaky' Emerick insisting he was a raindrop, and went on to have Graham Nash and Dave Mason singing beautiful harmonies (some with Paul), Jane and Mrs. Asher giving fine impressions of ghosts plus Michaelangelic incantations, Barry 'Chelsea Arts Club' Fantoni playing sax, John Mayall playing harpsichord,* Mitch Mitchell and Gary 'Walker Brother' Leeds on drums, and the one and only Jimi Hendrix playing lead guitar on whatever he liked . . . such is the power of love.

So in the spate of a few months two fine albums had been made, one with poetry, humour and music called *McGough-McGear* which received the *Melody Maker* Album of the Month award and sold next to nothing, the other, which received every accolade under the sun, made millions of money, was the basis of the *Yellow Submarine* cartoon, and was eventually turned into a multi-million pound film (even *without* the Beatles) . . . such is the power of good music.

JIMI

My first meeting with the 'Wild Man of Pop' Jimi Hendrix, other than seeing him down the Scotch, is well worth a few words. His name as a brilliant guitarist and husky singer was growing in stature every day, but his reputation as a wild, drug-taking womaniser was miles ahead. So when Paul suggested that 'Jimi Hendrix would be great on this (*McGough-McGear*) track' and got a verbal phone agreement from him to come, I was *more* than interested to meet this living legend.

* His favourite track was 'Mr. Tickle'.

Noel Redding (on right) and Mitch Mitchell on the left were on the *McGear* album. They're seen here camping it up with Jimi looking the gentleman he was.

Expecting hundreds of roadies, lighting experts, groupies and joint roller . . . I was surprised when Mr. Hendrix turned up half way through a session at De Lane Lee Recording Studios, Kingsway, London, on his own, carrying a small guitar case.

As the 'musicians' were doing us an impossible, unpayable favour (and being from Liverpool where *everybody* drank) I thought the least I could do was to get a stock of ale in for the lads. On Jimi's arrival, as we were right in the middle of mixing a track, I offered him a selection of the boozy table.

'No thank you, I'll just sit in the studio if that's cool . . .' And *this* is the wild man of Borneo? *This* my dear readers was a gentleman, and on the other occasions that I bumped into him before his death I confirmed to myself that not only was he a gentleman, he was also a gentle man.

When Paul and I had finished the track, we went into the studio where Jimi was sitting on the floor, guitar in hand, and we discussed where we wanted his guitar solo on the new track. He seemed to know exactly what was required, so we left him to it and returned to the control box.

'Ready Jim?' Paul asked over the studio two-way mike.

'Ready.'

'Play him the track,' Paul instructed the tape op.

Everything was going very quietly until it got to the solo bit where Jimi was due to play. Suddenly, an electrifying surge of energy hit the room which built up till it reached an impossible peak and was then sustained through the whole song, up through the ceiling, across the universe, and into the middle of next week. In a few seconds he'd taken the song by the throat, transcended it by the scruff of the neck with his guitar, and sent it hurtling into the infinite.

'Will that do you?' Paul asked me with a smile. Having been in Abbey Road for four meticulous musical months making *Sergeant Pepper*, snap decisions came easy when such brilliance presented itself.

But Mike McGear hadn't been in EMI for anywhere near as long, wasn't a musician (never mind an experienced one) and youthfully —stupidly—argued with everything.

'It didn't come in exactly where it should have, and shouldn't he have stopped a bit earlier?'

'You've got to be joking.'

'No.'

'Let's go out and ask Jimi then.'

Jimi, being the gent he was, said that he'd be only too pleased to have another go.

'*I* thought it was great,' said Paul, 'but if you've got the time and don't mind, we could go for another take I suppose.'

'Surely.'

When we got back in the control room, Paul said, 'I think you're crazy. But let's roll . . . take two.'

Over the next half-dozen takes, Jimi got nearer and nearer to what *I* wanted but further and further from the truth (you can contain a tiger in a cage, but eventually it's better for him and you to let him free to roam in the wild).

In the end I conceded, 'You were right, I'm sorry, it *was* the first take.'

'Great,' said Paul. 'I'm dying to hear that one again.' (Flicks mike on.)

'OK Jim, that's the one . . . come on in,' and to the tape op, 'Play back the first take will you?'

'The *first* take?' said the op, 'But there were no tracks left so I've been wiping over every solo . . . we've only got the last take there.' Our stomachs hit the floor . . . Paul for missing such musical genius, me for being so bloody-minded.

When Jimi came in and asked, 'Was that the one?' we didn't have the heart to tell him anything, but simply said, 'Yes, that was the one . . . it's beautiful.'

The climax of the *McGough-McGear* album for me was a track which eventually never made the LP.

As it was entitled 'Oh to be a Child' I thought it only proper to use childlike instruments and so hired the 'Haydn's Toy Symphony' collection from a London music store.

To create a playground atmosphere, as opposed to the dead studio sound, we opened the studio doors and arranged the microphone in the corridors. Then my greatest joy was to witness Jane 'Serious Actress' Asher, Graham 'Holly' Nash, Mitch 'Experience' Mitchell and Noel 'Clonakilty Cowboy' Redding, John 'Blues' Man' Mayall, Dave 'Traffic' Mason and Jimi 'Wild Man' Hendrix walking up and down the corridors banging toy instruments like big soft kids.

WUNERFUL RADIO ONE

When the nation's number one radio channel was first rumoured I applied for a job with BBC's 'Wonderful Radio One'.

The first obvious idea was to tape me and my wonderful famous (and infamous) friends from the pop business, indulging in wonderful show biz nonsequiturs, so when Graham Nash suggested I drop by to meet the Supremes one day, here was my first chance of a 'scoop'.

The bureaucratic BBC tape machine lending department being closed, I went along to meet the girls anyway. Diana (same age as me) and the 'MoTown Mop Tops' were extremely well turned out, sexy, polite, beautiful, as well as being highly professional (and this was *off* stage). But none of them fancied me, so I went home to bed.

The following midday I awoke, collected my Uher BBKING 9732487630¼ tape recorder from the Beeb lending library (plus putting my monicer on the statutory 'signing out' form) and presented myself at Graham's wunderful London mews house door, just in case the Super Premes were still around.

Rubbing his eyes with an Indian rubber Ravi Shankar had given him, he opened the door, and inside his apartment I discovered an even sleepier head . . . Dave (ex-Traffic) Mason. Dave shook my hand with one of those funny handgrips that only Masons can do, and I explained why I'd come.

'Sorry, but the girls have gone back to the States . . . will we do? And if you're the new radio one jock, we'd better celebrate right away,' said Graham, going to the fridge and producing a couple of bottles of vintage champagne and a few spliffs. After a couple of glasses of bubbly (or one and half bottles . . . I can never remember) Graham and Dave dressed and Grae said, 'Right, come on let's do the wonderful interview.'

'Where?' I asked.

'Push the button and we can go from here, there, or everywhere,' (Grae was a Paul fan too). 'Who knows we might end up at the Hungry Horsh.'

I pushed the button and we started in the general direction of their car, with half a bubbly bottle and a few more spliffs to keep us company.

'Are you sure we're all right to drive in this wonderful condition?'

I hazarded a guess. 'Sure, we can only be done for floating.'

'Correct', I had to agree.

As we motored merrily along, blowing the odd bubble, the questions came easily and were answered naturally, until all of a sudden BLA! BLA! BLA! BLA! hit the lazy afternoon air. A cop car was screeching to a halt alongside, filled with very heavy (and not so wonderful) looking policemen. I looked around to see the cause of the commotion and discovered we were driving down a one-way street the wrong way (not *again*)!

I could see the headlines: 'Mason, Nash and McCartney* on Drunk Drugs Driving Rap! Scaffold and Holly in London Traffic Bust'.

I don't know whether it was the superman in me, or my wonderful Liverpool supercool but I wound down the window like greased lightning and just as the boss bobby was about to leap from his car and breathalise us, I shoved the mike (and the Mike) out of the window and slurred 'Excuse me, officer, but I'm doing interviews for the new BBC Radio One programme, what do you think of it so far?'

As the Beeb launching was getting mass coverage from the media he had indeed heard of it (thank God) and stopped in mid track.

'No comment,' said the shy, stage-struck constable, slamming his door and zooming off into the distance.

'What a wonderful day,' said I—'You were shaying gentlemen?'

Needless to say I didn't get the job—Tony Blackburn did! Radio One opened on 30th September 1967 with Ronan O'Rahilly's Radio Caroline style jingles and top forty format, and is still there to this day . . . full of wonder.

ESHER ESHER ALL FALL DOWN

In the carefree, couldn't care less, psychedelic LSD, day tripper London period, I would leave our kid's St. Johns Wood home in my khaki coloured Scimitar sports car (the first one bought from Reliant at the 1967 Motor Show and not at all 'flower power' . . . more 'tank power') to drive down to 'Kinfauns', George and Patti's Esher home.

With explicit 'secret' instructions from George how to get lost, I soon arrived outside the high walled superhome and gave the 'secret' horn beeps. Before you could say 'open says me' the door had swung open and I was over the moat and inside the low slung castle.

After pleasant reunions I was shown around the 'bungalow George' home by Patti, through the Dali inspired extension, complete with huge round window, and out to the heated swimming pool.

We enjoyed a peaceful day lounging round the pool and a quiet Ravi-Byrds evening in, with large whisky and Cokes (Jim Macmeasures) poured into the early hours. By this time I was quite drunk (for

* 'McGear' wasn't known in London . . . yet.

the second time since August 1961, or was it the third?) and staggered to my bed.

In the morning (sorry mid-day) I shakily presented myself to the company, and after breakfast cum dinner brunch, George asked if I'd ever been to John's house. As I hadn't, he offered to drive me over to Weybridge after my Alka Seltzer.

We got into his new Ferrari bumptiay car.

'A bit of a change from the Ford Anglia,' I observed.

The big time!

'A few things have changed since those days, Michael.'

'I had noticed,' and off we BROOMED! down the drive, leaving my stomach back at the house.

I don't know if you've ever been in a Ferrarisuperfasterthan it should, but believe me they don't go slow, just like AC Cobras. So after five minutes rally-driving gear changes, I asked Wee Georgie if he would slow down a bit, as I wasn't feeling too well.

'We'll be there in a minute,' he answered, changing up to thirteenth gear, and passing four hundred Ford Classics.

Just before crossing over John's Wey-bridge I could contain myself no longer and enquired, 'Do you want it on the floor or on the window . . . I can *try* for the ashtray.'

'The Butter please, it's a new car.'

With that, he shrieked to an 'on the penny lane' stop and I nearly went through the windscreen.

In the tastefully arranged stockbroker belt (just near the buckle) I puked my ring up.

'Feeling better?'

'I think so.'

'Good, it's at the end of this road.'

After passing a gigantic black Beatle boot in the driveway John made us welcome and showed me round his home, leaf filled swimming pool . . . the lot . . .

'Hiya, Cyn.'

'Hello, Mike, you're looking rough.'

'Don't remind me.'

'Dya wanta see my new car.' asked John.

('Oh God not another drive,' I thought).

'Well just a little look, because George pours drinks like me dad and I'm feeling a little delicate.'

'Sure, it's in the garage.'

And he proceeded to show me the most extraordinary car that anybody had ever seen. It *used* to be a white Rolls Royce, but a gypsy graffiti artist had sneaked in during the night and painted the most elaborate fairground flowers and zodiac designs in yellow, orange and red all over it.

'What d'you think young Michael?'

There was nothing else to say about this ultimate in psychedelic whims except 'It's bloody fantastic!'

'It cost me a grand (I trust he meant the graffiti) and there's a telly in the back as well . . . go on in.' He opened the door and I climbed inside. His mistake was closing the door, because in my state, the sudden claustrophobic feeling of sitting in a smoked glass, black wall-to-wall carpeted psychedelic coffin nearly made me christen his tiny tot telly set . . . I staggered out for air *just* in time.

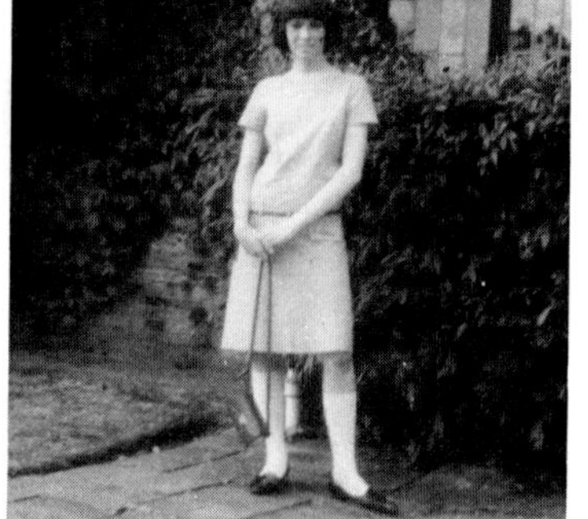

Me looking extremely delicate outside John Lennon's home that day.

'I think I'll go home now,' I probably said, and definitely did—back to Liverpool, and that was the nearest to 'a trip' I ever got.

When the Rolls was released to the press, Mr. Fallon (coach builder) was quoted as saying 'It was Mr. Lennon's original brilliant idea, the design was his, he's ever such a nice man'. (And so he is. After all, he's been good to me, Michael).

'ALL YOU NEED IS . . . OUR WORLD!'

As the *McGough-McGear* album took over a year to complete there was plenty of time for lots of little things in between. One of the little things was a satellite television concept to link up thirty one countries for two whole hours on a Sunday night in June 1967. At a cost of three quarters of a million (and even in those days, that was a couple of bob) it was to be the biggest 'live' TV show ever made.

Called *Our World* it would be seen by a staggering five hundred million people (that is . . . if they had a telly). Transmission was from Abbey Road's large number one studio and as I wasn't doing anything particular that Sunday I thought I'd pop along and give the BBC a hand.

Lo and behold if I didn't get in there and my brother had beaten me to it! 'What an opportunist,' I thought to myself, 'and not only that, he's brought along the other three as well as Mick Jagger, Eric Clapton, an entire orchestra conducted by George Martin . . . *plus* a few hundred festive people and a couple of relatives to boot!'

You'll be glad to hear I didn't boot anybody, or walk right out of that place, but instead swallowed my pride and stayed for a while (who knows, one of them might get nerves, and I could step in at the last moment).

When the 'live button' was pressed I did my best to liven things up a little by throwing streamers, pulling faces behind the cameras, holding cue cards up with 'Smile' and 'Laf now' on them (you know, the usual childish practices), and was most impressed to see that Anne Danher, one of my relatives, immediately grasped the idea and scrawled, in lipstick, a message to our Aunt in Australia . . . 'Come Home Milli, All is Forgiven'. I made sure they got *that* on camera . . . and I even nipped in front of the cameras and the Beatles to give a little wave myself, once in a while.

Thinking the BBC title of *Our World* a little trite, if not banal, I decided to change it just before we went on the air, which brother immediately picked up on and made it the theme tune for the programme. First the orchestra played a little French introduction, then the Beatles sang along lovingly, then cellos joined in, then John Lennon took the lead, then after a George solo everyone else slowly joined in . . . Mick, Eric, Anne, Milli (I even sang along myself at one stage!) until slowly all the people at home broke into song and finally the whole world was singing my song . . . *All You Need is Love'*.

What do you think of the title? Not bad eh? Well it seemed to go down quite well on the night . . .

Maharishi Mahesh Yogi

Lecture

at the Hilton Hotel, London, W.1.
Tonight at 8 p.m. **ALL TICKETS SOLD.**

Public Lectures

Wednesday, 30 August, at 8 p.m.
John Phillips Lecture Hall,
Normal College, Bangor, N. Wales.
Admission Free.

Friday, 1 September, at 8 p.m.
Concert Hall,
Amsterdam, Holland.

All enquiries to :—
S.R.M. Foundation of Great Britain,
20, Grosvenor Place, London, S.W.1.
Telephone: Belgravia 8994.

FROM RISHIKESH . . . TO VEGAS

Back in February 1967 Patti (Boyd) Harrison had been initiated into what we now call transcendental meditation, and when the SRM Guru who spread this particular brand of relaxation was about to lecture in London on 24th August, Patti told George and George rang Paul to inform him.

He imparted the information with such persuasiveness that neither Paul, Jane, myself, John or Cyn could refuse (Ringo was having his fab pic taken at Queen Charlotte's hospital with his five day old son Jason at the time, so he gave it a miss). The rest of us picked up our mental crutches and presented ourselves at the Hilton Hotel, Park Lane (a nice little address for a Himalayan recluse, thought I).

Pictures by DOUGLAS EATWELL

Listening, left to right: Paul McCartney, Jane Asher, a friend, John Lennon, Cynthia Lennon, Patti Harrison, George Harrison

Me and friends in search of truth.

On our arrival we were immediately shown to the front row (where else) of about a thousand very 'respectable' people in the large ballroom, with a few obviously religious baldy freaks sitting at our feet. Beyond them, in front of the stage, was the usual battery of press cameramen, busily 'cricking' away (obviously no flashes allowed).

Never having seen an Indian holy man before we didn't know what to expect, and when a tiny little brown skinned man with a long white skirt came in and the whole thousand stood up, I was even more confused. His eyes were bright and brown, he had long straggly hair with a small white goatee beard, and his very strong-looking arms were holding a bunch of red roses, carnations, or maybe both. He climbed on to what seemed to be a goatskin rug, composed himself into a lotus position and just sat there smiling with his trouble-free, happy face. His presence was electric and just looking at him made you want to smile too. It was like watching a happy child . . . you couldn't help but feel good.

His name was Maharishi Mahesh Yogi.

He talked in a high pitched Indian accent about the benefits of meditation twice a day, but the highlight of his performance for me was when he stopped talking and said, 'Now we will meditate for . . . ten minutes, yes?'

There was a thousand-breathed calm as he closed his eyes (as, apparently, did all those people behind us) and he *seemed* to go into a deep trance. His whole body relaxed, his breathing slowed down so much I thought it had stopped and he just sat there serenely for the ten minutes, with the only sound (other than the distant Park Lane traffic) being that of the noisy C..R..I..C..K..et cameras, still snapping Beatles and 'friend', in the tranquil summer air.

'This', I thought, 'has got to be the best act in the business . . . if he took this to Vegas he'd make a fortune'.*

Exactly at the allotted time, he began to stir . . . he wasn't asleep after all. Then, just as suddenly as he'd arrived, he placed his hands together in the prayer position, said 'Jai Guru Dev' and was gone. The whole thing made an extraordinary impact.

* Rather like the Queen . . . with the least possible effort she gets the most positive response. For instance at every gala performance with the Queen in attendance, whoever the top stars are, Her Majesty always gets the most applause, simply by being there.

The lads were whisked off to meet this 'Magicrishi' for about an hour, during which period Mick Jagger turned up and proceeded to sit on the same seat as the Maharishi! The meditating people were 'definitely not amused' . . . all, that is, except the present British leader, Vincent Snell, who thought it was hilarious. Later on that evening, brother, Jane and I were alone once more at Paul's home.

None of us could really *'say'* anything, the whole thing was so overpowering. In the middle of London, in the middle of the Hilton Hotel, something so simple!

'Somebody asked him what he thought about the flower people,' said Paul.

'What did he say?'

'Interflora's a very good firm.'

Another phone call soon informed us that the Maharishi was holding private audience in a secluded Kensington house and that we were welcome.

On our arrival 'his holiness' wasn't present so we just stood around waiting . . . me facing the door, (no fool I).

I don't know how he did it to this day, because I kept looking to see if he'd arrived, but I slowly felt the back of my head being drawn as though by a magnet and when I turned round there he was, sitting in the corner with a sort of glow round him (it's all in the mind and the white sheet you know).

It soon transpired that the audience wasn't just for us, but also for a few of our more elite top British journalists and we soon found ourselves in a cross-barrage of 'in depth' questions.

Some of the queries and comments were rather hard hitting to say the least but the 'boss' simply bounced them back with remarkable simplicity, deadly accuracy, and enormous joy. John was particularly in his element because here, at last, was someone on his own quick witted level with an equally 'Liverpool' sense of humour, who might even solve the world's problems at the same time.

After the Maharishi had demolished the sceptical media (you could see some of them writing it down with extreme reluctance because what he was saying *seemed* to be the truth, but would the truth mean good copy?) we all retired for the night.

The next day we were happy to hear that our new found hero was holding a more gentle gathering to which we were all once again invited. This turned out to be a far more relaxing affair with 'M' eating a small rice meal with his fingers, in a most normal ungodlike way, and we were able to ask him questions without having to intellectualise or be funny for the press.

I asked: 'Have you got a meditation centre up north?'

'Up north, what is this up north?'

'I mean Liverpool?'

'Ah, Liverpool' (brief pause for thought, and quick aside to meditator hierarchy, 'Do we have a centre in Liverpool?' Quick aside back, 'I don't think so, Your Majesty.')

'We will have one soon.'

'Thank you.'

'Tomorrow we go to Bangor in North Wales. Is this not "up North"?'

'You can see it from our house.'

'Then come.'

Beatles' manager is found dead

News brings pop groups back to London

BY THE NEWS TEAM

At the end of our chat, the Maharishi gave me a single red rose and said he hoped to see me soon. I'm not sure, but I think that he thought I was one of the Beatles—not without reason, as I was sporting the statutory 'Pepper' moustache (Paul and John having *just* shaved theirs off: trust them) spoke with the same nasal accent, and was sitting next to Ringo.

'Luckily' I didn't go to Bangor, but brother, chums, Mick and Marianne did (with Lennon in the luggage rack of the train) and it was there, of course, that the news of Brian Epstein's death reached them (just before his own planned initiation).

If Patti Harrison's statement in February that 'the Beatles all belong to each other' was true, then this can be extended to saying that 'the only other person that got *close* was Brian'. In the early days he'd given the type-written orders and they'd all jumped to it, because it worked, and they earned lots of money as well as becoming famous. But not *that* close. *Nobody* got that close. Before, during and after Beatlemania, the lads were like four soul brothers on a deserted tropical island, upon which *nobody* was allowed to set foot. In later years Brian became the final arbitrator (like a young Dad). They'd got used to and trusted him—he was known as the fifth (business) Beatle—and suddenly, at the age of thirty-two—Boom—he was dead.

Maharishi's meditation certainly seemed to help the Beatles at the time of Brian's death. As it was, they lost themselves completely in the *Magical Mystery Fun and Mayhem Tour* TV film shortly afterwards. They then manifested an idea which had been a twinkle in their (and Brian's) eyes—the idealistic cultural business centre, Apple—before packing their bags and joining 'the boss' in India.

CALL SHEET

NEMS ENTERPRISES LTD. No.

PRODUCTION NAME: "MAGICAL MYSTERY TOUR" PROD. No.: NEM 1

STAFF CALL: 9.00 a.m. on location CALL FOR DATE: Sunday 24th September, 1967

SETS OR LOCATIONS: West Malling Airfield, Nr. Maidstone, Kent. Scenes as below. Tel.: West Malling 3750

ARTISTES	DRESSING ROOM No.	CHARACTER	TIME REQUIRED AT STUDIO	TIME REQUIRED ON SET
1. 'Ballroom' INT. Hangar No. 2.				
John Lennon		John	9.00	9.15
Paul McCartney		Paul		
George Harrison		George		
Ringo Starr		Ringo		
Mandy West		Hostess		
Derek Royle		Courier		
Jessie Robbins		Ringo's Aunt		
Shirley Evans		Accordionist		
Ivor Cutler		Phantom Courier		
George Claydon		Photographer		
Alf Manders		Driver		
Nat Jackley		Rubber Man		
Maggie Wright		Starlet		
Bill Wall		Passenger		
Arthur Kelly		"		
Elizabeth Kelly		"		
Michael Gladden		"		
Neil Aspinall		"		
Mal Evans		"		
Sylvia Nightingale		"		
Luke Kelly		"		
Elizabeth Harvey		"		
CROWD Peggy Spencer				
160 Ballroom Dancers				
CAMERA To include 3 Eclairs, 1 16 mm Arriflex, 20/1 zoom, Moy head, Chapman Crane				
2. "Ivor's Number" West Malling Airfield			From above	
Ivor Cutler				
John Lennon				
Paul McCartney				
George Harrison				
Ringo Starr				
Plus All Coach Crowd				
PROPS To include white organ				

SEE OVER

DATE	CASTING DEPT.	ASSISTANT DIRECTOR
23rd September, 1967	Nems Enterprises	Andrew Burkin

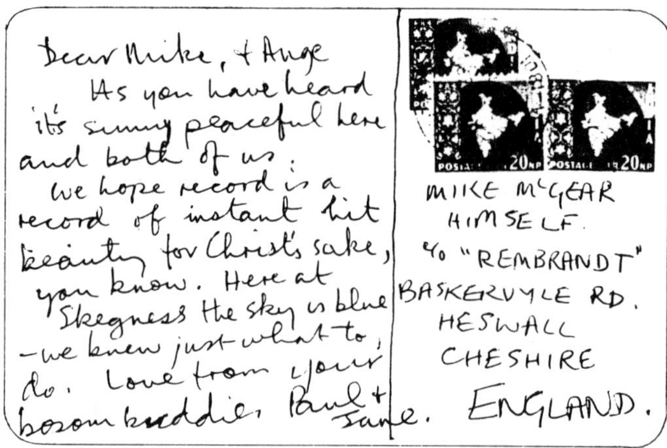

Dear Mike, + Ange
As you have heard
it's sunny peaceful here
and both of us:
we hope record is a
record of instant hit
beauty for Christ's sake,
you know. Here at
Skegness the sky is blue
—we knew just what to
do. Love from your
bosom buddies Paul + Jane.

MIKE McGEAR
HIMSELF
c/o "REMBRANDT"
BASKERVYLE RD.
HESWALL
CHESHIRE
ENGLAND.

This could have been their biggest mistake; with Brian gone there was an enormous gap which had to be filled and in my opinion they now became over-dependent on the Maharishi and his 'magic meditational medicine' to solve all their problems. Coupled with the after-effects of LSD and the loss of Brian, they were now meditating, not for the usual twenty minutes morning and evening, but for long *daily* rounds. Now this was fine with the boss around to check on their experiences, but when somebody started spreading rumours that the Maharishi was 'more than friendly' with a mere mortal girl, John and George not only chose to believe them, but also packed their bags and left for home. (Paul was mad with the other two because, even if 'M' had made contact with the lady, that was his affair, and only proved after all that he was human just like the rest of us.)

Now this was dangerous for John and George, to come back from months of long 'rounding' and re-enter our crazy western (so called) civilisation . . . that's heavy, with a capital disaster. Nowadays, with the strict rules and scientific verification surrounding TM (as it's now known), if anybody has to leave in the middle of the meditation programme they will be required to complete stringent 'checks' to make sure they are alright, so you can imagine what effect such an action must have had on the Beatles and friends all those years ago.

You see now why I mentioned that 'luckily' I didn't go to Bangor or for that matter India.

Thank U Very Much (for the Aintree Iron)

Having been in the wings (excuse pun and plug) while such a phenomena as brother and group had became universally accepted, it was with joy, coupled with apprehension, that I watched the growth of the Scaffold's first British hit.

On the one hand was the realisation that whatever I did I could never even scratch the surface of my elder brother's unbelievable success (in fact *nobody* could) and on the other hand came the desire to be loved by as many people as possible in the shortest possible time, which produced a bit of a two-headed, contradictory, monster problem.

In retrospect I realise, of course, there is no problem. All you have to do is coast along with life, be at one with it, and enjoy the fruits when (or if) they come your way. But that's in 'here and now' hindsight, with a few scalps of wisdom tucked under my belt.

But there and then the problem was, did I want success? You're bloody right, I did . . . but at what price, and how?

The way for Scaffold was pretty easy. Ee just had to fulfil the demand for simple singalong comedy songs for a mass whistle-along audience. We'd tried the other theatrical, esoteric, word imagery way which succeeded with university and small theatre audiences, but on a broader front wouldn't hang on the *Beyond the Fringe, That Was The Week That Was* and (later) *Monty Python*, washing line. Not that we didn't get good crits. We've got drawers full of excellent reviews, ref:

> 'The Scaffold is, I am sure, destined for a brilliant future' *The Stage*, 1964.
>
> 'Brilliant, cruel, heart-breaking, but not without compassion' *Financial Times*, 1966
>
> 'Fresh, highly original . . . they have succeeded in breaking the mould which *Beyond the Fringe* imposed on its successors' *The Scotsman*, 1966
>
> 'Not so much an entertainment, more a kind of intellectual battering . . . once you're reduced to mental pulp you can really enjoy one of the best late night revues' *Edinburgh Evening*, 1967
>
> 'It's difficult to imagine a more self-sufficient comedy unit than Scaffold . . . one and a half hours of hilarity . . . I haven't seen a funnier show than this' *London Morning Star*, 1968

Even as late as 1976, the *Evening Standard* was calling us 'the top pop/comedy group' but all this euphoria didn't pay the rent, so we had to find a way that would broaden our appeal without 'selling out' to cheap commercialism.

We chose . . . cheap commercialism! And I must take the blame for our first fab fave rave monster hit. Its origin started in my love of photography.

When I found out what could be achieved with natural lighting and fast shutter speeds on cameras, my interest in photography grew in leaps and bounds, so when one of the kings of cameras, a Nikon, arrived as a birthday present one day, I immediately rang my brother to thank him for the gift.

The reply to my call took some time and whilst waiting, I hummed a happy toon to myself. When he eventually answered there followed . . . silence. It's a customary superstar ploy, leaving all the onus on you, but being 'family' and in training for superstardom myself, I broke the silence and launched straight into 'Thank U very much for the Nikon camera, thank U very much, thank U very very very much, thank U very much for the Nikon camera, thank U very very very much'.

'Ah, great you got it then.'

'I'm afraid I did, and it's fabulous.'

'Yeh, we've all got one down here, they're gear, aren't they?'

'Not half . . . thanks *very* much.'

'My pleasure . . . tra well.'

'Tarar.'

As I don't play an instrument, I kept singing it over and over to myself till I'd recorded it on our old Grundig tape recorder,* and with crazy original verses like 'Thank you very much for the Saigon Angel' and 'Thank U for Gertie the gerl with the Garston gong', that was the start of the Scaffold's first top ten chart hit.

After we'd tried and tested it on the theatre circuits, as the climax of a Scaffold two-hour performance, to thank everybody for coming, paying, and lafing, we knew that, not only had we a good show ender, but a possible commercial record.

We'd been signed to EMI Records (I wonder why?) for some years, but as we hadn't quite outsold the Beatle's all-time record of five hundred thousand, trillion singles, EMI were beginning to lose interest. So when we went to them with our new 'possible hit' their enthusiasm was minimal as they saw it as just another comedy catastrophe like *Two Day's Monday* and *Goodbat Nightman* (a Batman spoof which also flopped).

We had faith in my song so we took it to producer George 'Goon Show' Martin who, like all good producers, gave it open ears and the nod of approval.

On the day of recording, brother Paul dropped into Abbey Road's Dark Side of the Pink Floyd number three studio † during our session and even made some constructive suggestions on the musical side (as usual) and suddenly *Thank U Very Much for the Aintree Iron* was in the

* The one used for early Cavern practices and the one on which I managed to wipe out (!) part of the Beatles first ever recordings when taping my kids in later years.

† We all used the same studios in those days, but the Beatles had priority. Their personal preference was number two.

bag. But not without a fight! Before the recording Paul had a comment to make . . . '*Don't* use the Aintree Iron, it's too oblique.'

'But that's the idea.'

'No, I'm serious Mike; it's a good commercial song, but that line gets in the way of its success.'

'But the whole song says thank you very much for the family, love, the birds and bees, etc., I think I can get away with *one* oblique line (I forgot to mention the other oblique line . . . ta very much for the napalm bomb!)'

'But "Aintree Iron's" the key to the whole song.'

'That's the idea.'

'Well, have it your own way, but don't say I didn't warn you.'

As I say, EMI were less than enthusiastic about their big non-selling record act and by some extraordinary coincidence (and there's no such thing as that) had cancelled our contract, even while the 'hit' was still hot in their building. So, there we were, in the unique position of having an obvious potential hit record but no record company.

Our manager, not being backwards, accepted the letter of termination from EMI and then rang EMI to ask would they be interested in the first Scaffold hit, at an obviously much better percentage and a fab new contract.

Sometimes God is on your side, or so it would seem.

EMI Parlophone bought the disc and the exciting build-up procedure to a 'hit' record was adopted: Press agent to handle the media, thousands of *Thank U Very Much* badges and stickers printed, lead sheets drawn-up, promo film made when 'The Product' started to do some business, and the weekly sales figure, denoting an eventual chart entry, closely watched.

Then came the mass playing, the mass buying, and the mass hit! Just like that. we were even on *Top of the Pops!*

For the first time, I was in the charts, and not only that, with brother Paul too! His *Hello, Goodbye* was zooming up the same chart. Another proud moment for the McCartney Mafia.

When the song became a nationwide hit and the Prime Minister's favourite pop song, *Thank U Very Much for the Aintree Iron* was on everybody's lips, and Paul had the temerity to ring me up. 'You were right about the Aintree Iron; I was wrong.' (It takes Big Boys to do things like that.)

So there we were (where were we?) suddenly stars! Ladies would run up to me in the street and say 'I never knew I said it so much'* or 'I can't say "thank you very much" without adding "for the Aintree Iron".' Not only that, London taxi drivers recognised us, so we *must* have been famous!

Not that we didn't *try* the more esoteric, arty farty, satirical records . . . we did, but they just boomeranged back in our faces (the mass public it seems don't like clever clever songs, they prefer it straight from the heart . . . and who can blame them?). We gave them the gentle summer satire *Do You Remember*, the deck of cards spoof *Pack of Lies* and the subtle C W send-up *Mummy Won't be Home for Christmas* (starring my middle daughter Theran) plus the humour, poetry, and song albums: *Live at the Queen Elizabeth Hall* with Dave Mason, Mike

* Wait till you hear my next catchphrase . . . er . . . come to think of it, I don't think I'll tell you.

Vickers, etc., *Scaffold L the P* (with Escher's *Klimmen en Dalen* cover . . . he wouldn't let the Stones use his precision drawings for *their* album but we were more cuddly) and *Fresh Liver* with the help of Neil Innes, George 'Zoot' Money, the Average White Band, amongst other fine friends. Alas, none of them were Top Ten Chart smashers.

A ROYAL BOOB

When *Thank U Very Much* became the catch phrase of Britain (as though it wasn't there before) it led, amongst other things to our being hired, at great expense, for a private function at London's Savoy Hotel.

When we arrived two press Lords, Sir Max Aitken (son of Lord Beaverbrook who founded the *Daily Express*) and Jocelyn (*Queen* magazine) Stevens greeted us and informed us that we would be performing, not in the main ballroom, but in its smaller annexe and that the occasion was the birthday of Sir Tommy Sopwith (he of Sopwith Camel fame).

Those were the days . . . our first chart topping pop ditty, boss bread, Savoy Hotel, as much ale as you could down, and the promise 'wink wink' of *Daily Express* and *Evening Standard* exposure (which Sir Max also happened to own and, to be fair, he kept his side of the wink for a while). Later that night, after dinner, 'us chaps' were assembled in the adjoining room, military fashion, backs to the guests (a birthday surprise I hear you whisper) and Sir Tommy was wheeled in (literally) from the ballroom with close friends in attendance.

On cue the birthday boys turned smartly to face the enemy, touched their forelocks, and politely performed their *Thank U Very Much* success. 'Thank U very much for the Sopwith Camel, Thank U very . . very . . very . . very . . . etc.'

As soon as the song was established Lady Sopwith burst out crying (literally) 'It's our song, Tommy, it's our song . . . OUR song,' and in between sobs, dabbed mascara soaked eyes, until its completion.

Sir Tommy, who was getting on a bit, was obviously nonplussed by it all, but nevertheless glad that his wife was so happy, and after dutifully rendering the hit we were heartily congratulated by the rest of the company 'Bravo, Jolly Good Show, DO IT AGAIN!'

'Thank U very much for Sir Tommy Camel, thank U very . . very . . very . . . etc. etc.'

We were a success and were immediately introduced around by one of the press barons.

'Lady Sopwith—Mr. McGear.'

'Mr. McGear—Lady Sopwith.'

'Princess Alexandra—Mr. McGear.'

'Mr. McGear—Princess Alexandra,' and suddenly, there on the end of my introduction was my first ROYAL!* . . . I must not blow it.

Casual conversation was made easier by the fact that Her Majesty's husband . . .

('Mr. Ogilvy—Mr. McGear.' 'Mr. McGear—Mr. Ogilvy.') was obviously elated by it all.

'*Did* you do it again?' asked Angus.

'Yes sir, thank you sir.'

'Jolly good.'

* I was only *next* to Dad when he was introduced to Princess Margaret.

I was introduced to Princess Alex just in time . . . Gorman was about to write her Royal number down in his little black book (references to 'dropping by for a cup of tea and a chat' etc).

After polite non-sequitors, the Princess and I somehow got round to fashion. For the evening she and I had both chosen to wear black velvet . . . she a velvet blouse . . . me a large black velvet tie.

'What a charming tie,' said the Royal She, reaching to feel the quality.

'It's just like yours,' said the not-so-royal he, reaching to feel a right Royal Boob (literally).

THE KOP

When Paul and I were children Dad used to take us to Liverpool's football matches. I must point out to non-Liverpudlians (there might be the odd one or two out there) that we have two football teams in my home town—Liverpool (team colours, red and white) and Everton (colours blue and white). As with Glasgow's Rangers and Celtic, they both have religiously loyal followers who would (and do) go to the ends of the earth for their team.

Having been brought up in Everton, my Dad was naturally True Blue, but this didn't prevent him (a true democrat) from taking us to both teams' matches.

I'll never forget when he took us to our first match at Liverpool's Anfield Road ground, complete with scarves, overcoats, gloves, vacuum flasks—the lot*. In the middle of the black and grey Anfield surroundings shone the bright green grass pitch. We were three diminutive figures in an ocean of united people.

'*This* is the STAND,' said Dad authoritatively.

'But we're sitting,' I observed.

'That's why it's called the STAND,' said Dad without batting an eyelid.

Never having seen a football match before I was spellbound to find how everybody got caught up in the web spun by the players.

No one more so than the huge Liverpool docker in front of us. He was so caught up and excited by the game . . .

'Fantastic!'

that *every* move his . . .

'Fan . . .'

team made, he would de-

. . . tastic!'

clare . . .

'FANTASTIC!' (and Liverpool's team made a *lot* of moves)

'If he says that *once* more,' Dad whispered to us, 'I'll knock his block off.' GOAL!

'FANBLOODYTASTIC!'

Dad let him off.

All through the game, one couldn't help but notice that a certain standing, swaying section of the crowd was slightly different from the rest. It was as though a whole block of the ground had been hired by my relatives. They sang as one, they chanted as one, they booed as one, they made humorous comments as one, they even thought as one . . . they WERE one.

* And this was at the height of summer!

'That's the Liverpool Kop', said Dad. 'Why do they call them the Kop?' we asked. 'They're named after a Boer War hill called the Spion Kop, and don't ask me why' explained dad.

When *Thank U Very Much* was becoming a British hit we were asked to do a promo film for America as, believe it or not, it was taking off in various states, but before it could be a *big* hit, it had to take off in the 'United' States. Hence the film.

One of the ideas our director Jim Goddard had was to film the Kop singing the last two lines of 'Thank you very much for our gracious TEAM' (team instead of Queen . . . get it?)—basically a good idea.

Roger was 'elsewhere' on the day of shooting (not that being an Evertonian had anything to do with it) so John and I presented ourselves at Liverpool's ground, on the afternoon of the match, with mixed feelings. There were only two of us, it was the dreaded Spion Kop, and what's more, what if they didn't like the song, or worse . . . didn't know it?

We took the gamble, and the film crew took the lead round the lion's den. Sure enough, a roar went up when we were spotted. I was terrified (after all it was *my* song). The idea was that when we got in front of the Kop the record would be played over the ground's loudspeakers and X million loyal fans would be filmed singing along to 'our gracious TEAM'.

Gorman had a very loud check suit on, we both had longish hair, and when we stopped, bang in front of the lion's open cage, the record didn't come on! The lions went silent. I went sweaty.

Then suddenly, as quick as a flick knife, they all roared together as one (to the tune of 'Ilkley Moor Bah Tat')

'Oh where dya get dat suit?
Oh where dya get dat suit?
Where did you get that sewt . . . .
'Getcher hur cut . . . getcher air cut'.

And we knew they were on our side. The simultaneous chanting of 'the brotherhood' was emotional, electric, and unforgettable . . . in a word, magic.

When the record finally came on, they sang better than the disc with the added joy of fifty million red and white scarves swaying on the line.

'It's a wrap loves,' one of the film crew might have said, as we made our way to the directors' box to watch the match. We must have been more than famous (you don't get in *there* without a passport from God).

Years later, McGough's true colours did eventually 'out' when we were asked to appear on the *This is your Life* TV programme for Bill Shankley, Liverpool's legendary boss.

As it was more convenient for the many sporting and showbiz personalities to meet in a central spot, a certain football ground was chosen for the filming of Bill's tributes, and let's just say it definitely wasn't in the city of Liverpool.

When it came to our spot, Roger couldn't bring himself to wear the red and white scarf (sorry Bill). But instead of letting the side down, he graciously allowed John (an Everpudlian) and me (a Livertonian) to drape our scarves over his shoulders . . . what a gent.

NOT SO MAGICALLY MYSTERIOUS
On enquiring as to Paul's whereabouts when I 'hit' London town in late 1967, I was told by Jane that both he and John were in Soho, viewing rushes of *Magical Mystery Tour.*

On arriving at the small cutting room in Old Compton Street, I found John sitting at the hand controlled viewing machine with Paul looking over his shoulder . . . brrrrrrrrrr. Just about to leave was a bespectacled local character called 'Rosie' who wouldn't say no to a drink and who specialised in singing to people in the street with a well balanced bottle of Guinness on his head (Tara would have been proud). As he floated down the stairs, Dick James, the Beatles' song publisher, floated up. Dick, best known for TV's *Robin Hood* opening music and discovering Reginald Dwight, was obviously concealing a lovely surprise, but waited for a break in the lads' (brrrrrrrrr . . .) viewing.

'I've got some exciting news,' he said at last. 'Barbra Streisand is making a new album and wants to do some of your songs.'

Now in anybody's language this was a fantastic accolade, and in publishing circles it was a dream come true. Barbra Streisand was becoming the biggest artist in and out of the business to record your songs, and SHE was fêting THEM. 'So if you could just write a few numbers for her . . .' Both Paul and John looked silently at Dick. John finally broke the silence.

'Fuck off.'

Brrrrrrrrrrr . . .

June 7th, 1968 . . . Wedding 1

During these halcyon, chaotic days I met my second love (sorry, third, after Mum and Celia).

I'd just driven home from London to Rembrandt on one of my many little visits, and Dad's horse-training brother was there having a 'Dad' drink . . . quadruple anything.

He invited me to a nearby country club party, but just having driven five hours non stop (spartan motorways in those days) and not relishing the thought of a posh country 'wah wah' club I nearly gave it a miss.

'There won't be any birds there will there?'

'Hundreds!'

'I'll get changed.'

At the 'do' I was quickly shown to a fellow star's table . . . Gerry (across the Ferry) Marsden, an old friend. He and Lennon used to do fabulous 'cripple' impersonations in the old days (three years previously!) and as we chatted, my eyes perused the room for a young lady.

Come to think of it I *was* twenty-three, a bachelor, relatively well-off, nationally famous, with a sports car *and* a Beatle for a brother. What more could a woman want!

She says *I* picked *her* up, I says *she* picked *me* up, but what does it matter, she ditched her steady boyfriend at the party and we zoomed off into the sunset . . . (but that's another story).

At first it wasn't an easy relationship, what with my hang ups *and* hers, but slowly, out of the turbulence blossomed the rose of my love for one Angela Fishwick (well I had to change a surname like that didn't I? Sorry Frank and Edie in laws!)

We got friendlier when she became my escort at the Magical Mystery Fancy Dress Party in London's Royal Lancaster Hotel, where the beautiful spectacle of Fred Lennon and Son publicly accepting each other for the first time by waltzing together on the dance floor, was a joy to behold. And friendlier when Dad, new wife Ange, my Angi and step sister Ruth, all went on hols to a warless Beirut. A French paper asked the question 'Arc Mike and Angi married?' and printed 'No, but it is the same,' (Ahlan wasalan). And *friendlier*, until in the end we got *so* friendly that the inevitable happened and my first daughter got the best view of our country church marriage . . . through her Mum's naval. (i.e. we were pregnant).

Not that we were even going to get married, but the thought of my travelling round the world as free as a bird leaving expectant Angi to local, behind-the-back gossip was too much for me (not that they would . . . our locals are straight). But once decided, where do you go for a bit of privacy? I was by now a household name and as Paul was coming up from London (with Jane) to be my best man, this wouldn't increase the chances of secrecy. But privacy we wanted and secrecy

Paul, Jane, Mike, Angi in the back garden of Rembrandt.

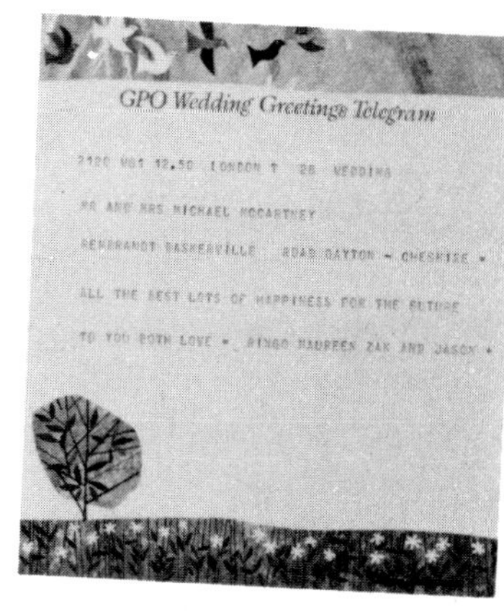
GPO Wedding Greetings Telegram

MR AND MRS MICHAEL MCCARTNEY

REMBRANDT BASKERVILLE ROAD ... CHESHIRE .

ALL THE BEST LOTS OF HAPPINESS FOR THE FUTURE

TO YOU BOTH LOVE . RINGO MAUREEN ZAK AND JASON .

Paul signing my life away.

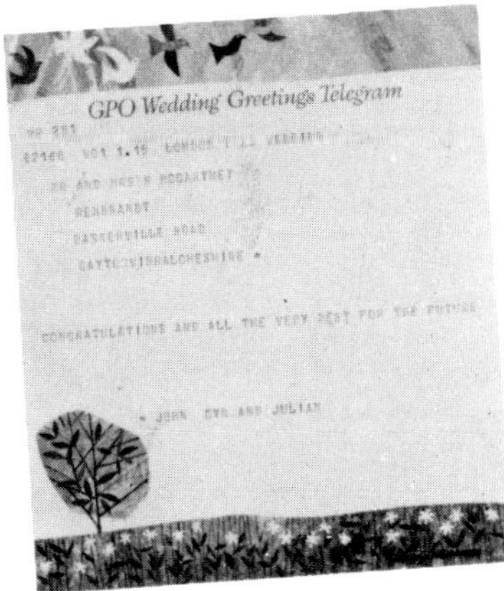
GPO Wedding Greetings Telegram

REMBRANDT

BASKERVILLE ROAD

CONGRATULATIONS AND ALL THE VERY BEST FOR THE FUTURE

. JOHN CYN AND JULIAN

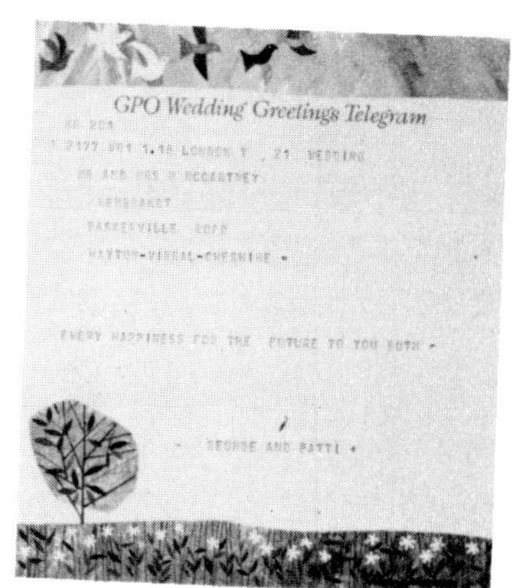
GPO Wedding Greetings Telegram

MR AND MRS M MCCARTNEY

REMBRANDT

EVERY HAPPINESS FOR THE FUTURE TO YOU BOTH .

GEORGE AND PATTI .

we'd get, so Angi and I went to Buddy Bevan, a distant Welsh relative from near Corwen in North Wales, who had married Dad to his Ange a few years back, and explained the position. We wanted nobody at the church but immediate family, not *a word* to a soul, never mind the media ('Understood Mike') and (PS) a harpist in the chapel if possible.

On the sunny morning of June 7th 1968, Paul, Jane and I set out for the well hidden, sleepy village of Carog, North Wales. I decided to set yet another trend by wearing my snazzy Scaffold showbiz white suit and thought that Piglet (a stuff and nonsense replica of Winnie the Pooh's friend, made for me by Angi) might like to come along for the ride. Piglet even insisted we call in at the New Carog Arms for a drinky-pooh, the naughty toy tippler.

Outside the peaceful, deserted country church we met my bride-to-be, checked on rings and the like, and entered the chapel. I shall now let my daughter Benna take over, from her naval eye view:

'Daddy and Mummy linked arms and walked down the little aisle. As there wasn't a harpist in all Wales, the lady on the organ played Solomon King's *She Wears my Ring* and when Mr. Bevan said some words to Mummy and Daddy, Daddy sat Piglet down on the front pew (hic!) for a better look. Then Mr. Bevan said, 'Do you take Mummy?' and Daddy said, 'I do,' and put a ring on Mummy's finger. Then Uncle Paul and Auntie Steph signed a thing called a register and we all went outside and there were all these photographers and press people. Daddy said 'How the bloody hell did *they* get there?' But it didn't matter now 'cos Mummy and Daddy were married and everyone kissed and went soppy . . . then we all went back to a big house called Rembrandt where all my new family were, and more press men came to take lots more pictures, and I was mad because we missed the fireworks 'cos Mummy and Daddy had to go on something called 'a honeymoon' to Edinburgh with Chris in the taxi car. Outside Edinburgh Mummy was sick because she was having me, but we all had a nice honeymoon and Daddy drank all the champagne 'cos Mummy didn't feel like any.'

Thank you Ben . . . go to your room.

And so saying the new McCartney family set sail for the real Sunset . . . our home for the next ten years, where we brought into this world three of the most beautiful girls imaginable, Benna, Theran and Abbi.

SUNSET

Formerly 'Lismore', our new dream cottage home was a little small at first, but with bits bashed down here, and bits built on there, Sunset slowly took shape around us. The gradual shaping up of our home was a much more satisfying way of settling in, with my lesson learned from Rembrandt where, on reflection, we'd had too much too soon.

Sunset, our back-to-front dream cottage.

Although only half an hour from Liverpool (a quarter, if you drove like hell) our new Lower Heswall home was like living in the house at the end of the garden, i.e. back to front (sounds right), so that we had complete privacy with beautiful sunset views over the North Wales coast, the River Dee and the Irish Sea. Not only that, it was five minutes from Rembrandt and Dad.

1968 '. . . OR SOMETHING'

1968 started with the *Eleventh Hour* satirical BBC programme in which we appeared alongside such fun names as Richard 'Oz' Neville, to name but one, and were given a 'Scaffold Might Take Over' crit. We might have indeed if it had stayed on the air, but it didn't, so neither did we.

In June, just after I was married, the Scaffs were booked into our first Albert Hall apartheid concert entitled 'Come back Africa', starring Sammy Davis Jr, Cleo Laine and Johnny Dankworth, John (guitar) Williams, Jonathan Miller (still a gentleman), Annie Ross and us. Marlon Brando and Dick Gregory couldn't make it (pity, they were one of the main reasons I wanted to do it).

Later that year we played the London Palladium (at last) and were introduced to Princess Margaret and her husband Tony Armstrong-Sidley-Jones.

The Palladium was just the start of an impossible work pattern which was building up to *Lily the Pink* (The biggest Scaffold Hit) with Tuesday December 17th, eleven o'clock BBC 2 *Talk of the Town Scaffold Special* meet . . . 18th December *Sunday Express* interview for two hours, plus twelve o'clock call for *Crackerjack* (CRACKERJACK!) kids' TV show (if number one) . . . 19th December *Top of Pops* band call studio four, TV Centre, and do nation's number one pop show 'live', as number one (plus white suits) . . . 20th December record *Liver Birds* TV theme tune at BBC with Pauline (Alderton) Collins, etc. etc. All this, and the imminent birth of our first baby (she'd got fed up with wedding commentaries). Angi delayed having 'it' till I could fly back to Liverpool and the Oxford Street Maternity Hospital for the birth, and when the child started to emerge it was upside down with the umbilical cord three times round its neck! Some of my relatives advised me that 'it wasn't done' to be there, but sod that, I went.

Now in every film I've seen of babies being born, the nurse holds the baby up by the feet, smacks its bottom, the baby screams, the mummy and daddy smile and the toddler is handed to the proud parents in swaddling clothes, but let me tell you it's nothing like that. It's far more real, much more beautiful and takes the parents into a much deeper relationship after the birth.

Luckily we had Dr. Francis, one of the best gynaecologists in England, on hand for the difficult birth. When our baby finally emerged I was told 'It's a girl!' at a quarter to three* in the morning, but the nurse held her up, smacked her bum and . . . nothing happened! She was taken hurriedly from the room and I turned to comfort Angi about our dead child, which was slightly futile because my wife was out of her mind on pain-killing drugs. (At the time, we hadn't heard of the epidural.) Thank God they brought Benna back into the room after cleaning her out and all was at peace with the universe.

* I remember the time by the 'U.S. Bonds' quarter to three single.

She was going to be a little boy called Ben so we just stuck a 'na' on the end and changed her sex.

When I got home on my own the amount of overwork finally caught up with me, and sitting in the lounge, I suddenly realised why people like Spike Milligan break down and go into asylums. I was a physical, emotional, and mental wreck.

God knows how we did it, but Angi, myself and baby Ben all made it to Angi's Mum and Dad's just three days later with my Dad, his new wife and daughter, plus Paul and family, for a slap-up Christmas dinner (on reflection, quite an occasion). The following day the nation's press took pics of tiny Benna for their front pages, and then the day after that we jetted off to a cabaret in Gstaad, Switzerland, (with arms full of newspapers).

Perusing the papers on the plane, I spotted a Beatle article in which the last 'quote of the year' came from Ringo: 'We'll never completely split and we've signed a lot of papers so as we stay together for twenty years or something.' God love 'im.

Ringo, on top of things—God love 'im!

IN THE LILY THE PINK

Lily the Pink, a children's-cum-rugby-sing-along song, went to the coveted number one spot and stayed there over the entire Christmas period and beyond.

If *Thank U Very Much* presented a problem, *Lily* presented a nightmare. Here was a song with such obvious commercial undertones that it really exposed the 'selling out' tag. Coupled with the fact that we'd had a monster the previous year, I was, at first, reluctant to record it (I must have been mad).

Being in the fortunate financial position of not having to do it made me even more wary, because if it wasn't done properly I had a theory that it could destroy us by reducing our credibility to nil.

John Gorman and I had heated discussions up at the Edinburgh festival as to how the commercial aspect should be handled, and in the end I agreed to back it only if the other side of the record showed our less commercial, theatre-humour-poetry side. In the end life's eternal compromise was reached; we democratically agreed to a double A-Side, with *Lily* on one half and a poetic love song called *Buttons of Your Mind* on the other. (It's nice to know I once had some scruples.)

As George Martin had gone on to other things, Norrie Paramour was to produce our fab new disc, and he *must* be good, his wife came from Liverpool. On the day of recording in Abbey Road, Norrie's new, well spoken, Crompton Court assistant showed great interest and gave lots of friendly advice. In later years he became rather well known in his own right, with such artistic endeavours as *Joseph's Amazing Technicolour Dreamcoat, Jesus Christus Superstar* and *Evita*. I refer, of course, to that cricketing luminary, Tom and Jerry fanatic, 'Bonzo' dog do dah owner, and 'Jennings of Fishfriers' . . . Tim Rice. Well, anyway, he was the can lad fetching cups of tea for Norrie, us, MD Mike Vickers, and any other passing superstars.

As Mike (Manfred Mann) Vickers was a friend of Jack Bruce's he'd somehow arranged for the ace Scottish bass player of Cream to join us on the session and being a fan of Mr. Bruce I gave him permission to 'ad lib' with the happy toon (I'd already learned from the Jimi H. episode). When he heard *Lily* in rehearsal he said, 'Quite honestly Mike, the only thing I can do on this song is *bum bum . . . bum bum.*' As he was absolutely right, I left him to it.

One of the kiddy verses had a line about 'Jennifer Eccles' having 'terrible freckles' and as this just so happened to be the name of the Hollies hit (what a coincidence) we asked Graham Nash to sing the verse, if he was passing the studio that is. Not only did he drop by and sing on the record, he danced on it as well, and to this day people still think that it was Roger McGough doing both. I'm not sure if it was as a direct result of singing with such superstars as the Scaffold, but shortly after this milestone in his career Graham left the Hollies to join Crosby, Stills, Nash and Carl Gustav Young in America.

At the end of a very hard-working but positive day, we had *Lily, Buttons*, Jack and Graham in the can, and Norrie, Tim and I were about to mix them.

As we'd structured *Lily* in the most obvious foot stomping, dance along way, I asked for 'lots more bass drum thud' for the final mix. (More lessons learned from brother and group, I'm afraid).

The engineer explained, 'Sorry, but as we've overdubbed so many effects, people and instruments since the basic tracks, *that's* all the level I have left on the bass drum.'

I was gabberflasted. 'But that's the whole idea of this silly song . . . to tap your toe to the *thud, thud, thud . . .*'

'Sorry, but that's all the thud I can give you.'

Undaunted I went to reception and asked for the keys to the Beatles' instrument cupboard behind number three studio.

'But nobody's allowed in there!' said the fine 'dark side of the Irish' commissioner.

'It's all right, our kid said it's OK,' I lied.

'And who might your kid be?'

'Ringo.'

As I had at last made it to the top on my own, I asked the Express to cool the Beatle brother bit . . . *this* was the result.

THEATRE . . . TV . . . RADIO . . . POP . . . FILMS . . .

GO-GO by JUDITH SIMONS

Beatle Paul's kid brother hits No 1 spot

BEATLE Paul McCartney was recording a new album with his "discovery" Mary Hopkin when I broke the news to him: The Scaffold, the Liverpool trio of which his 24-year-old younger brother Mike McGear is a member, was No 1 in the Hit Parade with "Lily the Pink."

McCartney commented: "That's terrific. I've always given Mike brotherly advice, because I reckon I know something about recording. But my advice to him has always been wrong!

"When the Scaffold recorded 'Thank U Very Much' I told him not to sing about the 'Aintree Iron' because it was too obscure—yet that became a talking point about the song. And I also told him I was not too sure 'Lily the Pink' was the right thing to record."

Humour

The Scaffold — the other two members are Roger McGough and John Gorman — specialise in humour and poetry, and their hit, about "medicinal compound," set to a tune known to Rugby clubs and schoolchildren, certainly would not seem a sure-fire winner!

Yesterday McGear, whose wife Angela is expecting a baby later this month, was planning a public house celebration with the group.

John Gorman said: "We are now working on a 40-minute show for B.B.C.2 and planning a cabaret act. At this rate we'll be breaking into pantomime!"

Big jumper this week is another song with childhood association. Up 11 places to No. 7 is Des O'Connor's "**One Two Three O'Leary.**"

Entering at No. 18 is another song with an off-beat subject, Diana Ross and the Supremes' "**Love Child,**" about a girl born illegitimate determined to avoid making the same mistake as her mother.

TOP 20

(Last week's placings in brackets)

1 LILY THE PINK Scaffold (3)
2 THE GOOD, THE BAD AND THE UGLY Hugo Montenegro (2)
3 ELOISE Barry Ryan (1)
4 THIS OLD HEART OF MINE Isley Brothers (3)
5 BREAKING DOWN THE WALLS OF HEARTACHE Bandwagon (4)
6 I'M A TIGER Lulu (10)
7 ONE, TWO, THREE O'LEARY Des O'Connor (18)
8 AIN'T GOT NO—I GOT LIFE Nina Simone (7)
9 ELENORE Turtles (6)
10 HARPER VALLEY P.T.A. Jeannie C. Riley (11)
11 ALL ALONG THE WATCHTOWER Jimi Hendrix Experience (8)
12 BUILD ME UP BUTTERCUP Foundations (17)
13 MAY I HAVE THE NEXT DREAM? Malcolm Roberts (12)
14 IF I KNEW THEN WHAT I KNOW NOW Val Doonican (13)
15 A MINUTE OF YOUR TIME Tom Jones (23)
16 RACE WITH THE DEVIL Gun (21)
17 WITH A LITTLE HELP Joe Cocker (9)
18 LOVE CHILD Diana Ross and The Supremes (—)
19 THOSE WERE THE DAYS Mary Hopkin (16)
20 URBAN SPACEMAN Bonzo Dog Doo-Dah Band (29)

By arrangement with New Musical Express

TOMMY COOPE

HOW to make cer show in three ea complete run - thr cameras at 9 a.m. before a studio Change the audie real at 8 p.m. An Anybody who do p.m. show is out The bigger they writes RON BOY

SCAFFOLD'S LILY IN THE PINK!

Hit No. 1—now 2

THE Scaffold's medicinal compound has put them at the top of the Pop 30. The Liverpool threesome made number one this week with " Lily The Pink," an up-to-date, cleaned-up version of the old services song.

This is their first big hit since " Thank U Very Much " just before last Christmas.

Now the group are to get their first major West End showcases — with appearances at London's Ronnie Scott Club and the Open Space Theatre, Tottenham Court Road, early in the New Year.

They open at the Scott Club on January 6 playing opposite tenorist Stan Getz's Quartet (see below). The engagement will last a month and over three weekends, the Scaffold will appear at the Open Space Theatre in late night shows.

These shows will take place on January 9, 10, 11, 16, 17, 18, 23 and 25. On January 24, the Scaffold appear at Liverpool's Philharmonic Hall in a concert with the Bonzo Dog Doo Dah Band.

They are also considering an offer to spend four months next year touring the American college circuit presenting their two-hour stage show. The tour is for over 100 dates.

'Ah well, that'll be foin.'

And off I tracked, opened the secret door, rummaged around the infamous instruments and nicked brother Ringo's bass drum. Taking it through to number three studio, I put it flat on the floor, draped my coat over it to give it a flat *'thud'* and asked them to 'send the track,' which they did. I just sat there all on my own on the floor for the whole song going *thud! thud! thud!*

The trick worked because when the record had been released I was in O'Connor's pub* in Liverpool when someone shouted from the end of the long bar, 'Your record's on the jukebox, Mike.' All I could hear was the *thud thud thud*, with not even a whisper of me lovely singin' voice an' all an' all.

* Having checked for the presence of any eight-foot high dockers.

There were two ways I knew that *Lily* was going to be *big*. One was when I took a demo disc to play to John 'underground' Peel. Although into heavy listening music, I knew that DJ John would give a fair opinion because he's basically Liverpudlian.

A young, curly headed boy called Marc Bolan (T. Rex to you) put the record on, and when it stopped after the first playing, Mr. Peel said,

'That's number one, Mike.'

'Oh bugger off,' said I. 'Play it again.'

'If you insist, but that's an obvious number one if ever I heard one.'

'I agree it'll get into the charts . . . but number one?'

'You'll see.'

Thank God he's a clairvoyant as well as a Liverpool FC traumatic, and although it took three months to get there, John's prediction finally came true when we became Top of the Christmas Pops.

The other time was when the Scaffs were in a nightclub somewhere after a gig. The customers didn't know we were in, or hadn't recognised us, but when *Lily* came over the PA, the night-time audience rose as one (just like the Kop) and walked to the dance floor as though in a zombie trance. Once there, they all let loose for the full duration of the song–like marionettes controlled by the music, the living dead came alive on the dance floor.

THE WEDDING II

Having obliged as best man at my wedding it was not unnatural for brother Paul to request that I should reciprocate at *his* the following year. Jane had left Paul's North London home, and Paul was wooing Linda Eastman, a New York freelance photographer.

It was March 1969 and I was doubling up with the Scaffold at two Birmingham nightclubs (one of which had all the dressing room lights placed in a cardboard box to keep the Pakistani conjuror's chickens alive). The week was made even more hectic because each morning we had to struggle out of bed at God knows what hour to be down in London for a Watney's ale TV commercial . . . 'White suits *will be worn*'.

On the evening of March the 10th Paul was on the line from London to my hotel room. 'I'm getting married to Lin tomorrow morning, d'you want to be my best man, and don't tell ANYONE'

Beatlemania still abounding, and Paul being the final Beatle bachelor, immediacy and strictest confidence were of the essence, so promises were made, and I settled down for a restless sleep. Thoughts of my new sister-in-law, heavily confused with Eastman Kodak cameras, filled the small hotel room. What would she be like? Would I like her? Would she like me?

In the middle of the night, in the middle of a dream, the sudden thought, 'What ring?' hit me, and in a panic I called London.

'Don't worry, I've got the ring, you just be at Marylebone Registry Office at ten o'clock. Now get some sleep.'

Miraculously my alarm called me on time and I struggled to the station with my secret locked firmly with all the other big secrets . . . in my brain and heart. Miraculously the train was on time, and I boarded with great expectations.

Considering how it would affect the Watney's people who were, after all, paying Scaffold a large sum of money, I could contain myself no longer and blurted out the secret to John and Roge as we chuffed away from platform nine, Birmingham New Street Station.

Now everyone was happy. Everyone, that is, except the train. It broke down and we were over an hour late!

Resigning myself to the fact that when we finally hit London the wedding would be well and truly over I nevertheless asked our chauffeur-driven Rolls to call in at the registry office just in case they were still there.

When we got there, throngs of people massed around the entrance so I leapt out of the Watney's wagon, explaining to my Scaffolders that Paul must still be inside and that I'd be back in the TV commercial as soon as possible.

'Tell them it's great publicity,' I added for safety.

As I ran up the Marylebone steps a wag was heard to shout 'Late again Mike', and I waved a regal reply.

Not only were they still there, but Paul asked politely, 'Where the bloody 'ell have you been, you're an hour late!'

'The train broke down,' I suggested. 'Have you been done?'

'We had to wait for *you*, buggerlugs . . . good job there were no other weddings on . . . Mal, give him the ring, and let's go . . .' or words to that effect, and Paul, Lin, diddy daughter Heather, Big Mal Evans,* Peter Brown and I entered the austere room of officialdom.

Not much later we emerged from the Holy Fate far less nervously than we'd entered, and kisses were swopped all round. My new sister-in-law and infant from the New World seemed just fine thank you doo doo wee wee.

On the way to the limo, parked smack outside the 'private' ceremony, all hell was let loose—crowds crushing, media flashing and

* Gentle Giant Mal . . . another gentle man, who was later blown to pieces by Magnum toting cops in a US motel bedroom.

Best man, by the skin of my teeth.—'Where the bloody 'ell have you been?' Paul asked politely.

questioning and kids screaming in agony that Beatle Paul had finally fallen.

We were eventually bundled into the Rolls.

'Second today,' thought I, 'can't be bad,' as it took off at frightening speed.

'Come to the house for a glass of champagne,' offered brother and sis-in-law.

'I'd love to, but I'm working,' said I. 'Driver, can you stop by that tube station.' And so, in one door and out the other (Buster Keaton would have been proud) I left the happy couple as they set sail for a happy future, plus, of course, a Honeymoon Salad ('Lettuce Alone'†) and caught a taxi to the beer ad.

I later found out that I wasn't the only one working that night. Paul had to finish a recording session with Billy Kinsley and the Jackie Lomax Band!

LET IT BE . . . ME

During the filming of the Beatles' final hours together in *Let it Be*,* I was passing their Apple offices in Savile Row after a Scaffold photo session and decided to pop in to show Paul my new posh leather coat, (one of the perks of being a Top of the Pops instantly recognisable Superstar).

As filming was in process in the basement studio, I slipped quietly behind the grand piano and started to play it—with the lid closed, of course, doubling up with Billy Preston on lecy (electric) piano.

The brilliant comedy effect wasn't kept in the finished film by Mike Lindsay Hogg, but it just goes to show what a new coat will do for you.

This was during Paul's bearded, back to the roots, existentialist scruffy period and donning his old herringbone overcoat after the filming we both left Apple and walked through the busy London streets, looking for a taxi to take us to his home and new bride. We hadn't gone far when there was a screech from a passing lady . . . 'Ooh look,' she said, 'there's Mike McGear!'

'OFFICIAL REPRESENTATIVES'

When one is called upon by one's country to represent her on an international occasion, what can one do but accept graciously.

In 1969 Scaffold were invited to be the official British Representatives in Esbjerg, Denmark, for 'English Week'—seven days of delicate industrial trade negotiations between the British and Danish Governments.

When we arrived, all the hotels were full and we had to travel for half an hour by taxi to an hotel on the coast . . . Good start!

After rehearsals in the giant ninety-nine seater Esbjerg Stadium, we strolled through the town centre with its heavily embossed Carnaby Street union jacks and just happened to fall into a typically Danish bar.

The local 'Carly Special' strength beer, was going down rather smoothly when a group of heavy-set British officer cadet sailors accosted us. They explained that they were in Denmark as part of 'English Week' too and would we care to join them aboard their destroyer for a few 'drinky poohs'.

† One of Uncle Joe's I'm afraid.
* Mother Mary's Song.

Not wishing to appear inhospitable (or end up in hospital) we accepted their kind invitation, up anchored and sailed down to the harbour.

Once aboard, their fellow officers soon persuaded us to change to shorts (drinks that is, not trousers) as spirits were something like half a pee for a double grog and soon the party was in full swing. Young ladies appeared from nowhere, songs, popular and ribald were sung, and we were shown round the ship by one of the less intoxicated officers . . . BANG!

'Mind your heads.'

'*Now* he tells us.'

It was getting very late, so Roge and I set about looking for John (Moon Dog) Gorman who had disappeared, but after several more bonks on the head decided he was a big lad and could find his own way home.

We thanked the captain and his men for a splendid evening and threatened to call by again when they next docked in Liverpool.

'When you find the funny one, will you throw him in a taxi and send him home, we've got a show to do tomorrow . . . tar Jack.' (get it?)

In the middle of the night back at the hotel (or was it morning . . . I can never remember) there was an almighty banging and shouting (and falling over) but we took this to be an over-tired and emotional Gorman because after a while it settled down, and the seagulls took over.

In the morning, over giant plates of fried eggs, potatoes and bacon, Danish style, a bloodshot-eyed Gorman came staggering into the dining room, holding what seemed to be a ship's sextant.

'I found this in my bed.'

'What happened to *you* last night?'

'Well it's not very clear, but what I *do* remember is this queer sailor chasing me all round the boat, shouting "You're fab gear . . !" "You're fab gear . . !" and in the end I had to shin down the mooring rope and leg along the quayside to get away.'

'And what about the sextant?'

'I just found that in bed.'

When we got back to Esbjerg the Destroyer had flown, so John had to wait a few months till she came to Liverpool. God knows how they got round the world without a sextant.

On returning the sextant, accompanied by our old henchman, roadie, wine bar owner extraordinaire, John 'Hewo' Hewson, Gorman learned the truth about 'the Esbjerg incident'.

When Roge and I had staggered safely down the gangplank into our taxi, the ship's officer had immediately ordered another cab for Mr. Gorman and on its arrival had sent an able bodied gunner to retrieve John. By this time Mr. G. was quite paralytic (or palatic as we say in the Pool) and when he heard the sailor shouting 'Your cab's here' John had replied, 'What?'

'Your CAB'S HERE!' continued the sailor, but Gorman misconstrued it as 'YOUR FAB GEAR' and ran away from the gay gunner, down the mooring rope and onto the jetty as fast as his sea legs could carry him. He was last seen running from the Danish cab with something under his arm.

All was explained. The Captain graciously accepted the return of his sextant, and another groggy good time was had by all, with lots more naughtical naughtiness.

The next morning Gorman woke up at home with the Captain's hat and telescope in his bed!

A.D.J. from L.A.

In November 1969 whilst the Scaffold were appearing at the tiny Bitter End Club in New York, we were asked to make a guest appearance on the Mike Douglas TV show. Being hypersensitive about the 'Beatle brother' tag (it being only a few years since their last live appearance in the States) the fact that we were to be part of yet another 'English Week' on the show placated us somewhat, and the further fact that it would be networked throughout America clinched the deal.

On the first class Parlor Car train from New York to Philadelphia the American public were their usual friendly selves and wished us (obvious foreigners) a pleasant trip to their country. Whilst we were propping up the bar, I scored top marks for spotting a citizen using a phone on the train. When we arrived at the TV station we were introduced to Douglas Fairbanks Jr. (ah, this *must* be English Week) and we were asked to take our seats in the audience! We'd done quite a few strange shows in our short showbiz lives but not many *in* the audience, but thought, like phones on trains, it must be an American custom.

Night-time in friendly NYC . . .

Transmission time arrived and everyone waited expectantly, especially us, as no one had told us what we had to do. Mike Douglas and Doug Fairbanks talked a bit, fenced a bit, looked English a bit, and then introduced their next guest . . . a DJ from LA 'Ah, he *must* be British,' we thought proudly.

At that time, the 'Paul is Dead' rumour was sweeping the States and getting enormous exposure. Now, settling into the guest chair a few feet away, was the disc jockey who'd actually started the whole rumour on his Los Angeles radio show.

He went through the whole con with Mike Douglas . . . Paul's back to front on the *Pepper* album . . . Paul's shoes are off on the *Abbey Road* cover . . . Paul's this . . . Paul's that . . . all proving beyond a shadow of a Paul that Paul was definitely DEAD!!

Now certain things are like a red rag to a bull so when they'd stopped rabbitting on and Mike Douglas asked me for my comments (seeing as I was just passing, six thousand miles from home, and coincidentally happened to be Paul's brother) I pawed the ground a little, then charged.

I pointed out that apart from it being too silly to waste valuable air time for me, the Scaffold and the American public, it was also a gigantic, well-planned hoax, based on groundless innuendo and straight lies, but most of all how could you, Mr. LA DJ, condone, or live with, the precise moment in time when millions of young loving trusting teenagers heard that their biggest pop hero was . . . dead! (It was as though the Kennedy and Martin Luther King murders were a hoax!)

HOLLYWOOD BOWL
HOLLYWOOD 2301 N. Highland Ave. CALIFORNIA
AUG. 23 1964
THE BEATLES
SAT. EVE. AUG. 23, 8:00 P.M.
PRICE $4.00
NO REFUNDS — NO EXCHANGES
RESERVED $4.00
J 17 38

There was a stunned silence. Showbiz was never like this, especially on a cosy afternoon, live, network telly to middle America.

Mike Douglas covered beautifully and we went straight into the commercials.

Even I hadn't realised the impact I had caused until we were all halfway up the studio's narrow staircase and the numbed DJ suddenly came out of his coma. Turning around he spat down the stairs 'You f. . .ing b . . . . .d, you call yourself a f. . .ing professional, you couldn't lick my ass, you f. . .ing B . . .' and various other expletives.

They dragged him up up and away from me, arms flailing, and that day I realised that I'll never be a really *true* professional because sometimes (just sometimes) there are more important things than 'professionalism'. I think they call it telling the truth. I wouldn't mind, but the cad wasn't even British.

FAMILY MAAAN

In between shows at Paul Colby's Bitter End* we bumped into Joe Cocker at the 'English bar' on 42nd Street, after completing a David Frost network spectacular with Diana Rigg, Lou Rawls, and the late Patrick Campbell, a most charming man with an engaging stutter. As we'd cured our roadie 'Hewo' of stammering many years previously we were toying with the idea of hiring Patrick for a few weeks on the road to see if we could do the same for him, but decided instead to join Joe for a jar.

With a little help from our friend we were quickly informed about a New York species called 'the groupie'. These ladies apparently gave their bodies and souls to their favourite group, not for money but for love: They had adhered to a strict hierarchical system with number one groupies going for the Stones, Beatles, Jimi, etc., number two aiming for the Monkees, Blood Sweat and Tears, etc., number three, trying for . . . etc. . . . etc. The fact that some of the groups had no interest in their young, sensuous, 'free offer' bodies was of no consequence (I mean, just imagine what problems they must have had with Elton in later years). They simply followed Dad's old adage of 'God loves a tryer' and tried . . . persistently (usually with no holds barred and no stone unturned) till they 'got their man'.

So, one evening when we discovered from Joe that the main groupie bar in New York was in the next Greenwich Village block to the Bitter End we left the 'ice creams only' atmosphere to Tom Rush and rushed

* Now retitled 'The Other End' where our fab Scaff pic still stands in state amongst the other Rock Giants, behind the bar.

down for a closer look . . . purely for sociological and academic reasons you understand. The thought that we'd be entering a den of iniquity full of lower class scrubbers was soon dashed, as the bar slowly filled up with some of the best dressed, sophisticated looking women of all colours, shapes and accents that we'd ever seen, and man these chicks looked cool! (Particularly after three weeks away from home).

The word soon spread that a Liverpool group was in, and, even faster, that one of the group was a Beatle brother. I know this, because the following serviette scribbled message was passed to me by a male friend as we were finishing our drinks . . . Scribble, scribble, 'Paul McCartney's brother is sitting at the next table' (folds serviette and asks for waiter deliverance).

Perusal . . . scribble, scribble, 'On my right? Draw me a diagram' . . . (folds serviette) . . . 'Waiter'

Perusal . . . scribble, 'You . . . X——HIM X' (folds serv and waitaminute)

Perusal . . . scribble, 'I'm going to be so super cool MAAAN, I'm not gone ta look!'

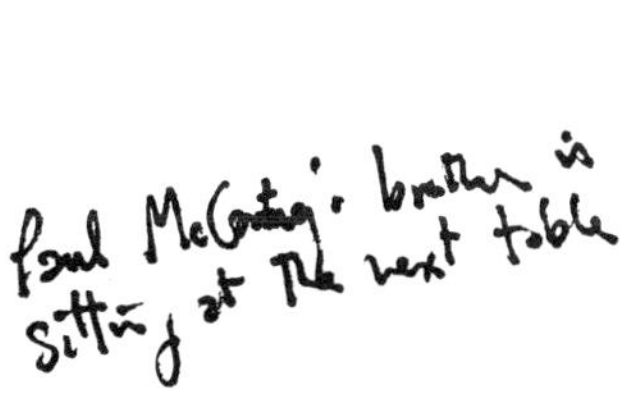

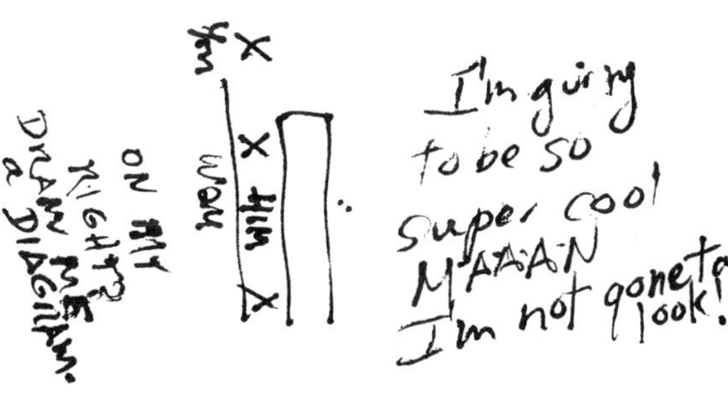

Groovie, groupie napkin . . . maan.

Now that's what you call a super-groupie and the sudden thought of 'Where have all these chicks been for the last three weeks?' was immediately squashed with the thought of my wife and one year old baby waiting at home for my return. Up until the disintegration of my marriage in 1979 I must admit that I was pretty damn faithful for ten years (and why not, that's what true love should be about . . . there's no *need* to be unfaithful).

After quaffing our ale, we sauntered back to the Bitter End where Tom was just finishing to rapturous applause (because he was good) and prepared for *our* nightly ordeal.

Just before 'curtains up' the door burst open and in walked two giant gorillas. 'Are you's de Scaffolds?'

'Might be, sir, all depends who you are.'

'Mr. C. Nostra for yiz,' and in strode an immaculately dressed clean shaven, thick set man with fedora hat, vicuna overcoat (over shoulder) and big cigar hanging from the mouth (just like in one of those gangster movies).

'OK you's guys, just thought I'd drop by and welcome you's to de Bitter End and New Yoik.'

It was our Record Company executive and colleagues (three weeks late for the opening night but nevertheless our record boss and chums).

After vice-like hand clamps all round, he exited as noisily as he'd entered with the two gorillas leading the way, ready for any 'action'.

'The Mafia?' asked Roge.

'Mafia, what's the Mafia?' said we.

'Nothing, what's the mafia wit you.'

This sort of quick fire, devastating, lively whacker whit was *nothing* compared to the stuff we gave our young American ice cream soda pop audience.

For them we aimed just above their heads for an hour of English poetic word imagery . . . very 'clever' but not very communicative. Most nights we went down with a big 'zero zilch'.

In fact in later years our humour went down better in Sweden than in New York . . . but back to *that* night.

Whilst we were performing I noticed a very attractive couple of girls taking more than the usual interest and after the show they were waiting outside the 'End'.

'Hi,' said the brown one.

'Hi!' said we.

'We caught your show,' said the blonde, Swedish-looking one.

'And you're crazy!' said brownie.

A few more interesting nonsequiturs were bandied round and we all walked along the rain-swept Greenwich Village pavement (sorry sidewalk), heading nowhere.

Just then a large white van stopped at the lights and through the waving windscreen wipers we glimpsed a curly headed bloke with hands madly drumming his steering wheel.

Him obviously enjoying the music inside his big warm white brain, and us obviously getting wet on the cold New York Street, seemed somehow inappropriate, so I sign languaged our predicament and he immediately responded by sliding open his door and letting us pour into his home on wheels.

The Stones were pounding round his front room, and when John Gorman felt the warm happy vibes (and being a lot of a show off) he started dancing and singing along at the top of his voice and feet.

Having no idea who we were, the young man with obvious vision (he *must* have been a man of vision—you don't pick up just anyone off New York Streets) introduced himself with a small printed card as Buzzy Linhart. CARD; 'GLAD TO SEE YOU and thanks for not smoking! (he'd just kicked the habit) Love Buzzy'.

The calling card of Buzzy Linhart, Bette Midler's No. 1 guitarist.

'You guys from England?'

'Fraid so . . . Liverpool.'

'Liverpool! Fantastic . . . dya know the Beadles?'

'Never 'eard of 'em.'

And off into the night drove three British satirical gentlemen, two brown and pink groupie beauties and one Nu Yoik, friendly, Bette Midler guitarist.

The lithe brown lady introduced herself as Devon and rolling up a cigarette offered: 'D'ya smoke dope?'

'No, it makes me sick, all that tobacco kills me . . . literally.'

'This is straight grass man, it's cool.'

'Well just a soupson then, after all it is Yom Kippur.'

'Pardon me.'

'I said John Kennedy's children smoke it, so why not us?'

'Right on . . . Hey what's your sign maan?'

Many nightclubs, grass puffs, and 'bottom ups' later, the girls had shown us New York and many fellow groupies, and Devon offered to take the limey whitey back to his Chelsea Hotel* in a yellow cab, as Buzzy, Scaffs and Blondie had buzzed off somewhere else.

The next thing I remember through the purple haze was her ordering my key from the desk and helping me into the lift . . . 'I'll just get you to your room.'

'Well isn't that nice,' I thought . . . 'What a gentleman'.

The next thing I remember was that all my clothes were off and I was safely tucked up in bed for the night.

'Night night mummy,' . . . no reply.

I suddenly realised that there was no reply because she was tucked up in bed beside me . . . stark naked.

A million heaven and hell thoughts hit me at the same time.

Saint: 'but you're a happily married father my son'

Sinner: 'well these *are* unusual circumstances, maybe just this once . . . the wife will never know'

Saint: 'you just feel like this because you've been away from home for three weeks'

Sinner: 'but she's a beautiful brown eyed handsome maiden, sod the three weeks . . . this is "here and now" . . . "attention" to *this* mynah bird'

Saint: 'she may be beautiful, but what if you get a dose, my son?' . . . But most of all, (and this was *me* talkin') if I don't do anything . . . she'll think I'm colour prejudiced!

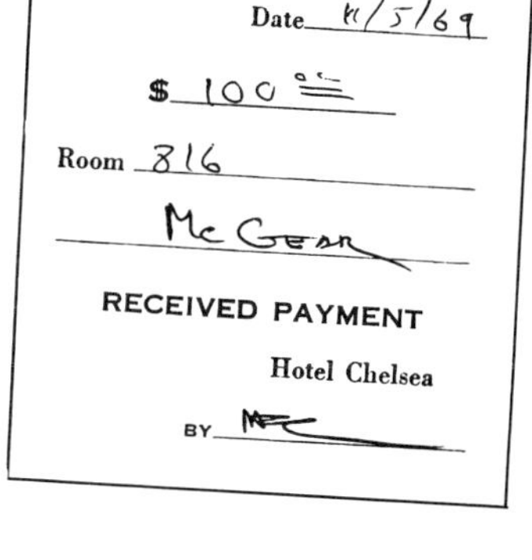
Date 16/5/69
$ 100 00
Room 816
Mc Gear
RECEIVED PAYMENT
Hotel Chelsea
BY

I decided to risk her fury and asked,'Do you mind if I sleep this one out?' to which she smiled an 'Oh god not one of them, back to the African Roots Liberals!' reply, and that's how I spent the night . . . cuddled in the arms of New York's number two groupie. Now that's the truth, though you'd never believe it!

* We chose the Chelsea Hotel because Leonard Cohen and Brendan Behan supposedly stayed there when in NY, and because Dylan Thomas (Bob's brother) supposedly died there.

Big Apple hats: Gorman with his back to us; Devon next to him; McGough far left and me kneeling on the floor of a clothes store in the Village.

NEW YOIK. NEW YOIK

John Lennon liked New York's abrasive, brutal, succinct, sometimes vicious attitude because it reminded him of a tighter, more together Liverpool. I prefer however to live without big cities . . . or, should I say, away from them. Not that there isn't a certain charm about their bullet headed frankness, but I can think of better things to do than going into the shop next to the Chelsea Hotel, 1234567th Street, and asking . . .

'Excuse me, (mistake number one!) but do you sell peanuts?'
'Sure we sells peanuts?'
'Could I have a bag please? (second mistake . . . 'please')
. . . and do you sell Coca Cola?'
'Sure we sells Coke . . . big . . . small?'
'Large please . . . and do you sell whisky?'
'Whisky! WHISKY! . . . do I *look* like I sells goddam whisky?'
'I beg your pardon.'
'You gets whisky down d'street.'
'Thank you, good day.' (mistake number three)
'Goddam motherfucker.'
Now what I *should* have said was . . .
'You got any peanuts?'
'Sure.'
'Gimme a bag . . . you got Coke?'
'Sure.'
'Gimme Coke.'
'Big?'
'Big.'
'You've got it.'
'You got any broken biscuits?'
'Sure.'
'Well mend them you motherfucker.'

When Buzy got to know us better, he couldn't get rid of us. Here he is with his bass player and us smoking his non-smoking cigarettes, next to Claes Oldenburg's bent saw.

THE 3D BEARS

And then there was the time we were walking round Times Square, window shopping.

As we passed a small sex shop, I spotted a 3D picture of—can you believe it?—Goldilocks and the Three Bears. It was just to fill the window out, and was nestled snugly amongst variously posed ladies and assorted sex aids (It could only happen in New York.

As I had a small eleven-month-old baby quickly growing older at home, and not having too much money, I walked into the shop and asked,

'Excuse me, but how much is that . . . (Teddy in the window? . . . no) how much is that picture of the Three Bears in the window?'

'De Tree WHAT!'

'There's a 3D picture in the window of Goldilocks and the Three Bears, is it for sale?'

'Are you some kind of poivoit?* . . . Gedout a here before I calls de cops.'

I couldn't get out of that one, but he did eventually relent and sell me the picture. It's up in one of my three girls' bedrooms at Sunset, Parkwest, at dis . . . sorry, this, second in time.

* Pervert.

-HE Queen's day of variety in the North yesterday ended with a night of variety that made the Royal train late.

By KENNETH TOSSELL

fter visiting Manchester and then going on to Liverpool to open the new Mersey Tunnel, the Queen saw the North's top variety talent at the Liverpool Empire.

'erves' threatened her holiday—
'natogen put her back on top

fold and Peter Adamson of "Coronation Street" were also in the show.

Ken Dodd was there, too, joking about the new Mersey Tunnel—"for the dockers to get from one strike to another quicker."

Introducing the show, Liverpool-born film star Rex Harrison recalled the days when he acted for 30 shillings at the local rep—and was advised by the manager to give it up.

A quartet of club comics, George Roper, Mike Burton, Stuart Gillespie and Steve Faye, did quick-fire two minute spots.

And Gerry Marsden sang his first number one hit, the Kop song "You" Never Walk Alone."

The Queen also saw excerpt from a mu about the late Mrs. Braddock, MP.

There's nothing nearly as nice as shaking the Queen's hand. Or should I say nothing as nice as *nearly* shaking Her Majesty's hand.

The Scaffold had been asked to appear at the Royal Gala Performance to celebrate the opening by Queen Elizabeth II of Liverpool's second Mersey Tunnel.

The name of the tunnel was a closely guarded secret with everybody trying to get their greedy hands on it. *We* simply rang the workman who installed the lettering above the tunnel entrance and asked what order they went up in.

'K.I.N.G.S.W.A.Y.' he said

'K I N G S W A Y? . . . thanks a lot, Tommy.'

'Get it down ya.'

On the last afternoon rehearsal at the Empire Theatre, we slipped the 'secret' name into our fab hit: 'Thank U very much for the Kingsway Tunnel, thank you very very much.' No one got it . . . great, plod on . . . Well *nearly* no one.

'Boys! boys! Stop there would you . . . a little word please.'

Sir Bernard Delfont, the impresario in charge of proceedings, rushed down the aisle taking us to one side.

'My boys, you're not supposed to know the name of the tunnel,' he whispered heavily.

'But we do.'

'. . . and you're certainly not supposed to put it in your song.'

'But we just have.'

'*Don't* put it in tonight boys!'

'Yes sir.'

I'm sure it was because Sir Bernie wanted to be the first to tell Her Majesty, but it didn't bother us so we let him do the honours and after the show, an urgent knock on the dressing room door called for 'Scaffold front of house please.'

'What for?' I shouted.

'For presentation to the Queen dear . . . in the foyer.'

'Stand in a long embarrassing queue to shake hands with the Queen? . . . no chance,' I thought, 'and anyway she thinks I'm a flasher'.

Being royal boot-lickers, my two colleagues disappeared out the door in seconds flat and looking in the mirror all alone in the drezy I had to ask myself, 'You are a contrary young man aren't you, what have you got against the Queen? *Answer . . . nothing.* You must be an anti-royalist then? *Not particularly.* Then why not be a nice sensible lad and join the Scaffold in line then? At least you'll be able to tell your children (of whom I had two . . . Benna Mary was joined by Santa Theran) that you once shook the Queen of England's hand'.

I got in line just in time, and as her Majesty walked slowly round, managed to squeeze my wife next to me for good measure.

Suddenly there, on the end of my hand, was the Queen of England's white GLOVE! (Not even skin maaan). We exchanged polite nonsequiturs (there's a lot of them about) and she turned out to be a charmingly natural lady (just like Auntie Dill). Next in line she chatted to Roger McGough, quick-thinking lively whacker wit. It was approaching the midnight hour and Her Majesty had to beatle back to London aboard her personal Royal Express sleeper.

Queen: 'I would love to stay, but I've simply got to catch my train.'

Roge: 'Why don't you get the next one?'

Ah well, never mind, apart from Roger's rapier sharp witticisms, I can at least tell my kids, 'Children, once upon a time your father shook the Queen of England's GLUV,' (fame indeed).

John Elton Dwight . . backing singer

In 1971, when Paul launched his new supergroup Wings on an unsuspecting public at the Empire Ballroom, Leicester Square, my knife and I (cut that out for a start) my wife and I were naturally invited. Controversy was raging because brother had dared to include his 'non-singing' wife in the band. But Paul felt, 'Sod 'em, it's my band and I'll have who I want in it.' (To tell the truth, I'm sure Lin would have preferred being at home cooking the spaghetti turkey dins, but this way she could at least be with her fella as he winged his way round the world.)

It was a 'luvely do' with all sorts of luvely showbiz folk mixing with each other to the dance hall music of Ray McVay and his orchestra. At one stage it was slightly embarrassing when two 'old flames' of mine came over to Paulin and our table with their new husbands . . . Brenda (you remember her) Stokepodgers and Sandie 'Those Feet Were Made for Walking' Shaw. But any awkwardness soon passed as we discovered that we were all happily in love with our new partners.

At the end of the evening, just before we were thrown out, I excused myself to go to the boys' room and in the middle of a Jimmy Riddle (as Dad would say) who should be joining my sentiments but Elton (ex-Bluesology) John.

'Hello Mike.'

'Hello Reg.'

'Elton, it's my new image.'

'Sorry Elt, how's things?'

'Fantastic, are the boys with you?'

'Rog and John? . . . no, I haven't seen them tonight.'

'They were marvellous sessions we used to do together.'

'Were they?'

'Yes, we always used to enjoy coming to Abbey Road for your sessions . . . they were so much fun.'

'Really.'

'You don't remember, do you?'

'Not a lot.'

'I used to be a session singer and we used to back you.'

'Elton John backed the Scaffold?'

'I'm afraid so,' said Elton, shaking his body (as Abbi would say). 'And if you ever want a pianist just give us a ring.'

'OK Reg . . . sorry Elt.'

When I got back to my Liverpool home I listened to all our Scaffold records to see which backing singer was Elton—sorry, Reg—and d'you know something . . . you can actually hear him.

Stop the coach I want to get off!

In 1973, after ten years in 'the business', a passing Liverpool poet got drunk (no, not Roge) under the auspices of a full moon and attacked me like a series of wild animals on the 86 coach coming home from Manchester. (Tiger stalking, snake over the back of coach seats, and final ape attack.) I stopped the coach, got off, and hitched a taxi over the water to Sunset.

As I was in the middle of a Grimms tour† I took a few days to come to a decision (last bastions of 'professionalism' I'm afraid) but in the end decided that there were too many cooks spoiling the Grimm broth, that they could get by without me, and that I would cease my flirtation with showbiz therewith!

Brian poet sent me a lovely apology by post, but my mind was made up. I had stopped being an entertainer.

My first children's/adult book, *Roger Bear*, was such a joy to write (a kid's (?) book which wasn't released in the States because its hero Rog was holding his best friend's *black* hand on the cover), and the reaction from the Press was very encouraging: Spike Milligan thanked me for my 'lovely book . . . your nice people, love, light and peace.'

Sacha Puttnam (son of film producer Dave Puttnam) said, 'I have read *Roger Bear* five times. Please, *please* write a second story.'
John Lennon said 'We loved yer buke' and Yoko added 'we'll read it next week.'

If Dave Bowie* was anything to go by, then this was to be my new career, and besides I could dedicate them to Benna, Theran *and* Abbi (Faith) my last baby girl in the pipeline, due (and born) on 2nd December of that year.

Just as I was easing into my new genteel vocation as a kiddie book author, brother returned from his *Band On the Run* African episode, and suggested we make a single (*Leave It*) to 'make some money' which eventually turned into the *McGear* album, and WHAM, BAM,

† The Scaffold eventually extended into a unit which comprised Gorman (John), Roberts (Andy Liverpool Scene), Innes (Neil Bonzo Dog), McGough, McGear and Stanshall (Viv Bonzo Boss) . . . GRIMMS.

* His manager Tony De Freis even rang from New York to demand another book, but I had to hang up as Angi was bringing my dinner into the lounge . . . cheeky sod, aren't I?

Top pop pool poser.

SOCKO, I was back in wonderful, there's no bizness quite like show-bizness . . . will I ever learn?

MR. GEAR

During the making of the album *McGear* in early 1974 with Paul, Linda, Denny Laine, Jimmy McCulloch† and Jerry Conway (Cat Steven's drummer), the control room door of Strawberry Studios, Stockport, swung open and in marched an entourage containing The Carpenters. They had just completed a successful concert in Manchester, and on hearing that I was recording, naturally rushed over to where the action was.

We were in the middle of a boring track which, under the sensitive ears of such pro's as Karen and Richard must have grown steadily more monotonous, but not for The Carpenters it seemed. They sat attentively listening in the corner for some hours, when I suddenly realised that it wasn't *me* they'd come for, it was my brother Paul! They were McCartney freaks.

Eventually both they and we had had enough. They departed for their Manchester hotel and we departed in Paul's Rolls Royce to our Liverpool homes.

Gliding along motorways the Rolls suddenly stopped rolling and came to a smooth halt by a lonely moonlit field.

Some minutes passed before I suggested, 'We've stopped.'

'Yeah,' said brother, 'We seem to have conked out.'

More minutes floated past the window . . . 'Shouldn't we get some help,' I hazarded a guess.

† The latter four being the basis of the second Wings formation, till Jimmy left. He died recently of a drug overdose, joining the seemingly endless list of Jimi, Bri, Janis, Moonie, Elvis etc. etc.

'Sposeso,' said Linda, and the three of us prepared to face the cold January night. Once outside we could see the distant lights of a small town and set across the fields in that direction. Eventually we found a telephone box which was actually working and I phoned a local taxi firm. It being an obvious 'one horse town' I decided to impress upon the locals the importance of the situation.

Beep . . . beep . . . beep . . . beep . . . beep. 'Good evening, I'm Mike McGear of the Scaffold'. Well they'd have never believed I was an ex-Beatle would they?

'Beg your pardon.'

'This is Mike McGEAR of the SCAFFOLD. We've just broken down on the way home from the STUDIOS and it's imperative we get home to Liverpool as soon as possible.'

'Certainly sir, just give me the details of where you are and we'll be with you as soon as possible.'

Concise details given, I rejoined my relatives, and on hearing the good news of a coming rescue party Paul decided we needed a little music to while away the time and went back to the Rolls for his guitar. Quite some time later he returned, I stopped snogging with Lin, and all three of us gave a magnificent moonlight concert to the long drawn out shadows of Frodsham, Lancashire, (with excerpts from 'the musicals', Buddy Holly, the Everly's and our latest *McGear* venture).

The time had passed long enough for cold bones and hungry stomachs to set in and still there was neither sound nor sight of a taxi. The importance of the situation had obviously not entered the ears of the local conveyance firm, so I excused myself from the entertainments and phoned again!

'Good evening,' I demanded. 'This is MIKE McGEAR of THE SCAFFOLD, will you be LONG as we've got to catch a FLIGHT TO ISTANBUL early tomorrow morning?'

'Oh is that Mr. GEAR of GEAR Scaffolding? We should be with you any second sir, sorry for the delay.'

Sure enough, on opening the phone-box door, the taxi appeared as if by magic, and all three 'SCAFFOLDERS' stepped down to our fairy pumpkin in time to Paul's guitar . . . just like in musical.

'ASK HIM, HE USED TO BE ONE'

As a result of the magnificent work achieved on the *McGear* album I was signed to Warner Brothers Records with a fifty thousand dollars advance (which neither my family nor myself ever saw as it was immediately set against record costs . . . it could only happen to me) and one fine day in '74 I was telephoned from Warner's Hollywood office to ask could I promote the long player in the States.

'No thanks,' I replied, and waited for the silence.

'Pardon me, Mike?'

'I'd rather not, if you don't mind.'*

'It'd just be a small tour from New York to Los Angeles, Mike, taking in all the major cities.'

'I'm afraid the States are a mite too big for me, can't you promote it without me?'

* My first New York trip, four weeks buried in the core of the Big Apple, travelling underground with my umbrella . . . *not* for the rain, but to fence off the muggers and stoned murderers . . . daily Horn and Hardart style food, and cockroaches in the showers of grotty hotels, was quite enough for this little lad . . . ta very much.

'Well, as you say Mike, America is a BIG country, and you're not known *too* well over here, as far as record sales that is . . . So we thought that if you were to meet the media and the people actually moving your product, it might be just that bit easier to break you *and* the record.'

(Pause . . . as I am proud of the album on which Paul and I have collaborated for the first time.)

'Well OK I'll do it, but only if it's first-class flights, limousines, and top class hotels with fresh flowers, and a bottle of chilled Dom Perignon in every suite.' (They'll never go for it!)

(LA pause, and hand-over-the-phone speech.)

'OK Mike . . . you've got it. Look forward to meeting you in LA.'

'Tara well.' (*Thinks: 'LA? . . . I'm going to HOLLYWOOD! . . . fan-bloodytastic!'*)

So with all my conditions agreed upon, I flew into New York's Kennedy Airport, which was so suspiciously quiet I guessed that the thousands of fans had gone to Laguardia by mistake. My 'personal manager' Derek Taylor‡ and I floated through customs (more first class jumbo champers I'm afraid) and from my black chauffeur-driven limo it was befitting that I should finally step into the hip intelligentia's Algonquin Hotel on my second coming.

Once installed in the old-fashioned (for New York), French-feeling, lugubrious surroundings (the hotel Bogart was forced to flee because of his *High Sierra* fans), Derek and I planned our attack on the Big Apple, with occasional 'swarees' up town to our Warner Brothers campaign headquarters.

It was on one of these 'swarees' that I met Dave WB. At first his young business-orientated mind stuck to the job at hand, promoting McGear across the USA, but it soon became quite apparent that although only a babe at the time of the Beatle Invasion, he had slowly become a confirmed Beatlefreak!

Glad to see a whole new audience of kids digging the lively whacker foursome, I nevertheless decided that breaking ME was going to be hard enough in the States, so when invitations came to view a bootleg Beatle film and to authenticate a '*signed* photo from the Cavern'†, I politely refused, but said that we might get round to it 'later' . . . mistake number one.

The promotional work included interviews with the top papers (*Newsweek**, *Billboard* etc. at the Algonquin (one delicious young lady came into my suite, threw down more Scaffold, Grimms, McGear records and literature than even *I* own onto the floor and said, 'Well Mike, that's where *I'm* at') and a tough visit to New York's TOP Radio Station, where I had to blag my way onto the airwaves, but got street-level recognition from two lads in white overalls who heard my 'product' on their portable radio and asked for bar room autographs after the show. All in all a constructive day's work, which included

‡ An old friend who had helped brother through his hectic hiatus and who was instrumental in Scaffold joining WB England.

† Smart Liverpool lads used to make fortunes by placing 'genuine Beatle autographs', 'piece of Cavern stage', 'Ringo's drumstick' adverts in American magazines and on receipt of the money send over the treasured forgeries. At least they *were* from Liverpool.

* Who print: 'He changed his name to McGear and for ten years he denied he was Paul McCartney's younger brother . . . he seems determined to retain his own identity, and on his new album he lists his brother and sister-in-law as Paul and Linda McGear' . . .

more 'maybelaters' to Dave Beatlefreak as the day progressed.

Business over, I was lounging in my suite when an invitation to visit John Lennon arrived via Derek, an old chum and mentor.

'Great, it'll be good seeing the old sod after all these years, but for God's sake don't let the Babybeatlefreak know where we're going!'

'Naturally, Michael,' came the squirish reply.

Later that evening saw the dynamic duo in John's penthouse flat overlooking the East River which he shared with Yoko's secretary May Pang, as he and Yoko had separated for a while. It *was* good seeing the man after so many years and he appeared completely at ease as he asked what I was doing in NY.

'Hawking the album *McGear* across the States,' I replied.

'Don't knock it son,' said John. 'I was plugging *my* new single on the same radio station as you . . . two days ago!'

He then told me that he'd just seen a flying saucer.

'Good,' thought I, having just left Liverpool. 'He's still got his sense of humour.'

'Honest Mike!' he insisted, even taking me out on to the roof garden for a better look. He then described in detail how he'd been sunbathing starkers (sounds right) when something, moving at an incredible speed, shot across the reflection in the window. Looking up, he saw what can only be described as a UFO (of the first kind) hovering over the East River. After pinching himself, he called May out to verify that he WAS going mental.

'Just tell me I can't see a flying saucer.'

'But there *is* a flying saucer,' said May, 'and it's got a red light on top!'

It hovered for a while over the business heart of America before shooting down the river faster than speed and out of sight. The next day several sightings were reported from the block of apartments opposite.

'So you *did* see a UFO?' said I.

('You F.O. yourself,' John might have said, but didn't.)

'Yup, I did,' said he.

Later in the evening, just as we were at our most relaxed, the phone went. May shouted through the apartment, 'Mike, it's Dave from Warner Brothers.'

I froze. How the hell did he get John's number?

'Who's Dave?' asked John. I explained, but not the whole truth.

'What does he want?' John shouted back.

'Something about a Bootle Beatleg film, and a Cavern photograph.'

My heart hit my boots . . . after such a long time not seeing John, this little Beatlefreak was now making it seem that *I* was the Beatle-dropper in front of an ex-Beatle, now surely ex-friend!

'Oh, tell him to come on over,' shouted John, completely understanding my predicament, and turning to me said, 'New York's full of these young freaks. I suppose we should be grateful there's a whole new generation sprouting up.'

(Now that's what I call a gentleman . . . Squire! But in retrospect I wonder, if only he hadn't seen so nice . . . On reflection, certain similarities can be drawn between the Babybeatlefreak and the person who wasted John's life on 9th December, 1980. I refuse to name the assassin, as remembering him only adds to his meaningless notoriety.

He is best forgotten, lest other immature minds copy his act in order to bring meaning to their own sad lives. Both were young, both were fans and both were overpowered by the Beatle image and phenomena, rather than seeing through the smoke screen of stardom to the actual *real*, people beyond. The difference between the two was that one shot with a film projector, the other shot with a far too easily obtained gun. But the tragic result is the end of a man finally at peace with himself, just getting his second breath, and the loss of the loving husband of a fine lady and the father to two fine sons. Crazy isn't it?)

When young Dave arrived (seconds later) plus even younger projectionist, he said hello to John and me, set up the Washington concert bootleg film, and projected it on to John's white wall. John, Derek and I sat on the lounge bed as the two lads stared enraptured at the film which *they* must have seen many thousands of times before.

John whispered to me, 'I've seen this one. . . . Neil's* got it.'

After the show was over, Davebeatlefreak, happy as Larry with his fresh Beatle injection, came over to Johnbeatle's bed, Cavern photo in hand, leaned over Johnbeatle's legs, and asked in awe, 'Mike, is this a genuine Beatle autograph?'

'Why don't you ask *him*,' I suggested, nodding to John. 'He used to be one.'

'Oh yeah,' said baby without batting an eyelash 'John, is this a genuine Beatle autograph?'

John mumbled something to the effect of 'without a doubt', and Dave, clutching 'authenticated' memorabeatlia close to his young body, exited, happier than Larry . . . or John . . . or Mike . . . or May . . . or Derek.

WASHINGTON CLAPO

When we arrived in Washington on Saturday 5 October, on my lightning 1974 tour of the United States of America, I received the daunting news that a Tom Zito wished to interview me for the *Washington Post* . . . no less! The *Post* having just reduced the President of one of the most powerful nations on earth to tears, I wondered if it was now my turn.

Not wishing to appear ostentatious I checked into the Madison, Washington's 'correct address' located at 15th and M Streets, practically opposite the *Post* office.

'Well, he won't have far to walk,' I observed.

'Just a mental note, Mike,' instructed my mental mentor manager, Degs Taylor. 'Tom isn't any run-of-the-mill journalist, he likes to get to know the *real* you. For instance, no limo tonight, he'll pick you up in his old Volkswagon.'

Oh great, I've got a loony. 'Where am I being taken?'

'Eric Clapton's in town, and Tom wants to combine a story on you and him for a possible front page *Post* story.'

'If you insist,' insisted I, and started to unpack yet again.

Around the appointed hour Mr Zito was shown into my adjoining suite and taking the bull (and my career) by the horns, I joined him with the opening line, 'I don't know if you're pro- or anti-Nixon, but I'd just like to thank your paper for what it did for mankind,' or words to that effect.

* Neil Aspinall—first roadie and Apple overlord, whose book I've yet to read.

'I can assure you, Mike, that everyone on the paper was behind *that* one,' answered Tom, a casually dressed young man, obviously off the record.

'Thank God for that . . . like a glass of Dom Perignon?'

'No thanks, we're a bit late as it is. Do you mind if we take my car?'

'Not at all, they've told me all about you.'

So, world-travelled, black Harrod's bag over shoulder, Tom drives me in his battered VW to the *enormous* Capital centre stadium on the outskirts of Washington DC.

The Albert Hall's big, but this is ridiculous, I think, as we enter the gigantic eighteen thousand-seater auditorium with the people on stage looking like Manchurian candidates.

Tom and I walk the odd mile down to our front portal row M seats, and there's the suggestion that we've just time to see Eric before the show starts . . . if we hurry.

'Great,' I think. 'It'll be lovely to see Patti again after all these years,' (Miss Boyd having just left wee Georgy for Mr. Clapton's affections) as we hurry through cavernous back stage hangers and well-armed police to Eric's drezy.

Having not seen Eric since the *All You Need is Love* Beatle's live television show (well all right, I *didn't* write, produce and star in it) and hearing several contradictory rumours about his state of mind, I am little apprehensive about my initial apporach, but plump for the old Liverpool genteel opener . . . 'All right Clapo, how's things ya PUFF?'*

Eric collapses into a smile, so I know *he's* all right. 'But where's Patti? She's the only reason I came,' (as indeed I once had a crush on her).

'Oh she's up in Canada, she can't get a permit, but I'll be flying up to see her after the show.'

'Give her my love and good luck for tonight,' I say as we exit back to our seats, where we are joined by Derek and a friend.

'How's Eric?' asks Derek (without his dominoes).

'Excellent,' says I, and the concert starts in earnest, with Eric, and Yvonne Elliman, and Karl Radle, and Robert Stigwood's growing Organisation.

During the magnificent concert the atmosphere changes quite noticeably. This is partly due to the marijuana joints passed up and down the rows by the audience (when one reaches me, one of my guests says, 'No Mike, this is much better stuff,' and produces prime California grass from his jojo wallet) and partly due to Eric's remarkably together performance. At the end of the concert, which includes some fine Bo Diddley nicks (sorry . . . licks), some Wee Georgy style guitar, as well as *I Shot the Sheriff*, everyone is *very* happy, and we all light a match in the dark auditorium as a sign of our appreciation to Clapo and his band. Looking round, it's like a giant birthday cake with candles which only God could blow out.

As we leave the stadium Tom organises somewhere to go, and we part company with Derek and party, threatening to meet up later. He chauffeurs me through various stages of Washington till we reach a definitely 'black' area and he stops. Getting out of the people's car, he stands me in the middle of two low-slung buildings from which music can be heard.

* Still Anglo-Irish word for homosexual.

'Take your pick,' says Tom.

I listen in stony silence (good stuff that California lawn) and in the end decide . . .

'The one on the right.'

'Good.'

'Why, what's the difference?'

'The one on the left's a white version of this club,' says Tom, opening the door to a long low lying room full of black faces . . . looking straight at us! Silhouetted in the doorway, and perhaps being white, the audience is now staring at us. (It felt rather like going into a Liverpool dockland pub with a dress on.)

'Let's hit the back,' I panic, but Tom doesn't seem to bother, and even nods to the young black guitarist who has noticed the change in atmosphere and comes out of his hypnotic blues trance to nod back to our Tom.

After a few whisky and Cokes, brought by an old black man very reminiscent of my Dad, the tension relaxes (well mine at least) and with the addition of Derek's party and more whisky, it disappears altogether.

'Little Bobby Parker' and his trio play the most beautiful music I've heard for some time. Music which sounds as though his Dad taught him, and his Dad before him, and his Dad before *him*, etc. etc. Now it was Little Bobby's turn and with the help of a little wah wah and a lot of soul he was turning on not only us pop poseur whities, but the working-class black audience all around.

In fact this was the first time on my travels across America that I'd felt 'at home'. The atmosphere in the tiny club was very reminiscent of one of our McCartney 'do's', so naturally I just relaxed into it.

Later on, when the joint was really jumpin, I witnessed for the first (and hopefully not the last) time, dancing between members of the opposite sex which I can only describe as 'very truthful'. It was the nearest to making love on a dance floor that I've ever seen . . . all to the tight rock 'n' soul party sounds of young Mr. Parker.

And the terrible injustice of it all . . . we'd just left one young whitie playing above-average guitarlics in front of millions of dollar ticket paying fans, and now here's one young blackie playing his *more* than average ass off in front of his working class brothers for peanuts.* I'm not saying that black is best, or east is west, I'm just sorry that Eric missed it, that's all.

At the end of the evening (or was it morning? I can never remember) and in quite a state I had to take my leave of the relaxed natural atmosphere, as I had to be up early once again to zoom to yet another state.

MARGUERITA MAYHEM

When I finally arrived in Los Angeles after my thunderbolt US tour, I was well and truly wiped out.

Non-stop early alarm calls, non-existent breakfasts, rushing limos to airports, first-class champagne or Marguerita flights across thousands of time-zone American miles, dragging my battered leather Harrod's bag across another endless airport and through more gun

* And this is nothing! Some of our biggest blues 'legends' can't even get work in the States!

Derek Taylor, Russ Shaw (Frank Sinatra's roadie's son—all he did was rushaw everywhere) and me still way up in the clouds at L.A. airport.

detection machines, the next speeding limo, checking into another 'Nob Hill' hotel, sipping *another* glass of Dom Perignon, accepting my first interview, then second, then thirst, then up, down and across town to a record plant to meet the workers shipping *your* albums, then tucked into bed with *more* Dom Perignon, non-stop early alarm calls, etc. etc. . . . It had all taken its toll.

But realising the importance of the mission . . . to get even a *little* toe in such an enormous door, and being a bugger for punishment, I soldiered on . . . and on . . . and ON, till we reached the Beverly Wilshire Hotel and I was informed that Donald, my chauffeur, would pick me up for a 'very important' interview with the *LA Times* (a 'very important paper') in quarter of an hour.

When we arrived at the Beverly Hills Hotel, where our interview would take place, Donald parked the car and I got out the wrong side into the driveway.

'That's a no-no, Mike.'

'That's a yes-yes, Donald. I just did it.'

We walked through the sumptuous Bev Hills Hotel over the bodies of decaying film stars, and I was introduced to the *Times* reporter, Dennis Hunt.

'No relation to Marsha?' I quipped, as slow as lightning.*

'Brother actually,' said Dennis.

'You're joking.'

'No, I'm Marsha's brother.'

'I've met your sister in London then.'

'Say hello from me next time you see her . . . would you like a drink, Mike?'

* Marsha Hunt, delicious singist from *Hair* (or 'HUR' as it still comes out) rumoured to have had a 'love baby' with one Mick Jagger.

'Marguerita please.'

The ale ordered, we launched into the interview, which was going like a house on fire when our drinks arrived.

'Cheers Mike,' said Den.

'Cheers Den,' said Mike, missing his lips completely and pouring the Marguerita down the front of his film star jacket.

I hoped that Dennis hadn't seen my extraordinary jet-lagged, over-worked over-hung behaviour, and covered by asking about Marsha's health.

The interview resumed, and I took another gulp at my drink, and God Bless me if I missed again . . . result, one Marguerita pool in my lap. I *really* had to regain full control over my senses. Checking the distance from the salt-covered glass to my dry thirsty lips, I took one last go, and . . . bugger me if I didn't miss again!

'Mike, I don't think that Marguerita wants you,' said Denis, as cool as a campari.

'I think maybe you're right, Den,' I replied, and ordered a scotch and Coke.

MOTTO: You can take a drink to a hoarse but you can't Mike it drink him if it doesn't really want you.

BILLY BANTER AND 'PARKY'

On the cover of my 1975 diary I have written 'Connolly . . . a powerful contender for life . . . an 'at''.

The man in question, Billy (W.C.) Connolly, a fine Glaswegian of a man, who sometimes waits for me with Sean Connery in Edinburgh's Caledonian Hotel but I never turn up, was first made known to me through an album entitled *Billy Connolly . . . Get Right Intae Him*. On the outer sleeve was a young, cheeky, bearded gentleman wearing only a black body stocking and a pair of Fyffe banana boots, posing in the Apollo Theatre, Glasgow. On the inner sleeve of the LP was the same man dressed in bishop's ecclesiastical garb, smoking a wee stoat and LPeeing in the dressing room sink.

On the black plastic disc inside the orange cover was one of the funniest, impossible to understand comedians I'd heard for a very long time.

At the time as I was trying my hand as a Liverpool 'Radio City' disc jock, and I religiously featured this album on my weekly show every Friday, and when some weeks later I discovered an ad in the *Echo* (Echo, Echo) informing Merseyside that Billy Connolly was attempting to fill the Empire Theatre (no mean feat for an 'unknown') I went along to the theatre box office in Lime Street to buy a ticket (something I hadn't done for many years).

'Alright Mick, come to buy a ticket for your kid's show?' asked one of the ladies.

'What show?' asked Mick.

'The Wings one.'

'No, I get those free, the one after that.'

'You mean David Essex?'

'No, not Mr. Cook, the one after *that*.'

'You mean Billy . . . er Connery?'

'That's me man.' (He even cost me two pounds!)

Paul and I with a fine Glaswegian of a man.

On the September night, Mr. Connolly not only filled the Empire, he also brought it down with his natural, relaxed, outrageous sense of humour and timing. 'This man is a BIG star!' thought I, and decided to lick his boots after the show.

In the Empire I always go to the same dressing room . . . the one the Beatles used before the war,* and this time was no exception. Sometimes there's no answer to my knock as the 'star' has got it wrong and is installed in another part of the building, but sure enough this night a 'Come in,' answered my rap-tap-a-tap-tap . . . tap-tap.

On my grand entrance, Billy not only recognised me, but said, 'Mike McGear! It's grayet (great) seeying ye again.'

'Again?'

'Yeh, we met years ago at The Ship† in Wardour Street when I was a Humblebum.'

Such is the price of fame I couldn't even remember a great star when I met it.

We were invited for 'drinkie poohs' at Billy's hotel, but chose instead to eat at Mr. Laus (one of the best Peking restaurants in Liverpool and indeed Britain) where we were joined by ex-Manfred Mann singist and fine gob iron player, Paul Jones (now, as well as a fine actor, lead singer with the Blues Band—no relation to the margarine group).

After yet another palatable Peking post prandial we dropped Paul off and called by Cono's hotel just in case he was still up.

The Big Yin was holding court at a deserted bar, and when I offered a more comfortable drinking establishment (namely Sunset) he took to the idea and we broomed over, under the Mersey, through the Birkenhead (or 'Berkhampstead' as Dave Essex prefers to call it) Tunnel out to Heswall.

Angi's mum was babysitting, and on meeting the hairy Scot, was immediately enamoured (he has that effect on lassies).

More drinkie-pooh beers with whisky chasers were offered, accepted, and drunk . . . interspersed with fine, discerning, razor-sharp wit and conversation. Not only that, Mr. Connolly had the ability to 'listen', a very fine quality in a chap . . . says I.

* The Beatlemania War from which several people are still recovering from shellshock.
† An old Liverpudlian Soho rendezvous.

In the middle of the night I called his name, 'Billy, I've just remembered a friend in Edinburgh gave me one of the finest malt whiskies in . . . Heswall, it's called Glenmorangie, (no relation to the wife) and there's a drop left, would you like it?'

'Nae Mike,' came the remarkable reply. 'I'm in no fit state tae appreciate it, just gimme *ordinary* whisky wi' a beer chaser, and that'll be fine.'

That's what you call class!

After a few more poohs we noticed that it was going light and decided to call it a day. I showed him to my den where a bed was dying for him to cuddle down into, and leaving him there I locked up for the night (morning).

A few 'chirpy' hours later, when his roadie rang to demand his return, I staggered in to yell the Big Yin.

There in the middle of my stone wall was an extraordinary sight . . . a pair of levitating socks! As there were no nails on the walls he must have scoured every brick in his tired and emotional state until he found the *one* that stuck out, to hang his socks on.

Since then, I've stayed at his house on the way to Paul's farm, we've crashed into each other quite a few times and it's been luvely seeing him quickly rising the dizzy showbiz ladder to the heights where he truly belongs.

New Victoria Theatre
WILTON ROAD, S.W.1
Telephone No. 834 0671
Manager : E C. CARTER

BILLY CONNELLY
EVENING 7-30
THURSDAY
OCTOBER 16
STALLS
£2·00
S32

No tickets exchanged nor money refunded
This portion to be retained [P.T.O

Some of the big boosts to his career have been his appearances on Michael Parkinson's TV chat show. His down-to-earth, insane normality with 'Parky' and anyone else who cares to listen has brought him thousands of converts. In fact, the only thing to top a Connolly telly performance, or better still a 'live' show, is the in-person, ordinary banter of the boy . . . Billy Banter no less.

But alas one of the programmes I probably won't be invited on is Mr. Parkinson's show.

I was down in London again and hearing that Billy was around, rang him at his hotel. 'Right, where are we meeting?' says I.

'Well, Parky's doin' an article on me for the *Sunday Times*, my boy, so I've got to meet him first, but then I'm going down to Tramp, are ye on?'

'Do we have to?'

'Well, that seems to be it.'

'Well, I feel like eating, so I'll pop down to Gerry's place (Gerald 'Billy Bunter' Campion's actors club in Soho) and I might see you later.'

When I finally got into the 'out' club and down to the 'in' table I saw that Mike Parkinson was still enjoying Billy's company, so I sat at the other end of the 'in' alcove . . . sulking.

Billy soon sussed this out and came to cheer me up. Soon there was me, William, and Mr. Parkinson in a line.

'Dya know Parky, Mike? Mike this Parky . . . Parky this is Mike.'

I can't honestly say to this day what happened, but it was like introducing two wounded bulls. For some reason he too was in a foul mood (sounds like a bloody farmyard) and said 'Yes, I met you a long time ago on *People and Scene at 6.30 Reports* on Granada TV.'

It wasn't so much *what* he said, it was the way he said it. Suddenly it was the war of the red rag to a bull roses . . . Lancashire v Yorkshire.

'No you didn't,' I replied.

(You don't say things like that to the country's most important chat show host, Michael . . . you might have a book out one day.)

'Yes I did,' replied Parky. (You *do* say things like that to a not-very-famous-in-his-own-right, ex-Scaffold, ex-Beatle brother, *and* get away with it).

'No you didn't.' (Jack Braithwaite of *Topic* magazine, posing as Johnny bloody Carson).

'Yes I did.' (If I had that young, long haired, Lancashire lout in front of a wicket, I'd knock his bloody bails off).

'No you didn't.' (Old fashioned Humbug 'established 1817' Parkinson . . . I can just see him on the bloody telly in twelve months time saying, 'There's nothing worse than a person of thirty-five writing their autobiography').

'Yes I did,' (and *his* bloody brother once came up to *me* at the height of Beatle mania and asked 'Can I have your autograph for me Mam').

'No you didn't.' (It couldn't have been for me bloody Mum, she was dead).

'Yes I did.' (Just give me the cheeky bludy munkey *and* Ali in a ring with one arm strapped behind me back . . .).

'No you didn't.' (Old grey-haired whistling twit).

'Yes I did.' (*You* can talk).

'No you didn't.' (Can't bat for toffee).

'Yes I did.'

Billy came to the rescue. 'If you two dinna shut up, I'll take you outside and sort ye both oot.'

The voice of sanity hit both the east and west of England mid-wicket . . . 'HOWZAT!'

'Well bowled, sir.'

When the blood had stopped boiling and the bill had been paid,* 'Parky' and I were last seen kissing each other behind Piccadilly (well, we shook hands at least), before departing in our chauffeur driven chariots (one limo . . . one taxi) for sunnier wickets. My taxi took me to . . . wait for it . . . Lords.†

'IT'S JUST THE WAY YOU'RE MADE, SON'

To say that 1976–77 were two 'interesting' years for the McCartney families would be a slight understatement.

On 18th March 1976 'Poppy' as my kids called Dad, finally gave up the fight and joined Mum on the other side of life.

At the height of one of his crippling arthritic periods he'd actually seen Mr. Death staring at him and had told him, 'Sod off, I'm not ready.' He had made a remarkable recovery, but this time it was all too much for him. Stepmother Ange confided to me that just before he died he said, 'I'll be with Mary soon,' and so indeed he now is . . . at least he knew where he was going.

My wife, Angi, and smallest baby, Abbi, were there at the end (Abbi asked, 'Has Poppy stopped?'), and when they told me he'd gone, I had to sit with him on my own for a while in the bedroom of his last bungalow home in Heswall (not far from Rembrandt*). I kept waiting

'It's the way you're made, son.'

* Certainly not by me—the last time I was at the same table with top pop group Slade, the drinks bill alone came to £300!
† England's number one cricket ground.
* Which brother Paul eventually bought from him.

One of my favourite family shots. It's the pic that I asked them to lay on Dad's coffin.

for him to wink at me, but he just lay there silently, the white sheet over his chest unusually still.

When it came to the funeral on the 22nd, I was a little late, and got into the car behind Dad's *just* in time to overhear one of my close relatives whisper, 'Mike'll be late for his *own* bloody funeral'.

'I hope I bloody am,' thought I.

It was no coincidence that Paul was on the continent at the time of the funeral (as I'm sure he'll tell you). Like Dad, who'd apologise for not being able to hold our stomachs when, as kids, we were being sick, Paul would never face that sort of thing. As Dad would say, 'It's just the way you're made, son'.

As Dad wanted to be cremated, we took him to Landican Cemetery not far from Heswall, where I soon realised just how many friends he actually had. They'd come from all points of the compass, and in all states of health, just to be there. Before they cremated him at ten thirty,

I asked one of the funeral men to put our family picture on his coffin, and that was that. (More tears, I'm afraid . . . last time, no more).

Such is (the majesty of) life, that the same evening, a half-hour 'Valderma Cream' Luxembourg Radio Show, starring me and my astrological chart, went out over the air with quotes and observations of uncanny accuracy about Dad and our family life, made by a complete stranger after simply studying my handwriting.

Shortly after, Stepmother Ange dropped two of Dad's things off at Sunset . . . one, the *A Hard Day's Night* painting of J. McCartney's Drake's Drum which now hangs in my den, and two, Dad's last keepsake . . . Mum's ring. Having never worn a ring (not even a wedding one) I tried it on every finger. The only one it felt *nearly* comfortable on was . . . the wedding finger! And that's where it rests until the day I die, when it will be passed on to the daughter it wants the most.

On the 10th April, the Maharishi finally caught up with me and I received my TM mantra from Sally Curphey in Liverpool, nine years after Paul got his from 'the Boss'. It didn't hurt a bit and I relaxed into it as regular as possible for two and a half years, until 2nd July 1979, three days before Theran's ninth birthday, when I stopped . . . just like that. *Self*-realisation being the whole point.

On 24th May, 'Wings over America' climaxed in New York's Madison Square Gardens to overwhelming success (good on yer Macca, particularly as George Harrison's tour of the States had met with less enthusiastic response just previously).

Soon after, my new single called *Do Nothing all Day* did absolutely nothing all year.

The day after Linda's 24th September birthday dinner party in Venice, Wings played a UNESCO concert in St. Mark's Square to stop Venice sinking, and with the weight of their equipment and staging, succeeded in sinking it a little further. As a momento Lin gave me a signed first copy of her *Linda's Pictures* book (PS I hope you've got it, it's a good book).

Linda's birthday party plus Mackids in Venice (good gondola!).

On 26th January, 1977 I was 'resting' at Sunset, when I received a phone call from brother informing me of a new baby in the Mac-pipeline. Without telling Paul, I wrote in my diary 'Paulin 2 have Baby James'. The odds of it being a boy were pretty high against (we both had three girls) and the odds of them calling him James were even higher. However, young James did emerge on 12th September, 1977, a fine bouncing baby(Do-do-wee wee wipe out)!

With only eighteen months between the departure of one Jim to the arrival of another, I had my first 'go' of baby James down in London at Paul's home. When the teeny lad was laid gently on my lap, there, before my very eyes, squirming and pulling 'Jim' faces was a mini Dad! Not that I am at all superstitious you understand . . . to my mind, if you step off a pavement into the road to avoid going under a ladder, a No. 86⅛ bus will only come along and knock you flat as a pancake anyway, so what's the difference.

On 1st April, 1977, the Scaffold performed their last live gig together. The show was called the *All Fools Show* (significantly) and starred us (with backing band Denny 'Wings' Laine, Zoot 'Big Roll' Money, Eric '10cc' Stewart, and Gerry 'Cat Stevens' Conway), plus Alan 'Animal' Price, an assorted Cleese/Palin Python team, and the EMI Go-Go Girls (of which all the best dancers were from Liverpool, naturally) with all the money going to charity.

This was probably why the Scaffold eventually parted company . . . we did everything for nothing! But it was a nice way to bow out as it was held at our old favourite venue, the Albert Hall, and was for mentally handicapped kids, so that'll be do.

The only reservation I feel about the Scaffold demise was that the *mass* public never saw the other poetic, word imagery, side to the lovable Liverpool lively whacker wits. But someday I shall let you see it, mark my words. (Like lots of Lennon's stuff, you're sometimes too far ahead for your own good it seems.)

Later on in April, I unconsciously master-minded the opening up of the Savile Row Apple Studios and the opening up of many memories.

I was looking for cheap studio time and space in London to complete some demo tapes for my recording company and when I heard that the half a million pound Apple Studios had been vacant for some years and were just sitting there silently decaying, I rang the 'man-in-charge' of the dead dynasty, Neil Aspinall, and asked cheekily to brush the cobwebs from Tutenbeatles' Tomb. Neil explained that permission could only be granted if I got clearance from one of his bosses and as the only ex-Beatle who kept in regular touch with me was my brother, I soon got a not too enthusiastic reply from the nearest member of my family. Well, would *you* be interested in digging down into the wounds of the most emotional, personal, mixed-up, legal break-ups in your and pop history's life? (Those nearest the shells obviously suffered the most.)

'Let sleeping logs die,' as Dad wouldn't say.

But not me. One of the problems of our present condition is the failure to come to terms with the mental blocks caused by our ugly past experiences (St. Michael's call to Adam's Apple, Chapter II converse LY). So knock the bloody walls down, Jim lad, ahar.

But most people, quite rightly, get a little tired of hitting their heads against brick walls, so what a luvely surprise it was when brother Paul regained his interest and said that not only could I use the Apple Studio ('Sod em') but also that, as I couldn't find a drummer, he'd come with me and play 'demo' drums, (Knock down the walls of ignorance to rebuild the walls [and bridges!] of knowledge structured in consciousness . . . first epistle of Paul's call to St. John, Chapter XI, verse 86a, platform 9).

As Paul didn't have a set of drums on him, Clive, an old Welsh friend, said we could borrow his, so we arranged to meet at 3 Savile Row the following day. The next afternoon Paul and I were the first there (the both of us early! That must be a record) and after viewing the roofless airy upstairs interior, by then completely ripped out, we opened up the underground tomb with a large selection of keys left by Neil. After switching off the alarm* we switched on the lights and sat in the old studio waiting for Clive and drum kit, plus assorted musical friends.

'When was the last time you were in here?' I asked Paul.

'I think it was . . . *Let it Be* . . . eight years ago.'

'Blimey, that's amazing, me too!'

I recalled that the last person I had bumped into at Apple before its closure was Ringo. I was having a record cut and Ritchie came in to say hello and goodbye. I was shocked to find he had grey hairs in his beard . . . *He* should worry, Auntie Jin got her first one at the age of twenty-five—a grey hair, that is.

But back to the story line . . . Paul, Denny Laine, Zoot Money, Viv Stanshall and I completed the demo and the next morning Paul flew off to the Caribbean to record his next album on a boat (where else, dear reader). Before he departed, farewell hugs were made and as he left his house, brother had to admit 'Great night that, last night . . . I had a ball.' (Wiping cobwebs clears the mind and eases the soul it seems.)

When I delivered the nowhere-near complete demo tapes to EMI records (tight budget and all that crap), the young man in charge of decisions (he left shortly after) said words to the effect that, 'Apart from other things, the drummer's left a lot to be desired, whoever he is, and therefore no more money can be spent on this project,' (i.e. you and your drummer are fired).

What I forgot to tell him is that the same drummer drummed on an entire album for EMI which sold over five million copies and earned over fourteen gold discs. It was called *Band on the Run*. Mind you, Decca turned the Beatles down fifteen years previously, and one of the Jones Boys the year before that . . . we can't *all* be right.

I didn't bother explaining to the young EMI mind ('Fools and children should never see or hear half-done work' . . . Florrie McCartney and Lee Eastman), I just walked out into the fresh air, out of Popbiz, and retired to the Pool for the second time in my short career. (Took everything 'seriously' in those days, didn't I?)

Shortly after the EMI single collapsed, so did my marriage. But in September 1977 I started to write this book in all seriousness in Tom Mitchell's (yes *the* Tom Mitchell) monastery in Gorebridge, near Edinburgh, having collected material, letters, newspaper cuttings, photographs, a little experience, and a lot of fond memories with the passing years.

* Body-snatchers had broken in the week before (a few hundred yards from Savile Row police headquarters)!

Just before starting it, I performed my last television show with Scaffold* (a year for lasts, I fear . . . the ups *and* downs of life's roller coaster). In true Scaffold style the programme, televised by Trevor Hyett from Liverpool's Kirklands (co-owned by our ex, roadie, 'Hewo' no less) was banned for its obscenity.

A sad '76 for both of us and a sadder '77 for me was brightened by Paul taking a catchy little ditty called *Mull of Kintyre* to the coveted number one Top of the Pops. Mulligan's Tyre sold two million copies in Britain, over four million around the world, and was the biggest-ever UK single, even topping the Beatles' *She Loves You . . . Yes, Yes, Yes.* ('It's just the way you're made . . . son.')

WHAT'S ON ROCKY

In early 1979, Granada Television interrupted my book writing to ask if the Scaffold would like to reform (after three years apart) as it was ten years since our hit song *Lily the Pink* had been a number one in the nation's charts and hearts.

After sussing out the other two, we reunited, made friends and turned in a fine anarchic performance on a programmed entitled *What's On*, a regular guide to what was happening, entertainments-wise, in the area.

Nobody seemed too bothered that we weren't appearing in the vicinity or even likely to be for some months, or even AT ALL that year . . . or EVER! But at least I managed to get in a plug about my book. (Well, nearly . . . John 'Tiswas' Gorman talked right across the plug!)

The fee was twenty-two pounds, fifty pence! . . . there was a query about expenses . . . and in typical Scaffold style Roger McGough and I missed the actual transmission, as a friend who owns a pub said to watch it on his bar TV, and we turned up late, and the telly was off, and our friend was upstairs with John Conteh's sister, and anyway you can't get Granada in this area, etc, etc, bla, bla, etc, etc. . . .

A few days later, on the day my wife moved out of Sunset†, a letter arrived from an old contact, Rocky 'Bodyguard to the Stars' Seddon from Shrewsbury Road, Garston, within spitting distance of 20 Forthlin Road.

Through the spittle, the letter simply said,

> Dear Mike, saw you last night on *What's On*. If you really want some anecdotes, how about the time I opened the dressing room door in Las Vegas to Edward G. Robinson. Tom Jones shouted from the shower, 'Who is it Rocky?' I replied, 'Edward G. Robinson'. He shouted back, 'Fuck off, he's dead!!!' Imagine the looks all round? Call me if you want anymore.

Regards and good wishes to John and Roger, Yours,
Rocky Seddon.

THE CHILDREN OF YEW TREE CEMETERY (Section 3A, Grave 276)

Mum's death having created a childhood mental block, I resolved one

* Well nearly last.

† We were divorced on St. George's Day 1979 (Good Lord they made him a Saint!) at eleven-thirty, in India Buildings, Water Street, Liverpool, with the judge asking at the end, 'By the way . . . How are the Scaffold?' (Honest!)

day to help clear the block by visiting her grave some twenty-two years late. 'Better late than never' seemed in its right place for the first time.

The only memory of where Mum had been buried was a blurred one from the top of a bus going to Uncle Joe's Anfield home, so I asked Aunties Jin and Mill exactly where her grave was. Death not being exactly the fondest of memories, they were as confused as me, until Jin finally rang up with the exact details.

'She's in Section 3A, grave 276, Yew Tree Cemetery, Finch Lane, Huyton, not far from Dinahs Lane (Jin and Harry's old home) . . . are you sure you want to go, son?'

'It's something I've got to do Jinny, after all it *is* twenty-two years.'

'Well, if you've *got* to, then God bless you, sunshine.'

So off I motor on my own, on a Sunny September Sunday, in my racing green, hand-painted (by me and Norm) FRY 8D vintage Alvis (number plate enscribed 'Esse Quam Videri' . . . 'To *be* rather than to *seem*.'‡)

When I finally find the cemetery, the gates are closed and I have to park the old lady outside, Inside, Steve, the grave digger's son, and I search the very run-down cemetery for Section 3A.

'It's Sunday, me Dad's off today, but I'll give you a hand.'

When we finally find Section 3A, it's even more impossible to discover grave 276, due to the apparent disorganisation, obvious neglect by people like me, and the heavy overgrowth.

Outside the gates in the distance I can see some children obviously admiring my beautiful old Alvis (as you drive around, young kids are seen mouthing 'What's that!' in wonderment, and old folks just nod, 'Ah, there's an Alvis,' with pride at good old British workmanship).

I smile at the thought and we continue to plough through the dead bodies. Eventually, we find 270 and 278 . . . the nearest to it! We can only discern that there is no headstone, but I want to be certain, as it is (or was) my Mum, so we traipse back to the gravedigger's lodge (passed the envious Alvis kids . . . they wave . . . I wave back) where we look into the cemetery records. Finally the correct page is found: 3rd November, 1956 (three days after Mum died) but the handwriting says 'Mary McCarthey, Western Hospital, aged 44'.

As I'm pointing out that she was Mary McCart*ney*, 47, and died at *Northern* Hospital, Steve's Dad, Vincent, arrives . . . boss gravedigger.

I explain my predicament and Vincent takes my number (3A . . . 276) and myself with unnerving precision straight back to where we'd been standing beneath a desecrated tree ('It's the vandals, they climb over the wall'). He's an obvious professional and verifies that the overgrown rectangle of earth on which I'd been standing for the last half hour is indeed where Mum lies buried in Owen Mohin's grave* with her Mum, Mary Theresa, three children, and the lady she left home for . . . stepmother, Rose Mohin! (All wounds are healed in death it seems.)

I ask to be alone, and sit for a while on an overturned headstone in the late Liverpool afternoon, thinking about nothing . . . just being.

As the sun sets, I walk past the lodge, thank the Caseys for their

‡ Not, as it may *seem*, a profound gurufic thought, but the motto of one of the world's most ruthless gun-runners (so I later found out).
* But not Owen; he's on his own somewhere else.

time, and walk to my car. The children have gone home to their Mums and Dads by now, and I open the car door. There, all over the inside of my old lady, is a present from the Yew Tree Cemetery kids . . . broken glass. They'd smashed the window in. A small crowd of children soon appear from nowhere as Steve and I brush most of the glass out of the car, and as I drive off, one of them shouts in broad Liverpool, 'You're dead lucky mister, dey usually nick de car, get pissed, and wrap it round a lamp post.'

Suffer little children to come unto me, verse? chapter? book of?

Well here we are (where are we? . . . as Dad and Auntie Mill would say) sadly at the end of the book. In the last few years even more people have joined Jim and Mary, including Uncle Harry and Johnny Moondog, giving even more importance to my living life to the full, here and now, philosophy. At this moment in time (as Cyn 'Let's Twist Again' Lennon never says) I still live at Sunset with my three beautiful, GROWING kids, and am about to dive, last time, no more, into the ocean of showbiz by producing my own and other people's songs, writing, and who knows, later on, we might even re-erect Scaffold.

I hope you've enjoyed travelling through my life and mind (I certainly have) and look backwards to meeting you (as Dad wouldn't say) in my next book, or better still in person. Or, as Uncle Bill would say to his Eagle Hotel regulars, 'All right yiz lot, you've read me bewk . . . now sod off, the lot of yiz.'